Art Music Activism

MUSIC IN AMERICAN LIFE

The Music in American Life series documents and celebrates the dynamic and multifaceted relationship between music and American culture. From its first publication in 1972 through its half-century mark and beyond, the series has embraced a wide variety of methodologies, from biography and memoir to history and musical analysis, and spans the full range of musical forms, from classical through all types of vernacular music. The series showcases the wealth of musical practice and expression that characterizes American music, as well as the rich diversity of its stylistic, regional, racial, ethnic, and gendered contexts. Characterized by a firm grounding in material culture, whether archival or ethnographic, and by work that honors the musical activities of ordinary people and their communities, Music in American Life continually redefines and expands the very definition of what constitutes music in American culture, whose voices are heard, and how music and musical practices are understood and valued.

For a list of books in the series, please see our website at www.press.uillinois.edu.

Art Music Activism

Aesthetics and Politics
in 1930s New York City

MARIA CRISTINA FAVA

UNIVERSITY OF
ILLINOIS PRESS
Urbana, Chicago, and Springfield

Publication of this book was supported by the
AMS 75 PAYS Fund of the American Musicological Society,
supported in part by the National Endowment for the
Humanities and the Andrew W. Mellon Foundation.

© 2024 by the Board of Trustees
of the University of Illinois
All rights reserved
C 5 4 3 2 1
∞ This book is printed on acid-free paper.

Library of Congress Cataloging-in-Publication Data
Names: Fava, Maria Cristina, 1960- author.
Title: Art music activism : aesthetics and politics in 1930s New
    York City / Maria Cristina Fava.
Description: Urbana : University of Illinois Press, 2024. | Series:
    Music in American life | Includes bibliographical references
    (pages 177–209) and index.
Identifiers: LCCN 2023031617 (print) | LCCN 2023031618 (ebook)
    | ISBN 9780252045714 (hardback) | ISBN 9780252056574
    (ebook)
Subjects: LCSH: Musical theater—Political aspects—United
    States—History—20th century. | Musical theater—New
    York (State)—New York—History—20th century. | New York
    (State)—New York—Intellectual life—History—20th century.
Classification: LCC ML3918.M85 F38 2024 (print) | LCC ML3918.
    M85 (ebook) | DDC 782.109747/109043—dc23/eng/20230801
LC record available at https://lccn.loc.gov/2023031617
LC ebook record available at https://lccn.loc.gov/2023031618

To Adriana and Nerino

Contents

Acknowledgments   ix

Introduction   1

1   Bourgeois Modernism for the Proletariat:
    The Composers' Collective   14

2   The Workers' Theater Movement
    and the Politicization of the Musical Revue   52

3   Keeping Politics at Bay:
    Composers' Forum Laboratory   95

4   The Living Newspaper Unit
    and Innovative Musical Approaches   120

5   A Leftist Myth:
    Marc Blitzstein's *The Cradle Will Rock*   143

Epilogue   170

Notes   177

Index   211

Acknowledgments

The completion of this research project would not have been possible without the help of scholarly and educational institutions, as well as colleagues, friends, and family members who offered me support and encouragement at every phase of its development.

I am grateful to Kim H. Kowalke for his invaluable assistance. His high standards of scholarship and his knowledge of the intricacies of American music and theater allowed me to look at the intersections between art and politics in the 1930s with an attentive and critical eye. For his aid in the writing process and priceless editing comments, I want to acknowledge Ralph Locke, who provided precious and continuous guidance. I can never thank him enough for his many 6:00 a.m. emails filled with thoughtful suggestions and research hints.

For their generous financial support, I extend my gratitude to the Musicology Department of the Eastman School of Music, the Eastman Professional Development Committee, and the American Music Library Association. A special thanks goes to the late Glenn Watkins, who sponsored the traveling grant that allowed me to visit the National Archives and Record Administration II in College Park, Maryland. Besides NARA, I am indebted to the State Historical Society of Wisconsin, whose Archives Collection hosts the Blitzstein's Estate that provided me with precious documentation. For essential research assistance, my gratitude goes out also to the New York Public Library for the Performing Arts, the Library of Congress, and the Kurt Weill Foundation. For his

x • *Acknowledgments*

invaluable help, I am also immensely grateful to David Peter Coppen, librarian and archivist at the Ruth T. Watanabe Special Collections of the Sibley Music Library, Eastman School of Music.

I thank with all my heart Carol Hess, who, when I began my Master's in Music History at Bowling Green State University, saw my potential as a scholar and educator. She helped me to think critically and to improve my English writing skills, but, most importantly, she became an invaluable friend who provided thoughtful inspiration and sustained my work even through the most difficult moments. Special thanks go also to Katherine Axtell for her helpful editing, Mary Ann Gilles for pushing me to look forward and believe in myself, and Maria White for keeping me always connected to real life.

I want to thank the various anonymous peer reviewers; their thoughtful criticism and positive reinforcement pushed me to challenge myself and strengthen the manuscript. At the University of Illinois Press I thank Gary Smith and Jennifer Argo for their assistance during production, but most of all I am indebted to Laurie Matheson, director, who always lent me her "fresh eyes" and helped me bring this project to the finish line.

I acknowledge my sister Gabriella, my brothers Germano, Paolo, and Massimo, and their families for having supported my pursuit of a dream of higher education in the United States, where I moved from Italy in 2000. I know that they missed sharing with me important moments in their lives, but I am grateful to them for never complaining and for instead encouraging my achievements. I hope to have made them proud. I also want to thank my in-laws, Laurie and Ronald, for having given me their support when I needed a family away from home.

I dedicate this work to my late parents, Adriana and Nerino, who instilled in me love for music, perseverance, and the courage to never give up. But the most important person, the one who kept alive in me the desire to share with others my ideas and research, is my spouse, Lauron Kehrer. They gently and understandingly shared with me the trials and errors as well as the successes of the last fourteen years. Their passion for the field and patience have inspired me to persist through many moments of doubt about my ability ever to complete this project. Indeed, this book is also the fruit of our relationship. Thank you, Lauron.

Art Music Activism

Introduction

> When someone says "Human beings esteem most that song/Which floats newest from the singer," someone might perchance suppose the poet means not new songs, but a new way of song, and praises that. Such a saying shouldn't be praised, nor should this one be taken in that sense. For they must beware of change to a strange form of music, taking it to be a danger to the whole. For never are the ways of music moved without the greatest political laws being moved.
>
> —Plato, *The Republic*, 424 B.C., translated with notes and an interpretive essay by Allan Bloom (Basic Books, 1991), 101–102

The Great Depression in America, with its heavy load of hardship and insecurity, turned the 1930s into a period of political and economic turmoil that escalated tensions between social strata. The economic downfall exacerbated conflicts between wealthier people and labor forces and strengthened the perception of a working class increasingly vulnerable to "dangerous" communist ideals. Articulated and latent dissent engendered ever-greater prejudice, discrimination, and suspicion against workers, especially immigrants and minority groups. Such explosive circumstances not only influenced social relationships but also helped American artists chart a fresh course that responded to the conflicts of the decade. Some creative minds documented current conditions of American life and thereby helped participate in the definition of a new American cultural identity. However, while John Steinbeck's novel *The Grapes of Wrath*, Thomas Benton's mural *The Social History of Missouri*, and Dorothea Lange's much-reproduced photograph *Migrant Mother* are now considered masterpieces that have become part of American history, no comparable musical composition written during the same period with the specific purpose of addressing contemporary life and sociopolitical unrest has become so powerfully iconic. Even

2 • Introduction

the most celebrated musical play of the decade, Marc Blitzstein's *The Cradle Will Rock*, tends to be addressed somewhat superficially, emphasizing the admittedly extraordinary events surrounding its premiere rather than its artistic value and social message. Yet music—particularly the fields of art music and musical theater—played a central role, not a marginal or anecdotal one, in the political struggles of the day. Creative minds adopted polemical positions, and new contributions pressed art into political and social service with works that probed socially relevant topics, and either affirmed or decried American customs and values widely touted as "traditional," essential to the nation's character, or even God-ordained. This book focuses on the challenges that artists active in the 1930s musical and theatrical fields faced when addressing these new themes. The task of maintaining the fragile balance between artistic ambitions and the need to engage audiences with a vernacular idiom that they could easily grasp, as we will see, was often insurmountable. However, when artists managed to find the perfect union between experimentation and populist intent, they were able to move audiences toward social change.

An increasing sensitivity to the needs and struggles of a suffering population and an attempt to engage workers of all industries in musical and dramatic pursuits characterized much artistic production in New York City in the 1930s. While the city's channels devoted to music and musical theater were in crisis, interest in radical politics and the growing importance of the labor movement intensified and offered composers new opportunities to bridge the gap with audiences and to write socially functional works. A new audience opened doors to American composers: the working class. Left-leaning musical institutions, such as the Workers Music League, the American Music League, the American League against War and Fascism, the Downtown Music School, and the art programs of the New Deal's Works Progress Administration, sponsored concerts, recitals, and lectures, and organized amateur choruses and orchestras. In striving to communicate with this new audience, a generation of young artists often moved with apparent ease from complicated intellectual heights to simplest forms of expression. The case of the Composers' Collective of New York, whose members had been trained primarily within elitist Eurocentric canons yet desired to promote social awareness in an idiom comprehensible to the masses, exemplifies this dichotomy. Similarly, the members of the Workers' Theater Movement offered productions loaded with artistic pretensions that were often equally reliant on naïveté, cheapness, and political propaganda.

Among American composers, perhaps none seems more strongly to represent the zeitgeist of the 1930s than Marc Blitzstein (1905–64). The composer contributed to the activities of most of the major left-leaning musical and theatrical organizations operating in the decade and deliberately attempted to define a new form of expression to unsettle political and social conventions. In striving to achieve his goals, Blitzstein embodied the tension between artistic aspirations and political commitment that typified the socially relevant music of the time. On one side, his political interests, as well as his fascination with vernacular idioms and musical theater, often put him at odds with what was expected of a serious composer, and he never assumed a leading role in American art music. On the other side, his background complicated his significance as "the social conscience of American music," using Eric Gordon's words.[1] His childhood was spent in the cultivated environment of a Russian Jewish family of bankers, in which socialist inclinations combined with typical concerns of the upper middle class. The young Blitzstein enjoyed all the benefits his social status conferred, including musical training from an early age and opportunities to travel and study with major composers and pedagogues such as Arnold Schoenberg and Nadia Boulanger. In 1928, when he met the German-born critic and novelist Eva Goldbeck, he began promoting the concept of socially relevant music.[2] His desire to engage with the working class eventually found fulfillment in his participation with the Composers' Collective of New York, for which he served as secretary from 1935 until its demise. In the same period, he was also active in the administration of the Downtown Music School. Blitzstein's political and social activities included not only composing and teaching, but also writing. Some of his reviews and articles—he contributed to *Modern Music, The Musical Quarterly, New Masses*, and the *Daily Worker*—are among the most vivid testimonies of the intersection between music and politics in the 1930s, and they articulated his ideas about music's social function. "The art is renewing itself," wrote Blitzstein in his article "Coming—The Mass Audience!" as he led musicians to take advantage of unprecedented possibilities for professional involvement.[3] Yet, as was true of most other left-oriented fellow composers, Blitzstein encountered difficulties in fully reconciling his elitist and affluent upbringing with the proletariat. These tensions, as I will demonstrate, are at the core of the most engaging and vivid manifestation of contemporary artistic musical endeavors.

Americans in the 1930s were hardly the first to utilize the fine arts in general, and music in particular, for sociopolitical ends. Since the time of ancient Greece, political leaders and theorists have remarked upon, and often exploited, music's capacity to foster change and communicate with individuals in profound and complex ways. While art's cohesive power perfectly suited the political and social needs of the time, the issue of communicability became paramount as artists involved in left-leaning musical and theatrical organizations felt pressed

4 • *Introduction*

to address the sociopolitical needs of a growing class of blue-collar workers. Lacking the tools to communicate with such a new audience, they searched for an adequate idiom and often found themselves entangled in experiments where artistic and functional goals clashed, as in the case of the musical revue *Parade*, where a dogmatic communist message obscured the character of this type of light entertainment, or the mass songs of the *Workers Song Books* whose musical language combined marching rhythms, simple melodies, and harsh dissonant modernist harmonies.

The acceleration of life propelled by technological innovations, which typified the first decades of the twentieth century, came to these artists' aid as it intensified the use of creative expression to promote political agendas. Technology revolutionized the concepts of space and time, and ideas could move nationwide through radio and other communication media. Blue- and white-collar workers claimed a more active role in American democracy. In 1936, Blitzstein vividly described this new picture of American society:

> The great mass of people enters at last the field of serious music. Radio is responsible, the talkies, the summer concerts, a growing appetite, a hundred things; really the fact of an art and a world in progress. You can no more stop it than you can stop an avalanche.[4]

Indeed, artists and broadcasting network companies, taking advantage of recordings, radio, and film industry, nurtured the middle class's demand for art, and in many instances imposed musical trends through national broadcasts (i.e., the Eurocentric programs of Toscanini and the NBC Symphony Orchestra). The alliance between technology and the arts proved so powerful that even the federal government came to exploit its ability to spread ideas. The Federal Project One of the WPA, which started in 1935, prompted de facto, government institutionalization of the arts and exploited technology to disseminate nationwide the work done under the aegis of the Roosevelt administration.

Blitzstein's commitment, as well as that of all other artists involved in the leftist movements of the 1930s, must however be considered within the broad historical context that shaped the environment in which they worked. Although the Wall Street derailment of 1929 provides a handy marker, the complex circumstances that initiated the artistic paradigm shift of the 1930s commenced in the aftermath of World War I and accelerated during the "Roaring Twenties," when the perceived dichotomy between tradition and modernization, morality and immorality, and the native-born and the alien launched a series of upheavals in American life. The ensuing conflicts prompted regulation of immigration, Prohibition, intensification of the Ku Klux Klan's activity, the red scare, and the Palmer Raids. These historical circumstances deeply affected the social conditions of the 1930s and are fundamental to understanding the Roosevelt administration's relief actions.

To reconstruct the American economy and restore national confidence, Roosevelt and his administration initiated in 1933 a series of programs called the "New Deal" with the goal of relief, recovery, and reform of the United States economy. Roosevelt's plan addressed the immediate needs of those Americans—nearly a third of the population by then—who had lost their jobs. The New Deal culminated in 1935 with the establishment of the Works Progress Administration (WPA), which created working opportunities for skilled and unskilled American laborers. Blue-collar workers, especially immigrants and minority individuals who suffered political, social, and economical marginalization in pre-Depression America, felt momentarily empowered; some embraced Marxist ideologies and joined the "class struggle." Left-leaning Americans, and to a certain extent the American Communist Party encouraged by the Communist International, exerted a considerable influence in this redefinition of the labor movement. Socialist ideologies became even more appealing than they had been at the beginning of the Depression after 1935, when the Popular Front stance shifted attention from communist issues toward the promotion of anti-fascism and social equality.[5] A network of membership organizations founded during the decade supported this leftist agenda, including the American League Against War and Fascism in 1933 (renamed the American League for Peace and Democracy in 1937), the American Youth Congress in 1934, the League of American Writers in 1935, the National Negro Congress in 1936, and the American Congress for Democracy and Intellectual Freedom in 1939. But this new direction exacerbated class conflicts and devolved into a bitter critique of Roosevelt's New Deal. These tensions triggered attacks from conservative blocs that halted the expansion of the agenda and eventually, by the early 1940s, successfully abolished most of its programs.

While active, the New Deal also provided much-needed relief for the workers in the arts and entertainment industry. With most Americans struggling to feed their families, thousands of entertainment workers had lost their jobs as various theaters, opera companies, and orchestras were forced to cancel or curtail their seasons. Even the Metropolitan Opera, a major institution, lost the support of many of its wealthy donors and, by the end of 1932, had to resort to a fundraiser organized by singer Lucrezia Bori and the "Committee to Save the Metropolitan Opera House" to raise money to keep the next season alive.[6] Primarily to relieve this situation, in August 1935, the chief administrator of the WPA, Harry Hopkins, launched a major project involving four commissions to promote art,

6 · *Introduction*

theater, literature, and music: the Federal Project One (FPO).[7] The WPA initially supported the project with $27 million and, as Eleanor Roosevelt commented in her column "My Day," for a few years the federal government served as patron of the arts.[8] The primary task of the FPO included the employment of artists and workers of the arts on relief rolls who could not find employment in the private industry. How to define the program of the FPO and reach these goals, however, became a sensitive issue, a lightning rod for social and political tensions. Each of the four projects had to face different issues not only peculiar to their own cultural histories but also to the personal experience of its members. The officers of the FPO sought a balance between channeling artistic creativity toward the promotion of patriotic feelings and allowing freedom of expression to government-subsidized artists. The task proved particularly difficult, in no small part because of its political implications: should the government finance artists who end up producing potentially subversive material?

The revolutionary threat was legitimate, as many of the artists, workers, and officers involved in the FPO already had expressed strong left-wing tendencies and considered the arts a fundamental tool for social and political change. Many conservative Americans perceived the Federal Theater Project (FTP), which produced some of the most innovative staging of the period, as particularly hostile because of its left-leaning inclinations. The project attracted many playwrights, actors, and directors who, during the first half of the decade, had affiliated themselves with communist organizations and had actively contributed to the leftist Workers' Theater Movement. Furthermore, the declared goal of the FTP's director, Hallie Flanagan, was to create socially relevant theater, a position that proved dangerous as the FTP, more so than the other divisions of the FPO, endured attacks by anti–New Dealers and conservatives who accused it of communist infiltration. Not surprisingly, by 1937 political pressures both within and outside the presidential administration had begun to undermine Flanagan's dream of socially relevant American theater, and the FTP folded in 1939. Aside from the issue of its presumed communist infiltration, the FTP arguably became less prominent also because it lacked an overtly patriotic program to balance its explicitly liberal and class-conscious activities—a feature present, as we will see, in the more popular, and less politically charged, Federal Music Project (FMP).

Perhaps no group of workers in the entertainment industry suffered more than musicians, whose anxiety—already heightened thanks to a prolonged period of job losses during Prohibition when live performances declined—mounted as technological innovations progressed and the Great Depression deepened.[9] In 1929 alone, mechanized sound production, first introduced in

1927 with *The Jazz Singer*, replaced some 22,000 theater musicians, and radio and records replaced live musicians in public venues.[10] By 1933, approximately two-thirds of the nation's professional musicians were unemployed, with between 12,000 and 15,000 of them located in the New York metropolitan area. The United States government estimated that, by 1934, this unemployment rate had climbed to more than 70 percent. Those musicians who managed to keep their jobs barely managed to earn a living wage. With its plan to subsidize unemployed individuals, the FMP not only restored some hope in a brighter future and faith in the federal government, but it also created much-needed jobs: by 1936, it had employed more than 15,000 musicians in newly founded orchestras, bands, choruses, and opera units nationwide.[11] This project, more than the other branches of the FPO, aimed also to stimulate community interest, educate audiences, rebuild Americans' self-confidence, and cultivate a sense of patriotism, proving that, in the words of its director Nikolai Sokoloff, "all of this music belongs to the nation."[12] During its first year of activity, 32 million Americans attended a nationwide network of 36,000 musical events, most of which were free, in theaters and open-air venues, but also in public schools, hospices, hospitals, orphanages, and many other places where music, and especially classical music, previously had held little or no sway.[13]

However, the artistic value of the FMP did not always match its statistical success. Issues of control and Sokoloff's conservative attitude toward musical repertoire tainted the FMP's achievement and provoked an ongoing debate about the relative cultural value of cultivated and vernacular music, which affected not only much of its musical production and the ranking of musicians on relief rolls, but also the dissemination of American contemporary music nationwide.[14] Sokoloff mainly encouraged programs involving classical music; his decision prompted questions concerning the use of cultivated music to underscore social and cultural distinctions among audiences, and it cast doubt on his actual knowledge of American audiences and their musical tastes. To overcome these charges and counteract accusations that because he was not born in the United States, he was not adequately American, he surrounded himself with an advisory committee that included some of the most famous musical personalities of the time, such as Walter Damrosch, George Gershwin, Howard Hanson, and Leopold Stokowski. He also requested that at least one-fourth of the season's programming feature American composers. Nonetheless, during 1935–36, he fed audiences countrywide with the already beloved and familiar European canon and the most accessible and popular American composers (e.g., John Philip Sousa, George Gershwin, Stephen Foster, and Victor Herbert). Thereby his division did little to promote the actual dissemination at a national

8 · *Introduction*

level of modernist American art music and, to some extent, it simultaneously undermined the educational mission of the FMP. Sokoloff's excessive desire to please audiences nationwide failed to satisfy the demands of living composers and their advocates and tended to exacerbate the tension between innovation and populism that typified much musical production of the 1930s. Moreover, the dissemination of government-sponsored events that barely encouraged cultural growth of the audience constituted, especially at this particular historical moment, a veritable menace: it raised issues of state control over artistic expression and invited comparison with totalitarian regimes in Europe, such as German Nazism and Italian fascism, which blatantly used music for propagandistic reasons.[15] This position became even more precarious in 1937, when conservatives attacked certain branches of the FPO for their overtly left-leaning activities.

Sokoloff, to protect himself and the FMP's programs, opposed even more strongly artistic radicalism and retreated into overtly nationalistic endeavors such as the American Music Festival organized in 1938. This three-day gala, officially in honor of George Washington, showcased FMP units in more than one hundred cities countrywide and emphasized its nationalistic aspect by featuring American themes and music of composers such as Sousa and Foster, genuine bulwarks of national pride. Similarly, the FMP premiered in 1938 in Los Angeles with the LA Federal Orchestra a rather unsuccessful nationalistic opera entitled *Gettysburg*, commissioned for the seventy-fifth anniversary of the battle and composed by Harris Hutchins Ruger with a libretto by Arthur Robinson. Within this scenario, though, the distinctive avant-garde musical inclination that had characterized New York City since at least the early 1920s proved able to combine artistic endeavors with liberal tendencies embodied in the New Deal populist program. Even the FMP—which on a nationwide basis tended to promote nationalistic impulses in a predominantly conservative way—contributed in the City to experimental and socially relevant aspects of music in more progressive ways. For instance, it provided venues for composers of new music to present their works to an audience, such as the New York City Composers' Forum Laboratory established in 1935 as part of the FMP's Music Education Division. Indeed, the activities of the New York City branch of the FMP resonated throughout the United States where often similar endeavors were replicated in other major cities, meeting with similar strong support as well as strong resistance.

The many relief activities promoted by the FPO prompted an unprecedented politicization of American art, as artists intent on probing fissures in American society turned perhaps most often to themes of alternative political systems and the role of individuals in group contexts. Predictably, social concerns also found a powerful voice in numerous plays promoted by authors already involved in the Workers' Theater Movement or left-oriented theatrical groups such as the Theatre Union. Manifestations of the economic collapse of the 1930s appear even in the works of mainstream playwrights, writers, and organizations that did not overtly espouse the communist cause. For instance, Maxwell Anderson's *Both Your Houses* (1933), Clifford Odets's *Waiting for Lefty* (1935), and Eugene O'Neill's *The Iceman Cometh* (1939) all portrayed social problems pertinent to the increasing national sense of desperation. Many novels of the period, as well, criticized middle-class social and economic values and opposed the way capitalist oppression dispossessed the working class: James T. Farrell's trilogy featuring the protagonist Studs Lonigan (1932–35) dealt with urban workers, and John Steinbeck's *Grapes of Wrath* (1939) portrayed the hardships endured by a family of farmers in Oklahoma battered by drought and changes in the agricultural industry. Moreover, in the 1930s, the arts functioned not only as a means to express the anguish of society, but also to affirm traditional values, a feature that the New Deal embraced to promote its activities. The arts helped many Americans to feel united as a nation, overcome their vulnerability, and find a common sense of hope for a better future. Americanism and regionalism signified artistic tendencies embracing values that, ironically, promoted at the same time individualism and collectivity, urban and rural life, conservative and liberal ideologies. The Regionalist art movement, led by Thomas Hart Benton (Missouri), Grant Wood (Iowa), and John Steuart Curry (Kansas), captured this multifaceted reality in artworks depicting large urban scenes and simpler rural landscapes untouched by industrialization. In some instances, regionalists sought to make political statements, but, especially during the Great Depression, their almost naïve naturalism and reassuring images of regional life helped to rebuild American pride.[16]

In music, artistic freedom and variety fulfilled the needs of a wide-ranging audience, which, according to Virgil Thomson, consisted of three well-defined types:

> 1) The luxury-trade, capitalist Toscanini public riding with sedate satisfaction in streamlined trains from Beethoven to Sibelius and back.
>
> 2) The professor-and-critic conspiracy for internationalist or "contemporary" music, which prizes hermeticism and obscurantism and makes a cult out of the apparent complexities in systematically discordant counterpoint.
>
> 3) The theatre-public of the leftist-front, a public of educated, urban working people who want educated, urban spokesmen for their ideals.[17]

10 · *Introduction*

Thomson's third type is indeed the "new audience" that Blitzstein and a large group of young modernist composers of leftist persuasion living in New York City addressed, an audience that called for more than folk music and songs of protest to express its concerns.

Yet, while discussing the music produced in the 1930s, scholars have often focused on folk music as a weapon in the class struggle and only marginally addressed the work of non-folk-oriented musical endeavors. For instance, *The Beautiful Music All Around Us* by Stephen Wade provides an analysis of field recording of American folk songs, and Robbie Lieberman's *My Song Is My Weapon* looks at the political use of folk song as communist propaganda.[18] An important contribution in this field is Richard A. Reuss's *American Folk Music and Left-Wing Politics, 1927–1957*, which, among others, considers the 1930s leftist influence on art music to argue that its decay coincides with the growth of American radical political interest in folk traditions.[19]

Other authors have specifically focused on how the Federal Music Project offered venues for performance and musical experimentation on the West Coast of the United States, such as Peter Gough in *Sounds of the New Deal*.[20] Leta E. Miller in *Music and Politics in San Francisco from the 1906 Quake to the Second World War* problematizes the FMP's conflicting aims of unemployment relief and artistic excellence in the West Coast city, and Catherine Parsons Smith, in *Making Music in Los Angeles: Transforming the Popular*, investigates how the FMP summed up the role of music making between the Progressive era and later generations.[21]

When addressing the 1930s on the East Coast, scholars tend to discuss the musical life and leftist views of the decade within a broader analysis of the intersections between music and politics in the first half of the century in the United States or address only specific moments in the life of a composer or the activities of one entity. These contributions are relevant to the understanding of some specific aspects of music in the 1930s—for example, those of Carol Oja, Elizabeth Bergman Crist, Melissa de Graaf, and Sally Bick, which focus on *The Cradle Will Rock*, Aaron Copland in the 1930s, the Composers' Forum Laboratory, and the New School for Social Research in New York City, respectively.[22] None, though, considers how the same composers were rather freely moving from musical to theatrical, from federally sponsored to private, or from politically to artistically motivated endeavors. Indeed, while the abundant discourse on the theoretical aspects of using music for political ends was not always matched with successful instrumental or choral music written for that purpose, we find the most convincing political value of music when associated with theater. *Art Music Activism: Aesthetics and Politics in 1930s New York City* covers this aspect and

Introduction • 11

discusses an array of music and musical theater activities of the decade as a coherent unit to understand the depth of their imprint on American society.

This book is divided into chapters that look closely at documentary and archival evidence to present scenarios in which music and theater combining experimentation and populist interests were successful, or failed, in advancing the promotion, circulation, and acceptance of left-leaning sociopolitical ideas in 1930s New York City. Each chapter investigates a case study highlighting how tensions between aesthetics and pragmatic goals shifted artistic interests while still producing works that were at the center of the sociopolitical and cultural life of the decade. The first two chapters introduce the topics and main actors of the kaleidoscopic story that unfolds throughout the decade. Chapter 1 investigates the goals of the Composers' Collective of New York and ties their work to the successful songs of protest of the American labor movement to demonstrate how the combination of musical experimentation, populism, and political propaganda did not always help the group to advance left-leaning political ideas nor to produce artistic masterpieces. Under the sway of the Communist Party, these composers led by Charles Seeger searched for a musical language that could communicate with the masses and give voice to their needs. They aimed to establish an American proletarian music and envisioned it as an emerging musical style comparable to classicism or romanticism, but two inherent problems, one aesthetic and the other political, prevented the radical movement from reaching its objectives. Still, the stylistic experiments of the Collective contributed to the artistic maturity of composers such as Elie Siegmeister and Marc Blitzstein.

Chapter 2 examines the political use of music within the American Workers' Theater Movement (WTM). In particular, it describes how an essential blend of experimentation and vernacular idioms succeeded in addressing workers' sensibilities and issues and eventually led to the politicization of the musical revue. A survey of the activities of the WTM in the late 1920s and how they affected the movement during the years of the Depression will demonstrate that whereas the labor theater aimed to help the communist cause, the movement was also instrumental in building a new politicized American musical theater. The role that the musical vernacular had in this pursuit is considered, with a discussion of the reasons that determined opposing critical successes of the musical revues *Parade* (1935) and *Pins and Needles* (1937), which arguably signaled the entrance of the "left wing" theater into the field of the Broadway musical revue.

The next three chapters explore how composers and theater practitioners active within the politically charged Composers' Collective and WTM became prominent actors within the artistic endeavors promoted by the WPA. They investigate the tensions these artists encountered in balancing creative aims with experimentation, accessible content, and sociopolitical message. Beginning in June 1935, the New York branch of the Federal Music Project offered a temporary answer to these composers' needs not only by giving them meaningful financial relief but also by encouraging experimentation in artistic content and form. One of these venues was the Composers' Forum Laboratory, which allowed American composers to present and discuss their own music with the audience. Chapter 3 shows, though, that many modernist composers, while in principle understanding that they had to respond with their music to the contemporary sociopolitical situation, were reticent about being overtly political. Through reception history methodologies, primary sources are analyzed, such as the transcripts of the Q&A sessions that followed each concert, to demonstrate that, even if solicited by an eager audience, composers never crossed the subtle line between music and politics. In fact, rather elitist musical activities such as these forums, even when involving otherwise politically engaged composers, rarely intersected with political activism, as most participants avoided overt declaration of their political affiliations or leanings and favored discussions on the definition of musical Americanism.

While the Federal Theater Project served as a site for artistic avant-gardism, a seemingly paradoxical union of experimentation and populist intents lay at the basis of its own being. Particularly representative of this trend were the productions of the Living Newspaper Unit of New York, which were notorious for powerful sociopolitical messages delivered with a combination of experimentation and accessibility and are the subject of Chapter 4. Drawing primarily on materials of the WPA held at the National Archive, the chapter demonstrates ways in which the living newspapers provided an often-unacknowledged medium to try new musical innovations. It argues that the experimental nature of the living newspapers offered a potential forum for testing some of the same original musical approaches that were at the center of contemporary musical modernism, including a growing interest in percussion and non-Western music. Chapter 4 also considers how the editorial team of *Ethiopia* challenged the stereotypical portrayal of ethnicity that had typified Broadway conventions. It then addresses how Virgil Thomson's score for *Injunction Granted* matched the denunciation of the struggle of unionism against capitalism and the court system with modernist percussive and incisive musical commentary.

Chapter 5 explores the role of Blitzstein's *The Cradle Will Rock*, a work that merged music and theater in a powerful example of political activism. This piece, successfully combining experimentation, vernacular idioms, and a sociopolitical message, was indeed one of the strongest manifestations of the labor theater. Scholars have often emphasized that *Cradle* freely draws upon a variety of American vernacular traditions and, most of all, Bertolt Brecht's epic theater and Kurt Weill's populist music. Yet the contemporary success of the play is mostly tied to the American Workers' Theater Movement and its search for new theatrical and musical forms to engage audiences in social change. *Cradle* stems from this experimental theater and represents the wrenching cultural shift of the United States during the Great Depression. Revisiting its reception, though, displays that the left-wing theater's exploitation of the piece masked its artistic merits. The use of *Cradle* as the quintessential example of workers' theater led to a myth that discouraged commentators from considering its artistic value. Comparing selected sketches from *Cradle* in their piano version with the original orchestrated version displays Blitzstein's musical ingenuity and the still constructive effectiveness of the script. But the political climate, as well as the left theater's manipulation of its premiere, prevented the work from obtaining the artistic acclaim it deserved.

In 1930s New York City, the combination of experimentation and populism did not always succeed in mobilizing the masses against the perceived threat of capitalism and in advancing the promotion of left-leaning sociopolitical ideas. In fact, even if the artists involved in this controversial movement genuinely believed they could make a difference, most of their musical and theatrical activities failed to provide workers with revolutionary and ambitious works. The book's epilogue addresses the tensions that led to this outcome, explaining why we do not have a "masterpiece" of 1930s American music reflecting the Great Depression—not only because works from this time have been largely dismissed on aesthetic grounds, but also because of how this musical experience has been received and discussed since then, especially how it was framed during the Cold War period. Still, with their politically relevant and at times exciting works, these creative minds paved the road for the socially conscious use of art that typified so many American artistic movements to follow.

CHAPTER 1

Bourgeois Modernism for the Proletariat

The Composers' Collective

Music penetrates everywhere
It carries words with it
It fixes them in the mind
It graves them in the heart
Music is a weapon in the class struggle.

—Epigraph to *Workers Song Book No. 1* (New York: Workers Music
League, USA Section of International Music Bureau, 1934)

The years of the Great Depression coincided with a widespread demand for
art that could instill and sustain faith in a brighter future and define a stronger
American identity. As discussed in the introduction, though, balancing these
populist needs with aesthetic demands was not always easy, and it often constrained creative minds into complex and challenging artistic gridlocks. Some
composers, such as Roy Harris, successfully sought to build this new national
image by finding inspiration in the mythology of the American West, while others, for instance Aaron Copland and Virgil Thomson, focused on a rediscovered
popular appeal influenced by American folk and hymnody-like music.[1] A more
difficult way was chosen by the members of the Composers' Collective of New
York, a group of young artists, many of leftist persuasion, stimulated by a desire
to give music an active role in the political struggles of the day.

The composers of the Collective, some of whom are little known today, came
from a wide array of musical experiences. They represented the many trends of
contemporary American music, from the modernist approaches of Henry Cowell, Elie Siegmeister, Marc Blitzstein, and Charles Seeger to the populist music
of Earl Robinson and Lan Adomian, by way of the more conservative styles of

Norman Cazden, Herbert Haufrecht, and Henry Leland Clarke. Looking for a musical language that could communicate with the masses and give voice to the people's needs, they aimed to establish "American proletarian music." For the composers trained in the modernist tradition, the goal was also to pursue the development of an art music that would be free of many of the (real and perceived) constraints of European traditions, an objective that went beyond the demands of the sociopolitical target. Indeed, as we will see in this chapter, the heterogeneity of the group contributed to exacerbated tensions between artistic and propagandistic intents. Modernist aesthetic and simplicity of message clashed in an almost irreparable conflict as the musical product of the Composers' Collective, the two *Workers Song Books*, missed the initial aims. The extent to which the composers of the Collective promoted these aesthetic ideas clearly emerges in the content of a substantial document—twenty densely packed handwritten pages—that were originally misplaced in the Marc Blitzstein Papers housed at the State Historical Society in Madison, Wisconsin. The content of this document, which offers detailed evidence of the outcome of a Symposium on Proletarian Music that the Composers' Collective organized in June 1935, supports the claim that the dichotomy between aesthetic and political goals prevented the radical movement from reaching its objectives and led, eventually, to the collapse of the Collective itself.[2]

The Composers' Collective and the Proletariat

The Composers' Collective of New York formed in February 1932 as a subset of the Pierre Degeyter Club (named after the composer of "The Internationale").[3] The composer and critic Ashley Pettis, then a strong partisan of left-wing causes who later distanced himself from his leftist past, described the function of the Degeyter Club in *New Masses*:

> In New York and many other cities, revolutionary musical organizations are springing up under the name of "Pierre Degeyter Clubs," which are uniting the forces of class-conscious and politically-minded musicians. The functions of these groups are expanding daily through Service Bureaus, so that the activities of our musical craftsmen are becoming indissolubly linked with the lives of the workers in making available the best music to workers' organizations.[4]

Indeed, the already existing structural organization of the Degeyter Club in New York, which had its own chorus and orchestra and organized courses, lectures, and concerts while also being affiliated with the Workers Music League, provided the Collective with a wide potential audience.[5] This opportunity might

16 • CHAPTER 1

explain the enthusiastic response that the Composers' Collective, organized by Henry Cowell, Leon Charles, and Jacob Schaeffer, received from some prominent young American composers who were moved to social action during the Great Depression. Charles Seeger, who not only joined the group but contributed to its organizational plan, recalls that in the winter of 1931, Cowell told him:

> You know, Charlie, you were worried about the connection of music and society back there in Berkeley; there's a little group of good musicians who are moved by the Depression and are trying to make music that can go right out into the streets and be used in protests and at union meetings. I think you might be interested in it.[6]

While one could argue that, for the first time in American history, a group of organized professional musicians were embracing the communist call for action and were promoting music for the working class, as we will see, the heterogeneity of the Collective's membership also represented its weakness.[7]

An exhaustive list of all the members of the Collective does not exist, because some participants never officially joined, and others took part in only selected activities. Furthermore, most likely copying the comradely use of "combat names," several members adopted pseudonyms: L. E. Swift for Elie Siegmeister, Carl Sands for Charles Seeger, or Herbert Howe for Herbert Haufrecht. This choice had, no doubt, multiple advantages: not only did it allow some of the individuals to keep their ethnic origins unidentified (e.g., Siegmeister and Haufrecht), but it also enabled them to conceal their inability to blend the serious modern and the politically engaged composer. For instance, Seeger justified the use of his pseudonym, Carl Sands, to keep his achievements in musicology and ethnomusicology separated from his political endeavors. He did not want to compromise his efforts to establish the New York Musicological Society, as—according to David K. Dunaway—Seeger "was aware of the fact that the Collective was a dangerous adventure."[8] The following list relies on the names mentioned in Blitzstein's minutes and papers from the period during which he served as secretary of the Collective:

Official members:
Lan Adomian
Irving Bardansky
Janet Barnes [alias Jeannette Barnett?]
Marc Blitzstein
Irving Brooks
Harold Brown

Norman Cazden
Herman Chalof [alias Carlos Shaloff?]
Leon Charles [founder]
Henry Leland Clarke [alias J. Fairbanks]
Henry Cowell [founder]
Robert Gross [alias Robert Gates?]
Herbert Haufrecht [alias Herbert Howe]
Julius Keil
George Maynard
Mary Menk
Evelyn Modoi [alias Eve Lynn?]
Alex North
Gene Oliver
Ashley Pettis
Wallingford Riegger [alias J. C. Richards]
Jacob Schaeffer [founder]
Charles Seeger [alias Carl Sands]
Elie Siegmeister [alias L. E. Swift]
Earl Robinson

Unofficial members:
George Antheil
Aaron Copland
Ruth Crawford Seeger
Hanns Eisler [when in the United States][9]

This list includes many composers who were familiar to contemporary American musical circles, albeit often as representatives of musical modernism, a trend that had very little if anything to do with the struggle of the working class. Among the founders, for instance, Jacob Schaeffer was known for his interest in Jewish workers' choral music; he had founded the *Freiheit Gesangverein* in Chicago in 1912, an organization that later counted branches throughout the world, including the best known of these groups, the Jewish *Freiheit Gesangverein* (also known as the Freedom Singers' Society), which was first established in New Haven in 1923.[10] Henry Cowell, on the other side, was one of the ultra-modernists, and by 1931 his theosophical approach to music—including his interest in tone clusters as a symbol of the pervasive presence of the divine in the universe—and experiments in timbre and pitch had already carved his role as one of the most innovative American composers of the twentieth century.[11] Blitzstein himself had at the time little if any experience with music for the

18 • CHAPTER 1

working class. He had written the first composition for the proletarian movement, "Into the Streets May First" on a text by Alfred Hayes, as a contribution
to the *New Masses* 1934 contest for the May Day song. A holograph and a draft of
the song, both in Blitzstein's handwriting, are housed at the Wisconsin Historical Society in Madison, but his name does not appear among those of the nine
participants, suggesting the possibility that he might not have ever submitted
this work.[12] Unless, of course, he was the anonymous XYZ whom Ashley Pettis
mentioned in his *New Masses* review of the pieces in the contest:

> Certain of the songs, such as those by Adomian and XYZ have marked excellence
> in the melodic and rhythmic conception, but from the standpoint of harmonic
> construction are perhaps too sophisticated and *modern* for singers in workers'
> groups for whom mass songs are written.[13]

While there is no evidence that Blitzstein was the composer who concealed his
identity under the *nom de plume* XYZ, we could certainly recognize in his song
some of the qualities that Pettis outlined. The opening fanfare-like melodic and
rhythmic figuration is perfect for a marching and grand mass song, but the harsh
harmonies are those of a composer who still thinks that the audience cannot
be pampered and who is not ready to give up the modernist idiom in the name
of the workers. We know for sure, though, that Charles Seeger saw the song, as
he wrote a letter in which he encouraged Blitzstein not to give up and to write
more proletarian music, considering that

> [t]he mass song, which is to be sung by large crowds not because it is taught
> to them but because they have heard it and want to sing it, has some definite
> limitations that you must know about before trying again.[14]

In the same letter, Seeger also invited him to actively engage with the Collective
and, soon after receiving this letter, Blitzstein became the secretary of the group.

Besides emphasizing the musical diversity of the participating composers, the
list of the members of the Collective shows a scant presence of female composers
and raises questions about the artistic role of women in society and as promoters
of socially relevant music. In the early 1930s, at the height of the Great Depression, female professionals in the arts suffered more than their male counterparts,
who were still considered the breadwinners, and many lost their jobs as composers, performers, and educators. This might explain why very few female composers were involved in the activities of the Composers' Collective. Economic crisis
apart, though, women had to face other challenges in an essentially patriarchal
and hostile musical environment where, already in the early 1920s, Deems Taylor
claimed that women were responsible for the weakness of American music, as

its educational rather than artistic aspect reflected their strong presence.[15] Issues associated with gender and the feminization of American music in the early twentieth century are at the core of scholarship reclaiming the role of female composers, but they are also vividly present in some contemporary accounts.[16] For instance, Marion Bauer describes the opposition women perceived when, in the Q&A session of a Composers' Forum Laboratory concert, she was asked why there are not many women composers and answered: "There are a great many more than you think. What many women composers need is encouragement and an opportunity to work and to be taken seriously."[17]

Unsurprisingly then, the musical stereotypes that women faced among male American musical modernists also shaped the relationship between male composers and the less than a handful of women listed in Blitzstein's minutes. One wonders if the not always covert hostility of male composers toward female composers within the leftist musical movement of the 1930s could be linked to the alleged role of women in American music and a desire to preserve the manliness of the political engagement. This reading would explain, for instance, the many micro and macro aggressions against Janet Barnes, possibly the most active woman within the Collective. The tension between Barnes and the rest of the members of the group is evident in the minutes of the meetings of the Collective on May 10, 1935, which show her frustration with the rest of the group as she threatened to leave on the grounds that she did not learn anything from being a member. She was also complaining of the treatment that the members reserved for a friend of hers, a singer named Mrs. Schwartz, who apparently was not successful in performing some of their works. The Collective solved the friction with a written apology delivered to Schwartz by Siegmeister and Blitzstein, but the action did not indicate a change of heart toward female musicians, who continued to face major obstacles throughout the 1930s with little or no assistance to support their work.[18] The harshest attack against Barnes's work came by way of Aaron Copland in a 1934 article.[19] Reviewing the content of the first *Workers Song Book* published by the Composers' Collective, Copland found ways to praise male composers even when criticizing their musical efforts, yet he did not show any lenience for the only woman featured in the book, and stated about her song, "God to the Hungry Child by Janet Barnes is immature and might well have been omitted."[20] He put the bitter and insensitive comment in parenthesis, as though it were an afterthought not even deserving the reader's attention. However, as we will see below, Barnes was a rather skillful composer, as this particular song demonstrated.

The unlikely assortment of the members of the Collective may at first sight seem puzzling, but it acquires meaning if we look at it in its context. To

20 · CHAPTER 1

understand why such a diverse group of composers joined forces to promote music for the working class, it is useful to briefly trace the sociopolitical circumstances that led to its foundation.

Michael (Mike) Gold, prominent communist columnist and novelist, wrote in October 1933: "Why don't American workers sing? The Wobblies knew how, but we have still to develop a communist Joe Hill."[21] By evoking the memory of Hill, Gold's statement ties proletarian music of the early 1930s and its mass songs to the peculiar early twentieth-century American singing experience of the Industrial Workers of the World (IWW).[22] The Wobblies used to spread their message through songs, which they collected in various editions of the *Little Red Songbook*. The inflammatory message of these songs, set to singable and mostly already familiar tunes, helped expand and solidify the union. The texts addressed separation of workers from capitalism and oppression of the working class, as well as the divisiveness of existing craft organizations and the horrors of industrialization.[23] Indeed, Gold had a point: Hill, an author widely credited with making the IWW a singing movement, became something of an icon, an emblem of the injustices that the capitalist establishment perpetuated against the American working class. Hill's enduring fame among workers finds substantiation in the popularity of the song "Joe Hill" that lyricist Alfred Hayes and composer Earl Robinson, both involved in the efforts of the Composers' Collective of New York, dedicated to him in 1936.[24]

The same propagandistic qualities also characterized the musical activities of the American Communist Party when, at the turn of the 1930s, it identified music as a major educational tool capable of building social awareness and indoctrinating members. The party actively promoted proletarian music and, in its two principal printed media *New Masses* and the *Daily Worker*, communist writers urged composers to address the working class in the hope that revolutionary music would move masses to action by awakening class consciousness. Moreover, the communist intelligentsia endorsed mass events (including strike rallies and union meetings) in which choral singing could serve as a means of galvanizing the group into a unified body, and it encouraged the understanding of mass red songs as weapons in the class struggle. Yet these efforts were initially unsuccessful, as workers and composers seemed uninterested in these goals. Already in 1927, in the "Letters from Our Readers" column of the *Daily Worker*, a reader voiced the negative consequences of this indifference: "It is hard for a movement to grow if it cannot express itself in song. Let the Workers School teach one more subject—teaching of the revolutionary songs."[25]

To foster choral activity among workers and exploit the educational potential of music, on June 14, 1931, members of the American Communist Party established the Workers Music League (WML) as a division of the US section of the

International Music Bureau. With branches in the major cities, the WML at first supported various workers' musical organizations representing different nationalities and ethnic groups. Eventually, it developed into the central organization of all music forces connected with the Communist Party and ancillary revolutionary working-class movements. In *New Masses* in July 1931, though, Gold had already started to complain that the most successful workers' chorus, the 300-member *Freiheit Gesangverein*, was singing pieces that were too complicated for the workers, and he claimed that "there are no workers' songs and music being written in this country."[26] Indeed, the American proletariat in music lacked both an original repertory and a suitable idiom. In its first attempt at producing proletarian music, in 1932, the WML had compiled the *Red Song Book*, a collection of original and contrafacta songs meant to act as a stimulus for the organization of workers' singing groups.[27] But, as Gold argued in *New Masses*, to create and organize a durable working-class movement American workers needed to follow the "great" examples of Germany and the Soviet Union and employ culture.[28] To achieve this goal, composers had to define a proletarian musical style aimed at a genuine worker's voice: a "new revolutionary music" that would express a "revolutionary content."

Cultivating this American proletarian musical style, one that could speak of and to the people, thus became one of the major concerns of the members of the Composers' Collective. Their main task and challenge consisted in finding a way to connect with the masses of workers. They all agreed that the mass song was the best tool to achieve their goal. The problem, though, became aligning the aesthetic premises of the composers with those of the workers, something that, despite their enthusiasm, many members were unable to pursue. Copland, in 1934, was still addressing this tension when he argued that "we as musicians will naturally listen to these songs primarily as music, but the workers who sing them will in the first instance decide how they apply to the actualities of the daily struggle."[29] Composers attempted to raise the musical level of the masses and simultaneously learn from them but, as we will see, not everyone succeeded in finding the perfect balance between artistic aspirations and political allegiance.

Defining Proletarian Music

The period of intense commitment to music as a weapon in the class struggle started in winter 1932–33 with a seminar led by Charles Seeger and Henry Cowell on the topic "Historical and Theoretical Factors in the Composing of Workers' Songs."[30] The meetings addressed the technique of writing songs as an answer to workers' needs and to redirect and refine their musical taste.[31] The material available in the Marc Blitzstein Papers shows that the Collective's activities toward this goal fell into three broad categories: they published two *Workers Song Books*; they organized concerts to promote their music in collaboration with the WML, the International Composers' Guild, and the League of Composers; and they coordinated a series of music courses in collaboration with the New School for Social Research.[32] In particular, attempting to share their interests with the working class, unions, and other left-leaning intellectual organizations, the members of the Composers' Collective developed guidelines for "proletarian music," a new initiative intended to educate workers' musical tastes and cultivate political consciousness. The Collective's weekly meetings focused principally on the definition of an American proletarian musical style, on reconsiderations of the validity of the "art for art's sake" modernist aesthetic stance, and on ways to fulfill the musical needs of the working class.

In a draft of a text intended for use in a promotional pamphlet, the Collective outlined the musical genres most appropriate for these goals:

A) Mass songs:
The need for mass songs dealing with most immediate burning social issues, serving as a unifying force, to be sung at meetings, parades, demonstrations, and on the picket line (ex. United Front, Strike against war, Scottsboro Boys).
B) Choral songs:
The need for choral music to be sung by the ever growing number of amateur as well as professional choral groups both at concerts and at meetings, dealing with themes taken from the life and problems of the workers, farmers, youth, professionals of the country (ex. Flying Squadron, Ballad of Harry Sims, Sistern and Brethren).
C) Solo songs:
The need for solo songs dealing with these same themes, to be sung by trained as well as untrained singers at all gatherings, meetings and festivities to replace the sentimental, exotic, highly-subjective "popular" or "art" songs which serve to concentrate attention on purely personal and private emotions to the exclusion of realistic social questions (ex. Angelo Hernion, Death-House Blues).
D) Instrumental music:
The need (less immediate, perhaps, but no less important) for instrumental music (piano, chamber music, symphonic works) to express deepest feelings of the people. In the words of Romain Rolland (in his letter of greeting to the recent Congress of the People's Music Federation in Paris) "a music of the masses, a sort of musical fresco, in broad strokes and powerful sweeps, a music which embodies and arouses the people to joy and fury." Shostakovich has given us the first examples of this sort of music in his May Day and October Symphonies which are annually played in the Soviet Union on these dates and whose function it is, according to the composer, to unify in one spirit of solidarity great masses of people.[33]

They argued that this revolutionary music, in particular mass songs, would move the masses to action by awakening class consciousness in workers.

Initially, the communist tradition of workers' songs, especially the German examples of Hanns Eisler, became their principal model. Eisler's marching songs, written between 1926 and 1933, had gained some attention around the world; *"Roter Wedding," "Der heimliche Aufmarsch," "Stempellied," "Kominternlied," "Solidaritätslied,"* and the *"Einheitsfrontlied"* became emblems of the socialist movement. These functional teaching and fighting songs, expressions of a collective body, evince Eisler's reaction to the degeneration of music as a bourgeois commodity. They display a diatonic and texturally clear, almost folk-like, musical idiom that features economy of musical material. Usually in the minor mode (because Eisler felt it matched the threatening quality of the fighting workers), they present a dialectic between words and music. In his instructions to the singers, Eisler urged that they avoid the concept of "beautiful performance" and instead strive for rhythmic and precise singing, for clear declamation of the text without expression or sentimentalism, as his music already embeds the political message of the words.[34]

The composers who joined the Collective to offer with their music a solution to the political and economic problems of the Great Depression, though, voiced quite different musical aesthetics, from traditional conservative to radical modernist. Ironically, most of them shared a certain disdain for popular music, and the "good music" they intended to write for the masses derived from European art music. Their personal degree of involvement with the Communist Party varied, too. Some were card-carrying members but most never formally joined. According to Seeger, most of the members of the Collective really had little sympathy with "collective" music:

> The Collective members wouldn't listen to folk music; they were professional musicians, unconcerned with that low-grade stuff. Nobody in the Collective was interested in folk music. They didn't know anything about it, except from reading the first chapters of school textbooks, which began with the study of Greek music and folk music and then go on into Music. There was very little thought in the Collective of people singing our songs. The emphasis was on writing things for them to listen to. We didn't have much they could sing themselves, except songs with piano accompaniment, and there were lots of those.[35]

If these composers were not ready to write for the masses, then someone needed to teach them how to do it, a task that Seeger, even if aware that most members were unprepared to fulfill the workers' needs, took upon himself as the ideological and theoretical mastermind of the Composers' Collective. He penned the group's principal ideological statements, which were published in *Modern*

Music, the magazine of the League of Composers, and in the *Daily Worker* between January 1934 and June 1935.

In the article "On Proletarian Music," Seeger urged composers to address the working class and its struggle and promote the growth of an "American proletarian musical style":

> The proletariat has a clear realization of the content it wishes to have in the music it hears and in the music it will make for itself. It is a content expressing, and contributing to, the success of its struggle—a revolutionary content. But it has lacked, so far, a musical technic [*sic*] for the expression of this content. It has relied upon and found some use for trite and debased echoes of the existing bourgeois idiom.[36]

Echoing the view of the American Communist Party, he promoted music as an effective educational tool to foster social awareness and to indoctrinate. He envisioned "proletarian music" as an emergent musical style that would eventually evolve to be comparable to classicism or romanticism. He posited three phases for its development. The first stage would coincide with the definition of a style and the production of music *for* the proletariat. A "proletarian" composer would eventually have to avoid any similarity with bourgeois concert music. But a change in musical style could not happen overnight, because American audiences were still deeply drawn to the products of European art music. At least at the beginning, Seeger suggested that composers try to "be as bourgeois as possible" because "the new grows out of the old, retaining what is strong and discarding what is weak."[37]

Growing criticism of the influence of capitalism in music would characterize the second phase. Seeger considered romanticism a product of a decaying cultural and political system, and he disapproved of the fragmentary nature of contemporary bourgeois music and its conflicting tendencies. At the same time, though, he recognized in modern music a certain revolutionary potential in that it replaced old formulas with new techniques. But the extreme reliance on technical aspects demonstrated that bourgeois music lacked a balanced connection between *structure* (the workers) and *superstructure* (the intellectuals) and removed composers from both content and community. The proletarian composer, on the other hand, would aspire to build a "balanced society," to give voice to the proletariat, and to infuse music with revolutionary content.[38]

Like most of the members of the Collective, however, the Harvard-educated Seeger had been steeped in traditional musical training. Subsequently he had joined many other young American composers in Europe, where they were exposed to, and seduced by, the avant-garde. Consequently, in seeking to reconcile modernist music and proletarian songs, Seeger eventually concluded that innovative techniques must be used to express proletarian content. For the third phase of proletarian music—namely, the creation of music *of* the proletariat—he theorized a new style that would employ revolutionary techniques (a product of the intellectual superstructure) to express revolutionary content (a product of the proletarian structure). His instructions to the composers of American mass songs were few: write the largest part of the work in an idiom familiar to the masses, and introduce new technical parameters one at a time, so that the challenges would not be forbidding. In the end, the actual features that would give music its proletarian appeal remained obscure in Seeger's prospectus and, consequently, in the songs produced by the Collective.

The *Workers Song Books*

The Workers Music League published the most representative examples of proletarian music written by the Composers' Collective in two *Workers Song Books* respectively in 1934 and 1935.[39] The two publications included original a cappella choruses, mass and choral songs, and solo chants with piano accompaniment, mostly settings of newly written, pointedly proletarian texts. While the music associated with the working struggle until the 1930s essentially relied on contrafacta and on folk, religious, patriotic, or sentimental conventions, the new original proletarian style intended to increase the repertory of revolutionary music and show a "healthy and militant spirit that has been welcomed by American workers."[40]

The genre that initially defined the work of the Collective, thus, was the mass song meant to be performed by workers of the many choral organizations that were proliferating among members of American unions and in factories. In a collective exercise typical of Soviet-style composers' organizations, the members of the Collective jointly evaluated new works for their potential as proletarian music. As stated in the foreword to the first *Book*, "hardly a work comes through this critical fire without bearing the mark of modifications or alterations, proposed by colleagues and accepted by the composer." Moreover, because the *Books* assumed the didactic mission of providing music to suit workers' needs, the Collective in the foreword also claimed that mass choral organizations in New York City tested all the songs in rehearsals and performances prior to publication. There is indeed evidence that the songs were tested by Schaeffer's Jewish *Freiheit Gesangverein*, but not always with positive results, as Earl Robinson stated in an interview with Carol Oja:

> Most of the composers attempted to be original, and they were by no means near where the working class was. One of the members, Jacob Schaeffer, who

26 · CHAPTER 1

had a big Jewish chorus, would counsel them to be simpler, because his chorus couldn't sing anything they wrote.[41]

Performances of works by the Collective's members were also not always greeted with enthusiasm by workers' audiences. Siegmeister recalled:

> After the official program was over, the fireworks usually began. Members of the audience would rise and fire questions at the composers: "Where is the melody in your work?"—"Why did you write that composition?"—"What has your music to do with us?" Those questions sometimes made me angry, but after it was all over I realized that we had gotten the most honest and direct music criticism of all.[42]

These unsatisfactory results should not surprise as some of the young musical talents struggled to turn to a much simpler musical style to meet the requirements of proletarian music. If on the one hand we find composers arguing that workers' music should be simpler, on the other hand many, espousing Seeger's theories, wanted it to be revolutionary and modern as was the new proletarian movement. This antagonism would explain some of the paradoxes emerging from the two *Workers Song Books*.

The first book, besides Pierre Degeyter's "Internationale," which had become the anthem of all socialist parties and widely performed around the world, includes the following mass, choral, and solo songs by five members of the Collective: Carl Sands (Seeger), L. E. Swift (Siegmeister), Schaeffer, Adomian, and Barnes:

The Internationale	Pierre Degeyter
Mount the Barricades	Carl Sands (1933)
The Scottsboro Boys Shall Not Die	L. E. Swift (1933)
Hunger March	Jacob Schaeffer (1933)
Song to the Soldiers	Lan Adomian (1933)
Three Workers' Rounds	L. E. Swift (1933)
"Poor Mister Morgan"	
"Red Election Round"	
"Onward to Battle"	
Strife Song	Jacob Schaeffer (1926)
Lenin Our Leader	Jacob Schaeffer (1924)
Song of the Builders	Carl Sands (1933)
Red Soldiers Singing	Lan Adomian (1933)
God to the Hungry Child	Janet Barnes (1933)
A Negro Mother to Her Child	Lan Adomian (1930)

A characterizing feature of most of these compositions is that they rely on the primacy of words and their message set to a syllabic text setting. In fact, one of the tasks of the members of the Collective was inciting the masses and calling them to take an active part in the class struggle, and the stress on words as the principal carrier of meaning distinguished American proletarian music. This propagandistic intent is also evident in the concluding section of the foreword to the first book:

> A great audience calls forth great song. You are a great audience—the greatest that has ever been. As your call becomes clearer, stronger and more persistent by united mass action, great songs will come forth—the greatest that have ever been. Individual men will write them down, but YOU will make them![43]

The militant quality of the words of some of these songs is striking, especially if compared to those of some of the most popular songs produced by American workers. A typical example of more traditional songs would be those by Joe Hill published in the IWW *Little Red Songbooks*. Giving voice to the frustration, hostilities, and humor of the Wobblies, his songs, many contrafacta but some with newly composed tunes, including "Don't Take My Papa Away from Me," "The Rebel Girl," and "Workers of the World Awaken!," became popular within the movement. "The Rebel Girl" offers a typical example of his production. The simple text shows that Hill had limited literary aspirations, as does the rhyming technique that in many cases is definitely—in the word's more usual sense— "wobbly," and is reminiscent of a ballad, in verse and chorus format. It tells the story of a different type of woman, one who does not live in a mansion or care for clothes and jewelry, but a defiant woman who supports the union and fights for freedom:

> There are women of many descriptions
> In this queer world as everyone knows
> Some are living in beautiful mansions
> And are wearing the finest of clothes
> There are blue-blooded queens and princesses
> Who have charms made of diamonds and pearl
> But the only and thoroughbred lady
> Is the Rebel Girl
>
> *Chorus*
> That's the Rebel Girl
> That's the Rebel Girl
> To the working class she's a precious pearl
> She brings courage pride and joy
> To the fighting Rebel Boy
> We have girls before

28 • CHAPTER 1

but we need some more
In the Industrial Workers of the World
For it's great to fight for freedom
With a Rebel Girl

[...]

Figure 1.1. Joe Hill, "The Rebel Girl" (Chicago: Industrial Workers of the World, 1915)

Bourgeois Modernism for the Proletariat • 29

The music, in G major with excursions to the dominant and the relative minor, avoids dissonances and skillfully remains within the limits of the typical harmonic vocabulary of American folk songs and ballads. It has a regular phrase structure, either 4 or 8 measures always ending with a clear cadence, and a martial and spirited tempo; it employs a catchy melody for a syllabic setting that moves mainly stepwise, while the range never exceeds an octave (see figure 1.1).

The composers of the Collective, though, moved away from these ballad-like songs of protest and instead started writing harsh martial songs portraying images of strength and physicality. As the very model of modern workers' music, Seeger cited, in "On Proletarian Music," the three-part round "Onward to Battle," words and music by Siegmeister (alias L. E. Swift), from the first *Workers Song Book*. The text of the round is much more direct and inciting to fight than the romanticized description of the rebel girl in Hill's song:

A- Onward to battle,
Join in the fight,
This world is our world
Let us unite.

B- Onward to battle,
Workers of all countries,
Let's unite.

C- Break your chains
And join our ranks,
Join in with us,
Come fight with us.

Each stanza is set to a different 4-measure phrase, and in the performance notes Siegmeister instructs the conductor to divide the chorus into three groups. After a full choir performance of the song in its entirety, the first group starts at A and sings the song twice; the second group begins at A when the first reaches B and sings the song twice, too; the third group starts at A when the first one reaches C. Once the third group completes the second run through of the song, without interruption, the full chorus sings the song one last time but at double the speed, always clearly enunciating the words.[44] Seeger described the musical features of the round:

There is, in a brisk tempo, alternation of four-four and five-eight meter that would cause difficulty for most bourgeois choruses. But workers' choruses that have tried it do not have any trouble. Roughly speaking, if something unusual is done in one department [i.e., rhythm] it is wise to risk little in others [e.g., harmony] at that time. This speaks of the music that workers will sing.[45]

Yet, while rounds are a popular form, usually set to a simple phrase structure with a repetitive rhythmic pattern, "Onward to Battle" reveals that the workers had to face more than one "risky" element and that here we find ourselves far removed from romantic bourgeois choral music (figure 1.2). The meter is more irregular than Seeger describes, as it changes in each of its 4 measures, 4/4—3/4—5/4—5/8. The F♯ in the key signature suggests G major or E minor, but the melody invokes a pentatonic scale; and even though we could place it within a tonal framework, the round disregards the conventions of tonal harmony and embraces modal ambiguity. If we are in G major, why did Siegmeister end the piece on the dominant rather than the tonic? Perhaps the composer thought that this would encourage the singers to keep repeating the round; but it has the decided disadvantage of providing no satisfying way to end a performance.[46] The round thus would seem a strange and challenging piece and hardly suitable "to be sung by huge masses everywhere there are class-conscious workers."[47]

Figure 1.2. L. E. Swift [Elie Siegmeister], "Onward to Battle," from "Three Workers' Rounds," in *Workers Song Book No. 1* (New York: Workers Music League, USA Section of International Music Bureau, 1934)

Seeger's "Song of the Builders" for intermediate chorus and piano—composed under the pseudonym Carl Sands—has also a revolutionary and combative text:

We are the builders, we build the future,
The future world is in our hands.
We swing our hammers, we use our weapons
Against our foes in many lands.

We are the builders, we build the future,
And he who hinders us must fall.
Come join us comrades, our task is mighty,
We need your help you workers all.

[...]

Yet even Seeger's own experiments may seem inappropriate for proletarian usage. The song, which is apparently in G major, features a simple and mostly stepwise melody based on a pentatonic scale (D-E-G-A-B). While its simple syllabic text settings and homophonic texture seem chorus friendly, the irregular meter based on the alternation of 3/4 and 2/4 could cause problematic accent shifts, even if often it reflects the text (figure 1.3). The chorus must sing this ordinary melody, which uses *forte* as a preferred dynamic, over a piano accompaniment saturated with dissonant clusters that elude any relationship to the key signature. To render the chorus's task even more challenging, the third is often missing in cadences, as though Seeger deliberately wanted to keep the mode ambiguous.

Another extreme case is Janet Barnes's atonal "God to the Hungry Child" for solo voice and piano accompaniment on a poem by Langston Hughes written in 1925, at the beginning of his activism in the Harlem Renaissance movement:

Hungry child,
I didn't make this world for you.
You didn't buy any stock in my railroad.
You didn't invest in my corporation.
Where are your shares in standard oil?
I made the world for the rich
And the will-be-rich
And the have-always-been-rich.
Not for you,
Hungry child.

Figure 1.3. Carl Sands [Charles Seeger], "Song of the Builders," mm. 1–19, in *Workers Song Book No. 1* (New York: Workers Music League, USA Section of International Music Bureau, 1934)

The text looks like an anomaly in this collection of songs, as it does not incite to fight; rather it denounces capitalism and, more precisely, religion as a supporter of the capitalist status quo: God tells the poor children that the world was not made for them, but only for the wealthy (figure 1.4). Barnes's setting, listed among the "easy" songs in the "Graded Index of Workers' Choral Repertoire" printed on the back cover of the second *Workers Song Book*, differs from the simpler melodies of the other songs with its vocal line crowded with tritones. In the most difficult sections, the right hand in the piano doubles the vocal part, but it can hardly help an amateur singer to intone a song that starts with a descending tritone (C♯-G). Moreover, shifts in meter and constantly changing time signatures mirror the melodic angularity and, in truth, the piece is indeed complex but also rather competent. Indeed, the resemblance to an art song more than a revolutionary chant speaks for Barnes's skills as a composer and challenges Copland's assessment of the piece.

In the foreword to the second *Workers Song Book*, the editorial commission of the Workers' Music League stressed the importance of music in uniting the working class in "its persistent march to power."[48] The commission emphasized the role of mass singing in the strikes and demonstrations that swept the United States in the early 1930s (San Francisco General Strike, Textile General Strike, and others), and stated that music was a significant factor in the growth and life of the American labor movement. To involve a larger spectrum of workers, this second compilation included many novelties for the time, for instance two original "Negro" songs of protest; songs dealing with the struggles of the United Front and against war and fascism; songs commemorating American class war heroes fallen in battle (such as John Reed and Harry Simms); satirical songs in the American folk style against American capitalism; popular workers' songs from Germany (including compositions by Eisler and Stefan Volpe); and outstanding fighting songs from the Soviet Union, Mongolia, and China.[49] The twelve composers involved, eight of whom were Americans, provided the following pieces "for mass singing on the streets and at all rallies, for choruses (from elementary to advanced) as well as for informal singing wherever workers gather":

United Front	J. Fairbanks (1934)
War Is Murder	Lan Adomian (1934)
Into the Streets May First!	Aaron Copland (1934)
Song of the Pickets	Earl Robinson (1934)
Forward, We've Not Forgotten	Hanns Eisler (1935)
Comintern	Hanns Eisler (1931)

Figure 1.4. Janet Barnes, "God to the Hungry Child," in *Workers Song Book No. 1* (New York: Workers Music League, USA Section of International Music Bureau, 1934)

Ours Is the Future	Stefan Volpe (1935)
Stop in Your Tracks	Lan Adomian (1934)
Look Here Georgia	Lan Adomian (1934)
The Ballad of Harry Simms	Lan Adomian (1934)
We Toil, We Work	Karl Vollmer (1935)
I Went to Atlanta (Negro Song)	L. E. Swift (1934)
Sistern and Brethren (Negro Song)	L. E. Swift (1934)
We Want the World	L. E. Swift (1934)
The Red Banner	arr. by J. C. Richards (1934)
Chinese Red Soldiers' Song	arr. by J. C. Richards (1934)
The First Red Cavalry	A. Davidenko
John Reed, Our Captain	George Maynard (1934)
The Flying Squadron	Saul, Martin, Robinson (1934)
Three Workers' Rounds	
"The Three Brothers"	L. E. Swift (1934)
"Not If, But When"	Carl Sands (1934)
"Charlie Schwab"	Carl Sands (1934)

The revolutionary character of the words is again striking. Still, most original compositions did not address the typical American workers' musical experience, rooted as it was in the ballad tradition, church hymns, and of course 32-bar Tin Pan Alley songs. Siegmeister's (L. E. Swift) a cappella piece for SATB mixed chorus, "We Want the World," must have challenged workers' choruses (figure 1.5). Continuous changes in meter characterize the piece (in the first 5 measures the meter shifts from 2/4 to 3/8, 5/8, 2/4, and 3/8), and a tonal center, if one is to be found, floats somewhere among B♭ major, F major, and G major. Another challenge for the chorus is the polyphonic texture, transformed into a homophonic setting only in the last 8 bars, where the revolutionary message reaches its highest point with the words "Comrades, we want the world, the world is ours, We'll fight to the end to conquer the world." Paradoxically, Siegmeister also composed one of the most singable songs published in the second book: the satirical round "The Three Brothers," written in a regular meter, 4/4, and clearly in F major, which pokes fun at the DuPont family for their carelessness in selling arms to everyone who can pay.

But were the songs of the *Workers Song Books* really what Seeger and the members of the Collective envisioned as proletarian in musical style? Indeed, when composers felt free to express their individuality writing for trained performers and not for educational or propaganda purposes, their music is more ambitious. Siegmeister and Ruth Crawford Seeger both attempted to achieve a fusion of

Figure 1.5. L. E. Swift [Elie Siegmeister], "We Want The World," in *Workers Song Book No. 2* (New York: Workers Music League, USA Section of International Music Bureau, 1935)

modernist art with proletarian culture by means of contemporary compositional techniques and a topical text, and the results perhaps correspond better to what Seeger called "proletarian musical style" than do the songs and choruses from the *Workers Song Books*. This is the case with the two *Ricercari* that Crawford Seeger composed in 1932: "Sacco and Vanzetti," and "Chinaman, Laundry Man," both with words by the Chinese dissident H. T. Tsiang. The texts uphold the proletarian ideal of "music as a weapon in the class struggle." But the style she employs for this angry oratory—including *Sprechstimme* and her trademark anti-lyricism—was surely anything but familiar and comfortable to most trade and factory workers of the day.[50]

Another remarkable example of so-called proletarian art music is Siegmeister's "The Strange Funeral in Braddock" for baritone and piano (1934), based on a "proletarian chant" written by the aforementioned critic and novelist Michael Gold. Dissonances saturate its angular vocal line, and performance instructions specify avant-garde techniques of vocal delivery: "harsh singing," "nasal singing," "nasal-mocking," "pitched speech," while the loud piano part comprises clusters and percussive ostinatos.[51] The piece had multiple performances in the 1930s in New York City. Henry Cowell included it in his *New Music* series in 1936, and it was Siegmeister's first published work under his real name. Despite this local interest, however, the composer had to face harsh criticism for his supposedly excessive use of modernist techniques that obscured the proletarian thrust of the text. In a private interview, Mordecai Baumann, the baritone who premiered the piece, recalled a discussion that followed what he remembered as a "very successful performance" in New York City. Someone asked Gold to comment on the composition. Shocking the enthusiastic audience, the writer responded, "I hate it!"[52] Thereby Gold articulated an aggressive opposition to the Collective's concept of proletarian music, which he would later express in articles and columns in *New Masses* and in the *Daily Worker*. Despite Gold's objections, a first recording was issued in 1936, performed by Baumann with Siegmeister at the piano; the work would become a touchstone of protest music by a modernist composer.[53] But these sporadic cases, while attempting to meet the aesthetic requirements of "art music," could hardly appeal to an American working class untutored in musical complexities.

Reconsidering the Role of Proletarian Music

The homogeneous style Seeger dreamed of appeared to be a chimera. In spring 1935, a radical change of direction intriguingly coincided with the beginning of Blitzstein's membership and his assignment as the Collective's secretary and member of the executive committee. The composer drafted a pamphlet to promote the agenda of the Collective, which now seems to have abandoned any attempt at defining a proletarian style of musical composition:

> To the musicians who make up the Composers Collective of New York it is obvious that music of to-day, if it is to survive at all, must have a strong social content (explicit or implied) and must be of use to the broad masses of people in their struggles for social and cultural emancipation. The manner in which this social content is to be expressed is left to the individual composer. The Collective has no set formula, no single style for the writing of this music. In its meetings and on its programs, radical and conservative, "popular" and "serious," jazz and the most intricate contrapuntal forms exist side by side; the most conflicting musical views and techniques meet in free and vigorous interchange.[54]

While supporting the need for music to promote community relevance to keep their art alive in a socioeconomically distraught America, the composers of the Collective could not agree on a single definitive proletarian quality for music per se. They only focused on its function with a description that neatly skirts any need (or temptation) to prescribe specific aspirations or stylistic parameters for future compositions.

Blitzstein struggled with this problem, as drafts for this pamphlet demonstrate (never mind the difficulties he experienced when trying to compose in a proletarian musical style).[55] He crossed things out and rewrote many sections, showing that he encountered tremendous problems in trying to give voice to the often confused and inconsistent goals of the Collective (figure 1.6). At first, he sustained the members' right to their autonomy of musical style, but then he argued against the "chaos and anarchy that reign in modern music" in favor of a "closer relationship between the composer and the great, hitherto untouched people's audience of America."[56] Even though he eventually discarded this passage, it articulates the real problem: Blitzstein, like many other members of the Collective, was more interested in forging a connection between the American composer and his audience than in increasing music's political impact. He wanted to move beyond the inconsistency and extreme individualism that, to his mind, had halted American modernist music:

> Only thru organization can the composers on the one hand and the people on the other affect that mutual contact, which is so necessary if musical art in this country is to be preserved and carried further. The composers must learn to know this new audience, to study its musical needs and requirements, and fashion their work so that it may fit these requirements; it is obvious that the throwing off of certain habits and traditions of thought that have been molded exclusively by production for the needs of the bourgeois concert hall and the re-fashioning of these traditions for the needs of the new people's audience is no easy task.[57]

2.

implied) and must be of use to the broad masses of people in their
struggles for social and cultural emancipation.The manner in which
this social content is to be expressed is left to the individual
composer.The COLLECTIVE has no~~txxingixxfarmxixym~~ set formula,
no single style for the writing of this music.In its meetings,
and on its programs,radical and conservative,"popular" and "serious",
jazz and the most intricate contrapuntal forms exist side by side;
the most conflicting musical views and techniques meet in free and
vigorous interchange.   THE COMPOSER AND THE AUDIENCE
        Yet,while many differences in musical style exist and are
freely encouraged,the bond that draws the composers in the COLLECT-
IVE together is the common knowledge that the only solution of
the ~~xxixix~~ chaos and anarchy that reign in modern music to-day
lies in the welding of a closer relationship between the composer
and the great,hitherto untouched people's audience of America.
The conditions of bourgeois concert life, the managerial and patronage
systems have combined to enforce the domination of big business,
~~of the bankers,munitions makers,~~the Astors,Guggenheims and Duponts
on the musical life of this countryIt is they who control,thru their
foundations ~~xxx~~ donations, and endowments,the orchestras,conductors
and composers of this country.If the composer was to survive at all,
and live at least partially from the product of his labor,it was
necessary for him to cultivate the company,the tastes and the subsid-
ies of the financial Bourbons ~~of Park Avenue and the upper sixties.~~
~~XIXXXHXIXXXXHXXXXHXXXXXXXXXXXXXX XXXXHXXXXXXXXXX XYXXXXXXXX~~
~~XXXIIXIHXXXIXXIIIXXXXIXXHXXXHXXXXXXXXXXXXXXXXXX~~

        In response to the tastes of this small elite,~~kixxxxxixxx~~
and due to lack of ~~xxxxixx~~ ~~xxxx~~ of contact,thru his work,with the
mass of people that comprise this nation,his music grew ever more
and more "smart",subtle and refined, and consequently completely
remote from the realities of life of the 99% of American people.
Is it any wonder that under these circumstances the modern music
~~xf~~ has become weak,~~ineffex~~ ineffectual,and a dead letter to all
except a few rare (and ever rarer) spirits who are in the know?
~~XXX TURNING TOWARDS~~ [THE NEW AUDIENCE]
        The COMPOSERS COLLECTIVE was formed to struggle against this
~~xxxtxxx~~ vicious system of leisure class domination of music under
which both the composer and the great mass of people who comprise
the potential American audience are deprived of their most elementary musical rights: the composer,the right to a real,living audience,
to whom to address his music,and from whom he can draw strength; and
the people,the right to claim the best composers in America as their
own,and to have music concerning itself with the real issues and
~~prablxxxxxfxthxxxixxxxfxthxxxpxxpxxxx~~ struggles of ~~kifxx~~ themselves
~~of the people~~ Only thru organisation can the composers on the
the one hand and the people on the other effect that mutual contact
which is so necessary if musical art in this country is to be
preserved and carried further. The composers must learn to know this
new audience,to study ~~its~~ its musical needs and requirements and
fashion their work so that it may fit these requirements.That ~~this~~
~~isxxxxxxxxtxxkx~~ the throwing off of habits and traditions of thought
that have been molded exclusively by production for the needs of the
bourgeois concert hall and the re-fashioning of these traditions
for the needs of the new people's audience is no easy task.~~All~~
~~activity.~~The COMPOSERS COLLECTIVE,by serving as a clearing house
for the exchange of experiences among the various composers, as well
as a means of establishing,thru its concerts,contact with a growing

Figure 1.6. "Notes on the Work of the Composers' Collective of N.Y.," *Marc Blitzstein Papers*, State Historical Society, Madison, Wisconsin, Archive Division, Box 7, Folder 6, Wisconsin Center for Film and Theater Research

Ultimately, as Blitzstein argued, contact with the "people's audience" and with the various workers' organizations that had called on members of the Collective to provide functional music prompted them to turn away "from the preoccupation with abstract esthetic questions to concrete work to satisfy the musical needs of the broad masses of American people"; this was a task, though, that proved to be almost impossible.[58]

The problem at the core of this inability to define a clear path for proletarian music may reside in the truth that many of the young modernist musicians active in New York City espoused the idea of proletarian music more as a social necessity than as a genuine belief. As Baumann argued, "At that time the left wing movement, because of the Depression, had a face on the political scene. . . . Every New Yorker in the Depression was a left wing person; they had to be, there is nothing special [in that]."[59] Composer Arthur Berger described this approach:

> Many of us started to feel embarrassed at excluding the masses when we wrote music that they found inaccessible or accessible with difficulty. We need not have been card-carrying Party members, and we had no wish to overthrow the American government. We had our infighting as followers of either Leon Trotsky or Joseph Stalin, but during the mid-thirties many of us viewed Socialism in Russia through rose-colored glasses. We were known as "fellow-travelers," and we mingled with the faithful at endless meetings where the subject of how to communicate to the masses was ardently thrashed out and the tendency of the artist to take refuge in "escapism" was bitterly reviled.[60]

Blitzstein himself felt trapped in this challenge. After all, he believed that music does not need to lose its avant-garde features to address a wider audience and that a composer had the duty to instruct the masses in the new musical idiom and to avoid patronizing them with a simplistic language. He also claimed not to be really interested in the political message but in the musical result, a position that sheds a clearer light on his unsuccessful approach to proletarian music, which seems to exist almost in an apolitical world of its own with its diatonic and catchy tunes often set against a sophisticated accompaniment with ambiguous modulations rich in dissonant harmonies. Eventually, Blitzstein clearly elaborated these ideas in a three-part article titled "The Case for Modern Music," which appeared in consecutive issues of *New Masses* on July 14, 21, and 28, 1936; but in spring 1935, he, like all other composers of the Collective, was still unable to define a clear path for proletarian music.

To define basic aspirations for and technical approaches to proletarian music, the Collective's composers eventually convened a "Special Symposium-meeting" on June 16, 1935, in which they discussed how best to apply proletarian ideology to existing musical forms and genres. Blitzstein's minutes of the Collective's meeting on June 7 contain the following description of plans for the symposium:

> Special "Symposium-meeting" June 16 3PM, at 47 E. 12 (continued at 42 Horatio St.)
> North, Cazden, Howe, Swift, Maynard, Sands, Blitzstein, Goldbeck, Robinson, Fairbanks, Leroy, Lynn, Bloch, Sokoloff, etc., etc., etc.

(Shirley Cohen—42 Horatio St.; Dorothy Finney, 845 Sutter Ave., Brooklyn; Mary Menk, 34 E. 11 St.; Sam Weingstein, 34 E. 11 St.; Miriam Shapiro, 780 Prospect Pl. Brooklyn; Arthur Abrams, 121 Riverdale Ave., Brooklyn)[61]

Subjects:
Sands: Proletarian Music
Blitzstein: The Idiom of Proletarian Music
Swift: The Mass Song
Howe: The Art Song
Maynard: Program vs. Absolute Music
North: Music for the Dance
Margulis: Texts

To be discussed later:
Howe: Instrumental Music
Robinson: Theatre Music
Cazden: Jazz[62]

Blitzstein's minutes of June 21 also mention the symposium, but now retrospectively:

> Decision that all members who were leading discussions at the symposium of June 16, or who were not able to read their papers because of time limitations, write up their papers for record purposes. (Notes on the discussion will be added.)[63]

There is no record of such papers within the Collective's materials in Blitzstein's archive at the Wisconsin Historical Society, but the notes he refers to (and that he seems to have taken during the symposium and never transcribed) are most likely the ones that were misplaced and misidentified in Box 9, Folder 11: "Lectures-Articles, October 1934—1961."[64] These handwritten pages reported the proceedings of a symposium about the meaning of proletarian music and its link with traditional musical genres. Although the notes bear no indication of date or location, the leaders of the debate and the subjects discussed conform to those of the "Special Symposium-meeting on Proletarian Music" mentioned in the minutes.

The symposium's notes, summarizing the presentations and the ensuing animated discussions among the meeting's participants, demonstrate that the composers could not even agree on general issues of definition, origin, idiom, form, and content associated with the "new" musical style. The notes highlight two major issues affecting the establishment of proletarian music as a new musical trend: the struggle in choosing between modernism and popular musical idioms, and the different level of political involvement and ideological commitment of various members of the Collective. Most of these composers found themselves in a problematic position: to follow the agenda for proletarian propaganda, they had to set aside their aesthetic premises, abandon absolute music, and focus on functional music, especially on vocal music with revolutionary texts (mass and fighting songs). This task proved especially challenging for those composers who, in fact, lacked genuine political commitment or who, for some other reasons, continued to focus on instrumental music. Of course, they found a way to justify the use of purely instrumental music by giving it a special function, as stated in Blitzstein's promotional pamphlet: "to bring into the conventional concert hall, where it would perhaps be difficult for mass songs or choral works on social themes to penetrate, the viewpoint of composers who have definitely aligned themselves with the masses."[65] Yet they could only agree on what it should not be, rather than on a stylistic blueprint to follow:

> It will not be a delicate, decorative, introspective art. It will not go in for super-complexities of technique for technique's sake, nor refinement for refinement's sake. It will not be "smart" nor merely entertaining and amusing, although it will entertain and perhaps amuse. Whatever form it will take, it will contain vigor, directness, optimism, a simplicity of emotional utterance, and a broad monumental sweep.[66]

The lack of a clear direction is supported in the striking difference between Seeger's and Blitzstein's conceptualization of proletarian music as the new direction for modernist endeavors and Earl Robinson's insistence that it must be rooted in the folk tradition.

Seeger, who had since the establishment of the Collective aligned proletarian music with the revolutionary aspect of musical modernism, insisted on defining it as the historical referent for all music characterizing this period, rather than only as exemplification of a specific set of stylistic markers or genres associated with the workers. Seeger was pushing the unrealistic view that his proletarian music could define American "art music" of the twentieth century and argued that future criticism would validate it as its "historical classification." To that end, he even attempted to depoliticize it by distancing his ideas from those of Soviet Union composers and admitting the risk inherent in the new style being identified specifically as "communist."[67] Blitzstein, while outlining what the content of proletarian music should be—that is, agitational and educational—also noted that it does not have a recognizable idiom, a characteristic mode of musical expression. However, he claimed that it should not be associated only with a simplistic language and proposed that composers develop an idiom that incorporates a wide range of complexities to please both popular and artistic needs. Evidently, both composers were more resolved to protect their artistic identity and integrity than to find ways to bridge the gap between art music and the working class. Robinson's opposing view of proletarian music, though, eschewed any association with musical modernism as he maintained that workers' music has always existed and is therefore an indigenous artistic expression. He believed that proletarian music resides in folk music and thus lends itself to participatory performance by groups of untrained musicians.

The participatory, amateur, and folk qualities of proletarian music thus became the major dividing aspect and the most contentious topic of the symposium. Seeger, rebutting Robinson's claims, argued that relying on folk music could be problematic, as bourgeois musicians have collected folk music and, while maintaining some of its originality, they purged it of what might be politically and morally subversive. The minutes do not mention Hanns Eisler by name, but the German composer's ideas about folk music seem to inform both positions. Eisler made his first trip to the United States from February to May 1935, returning in October of the same year, and gave guest lectures on workers' music in some of the main cities, including New York, Pittsburgh, Chicago, San Francisco, Los Angeles, Saint Louis, and Detroit. Among his aesthetic principles, he proposed choral music as the ultimate expression of the workers' music movements, considering it the perfect genre to serve social and functional purposes, activate members for struggle, and encourage political education.[68] He saw vocal music as the ultimate means to support the working-class struggle for a radical change in capitalist society, and he promoted the mass and fighting songs of the modern working class, thus supporting Robinson's stance. In line with Seeger, though, he also cautioned against the indiscriminate use of folk songs and recognized two different types, the *genuine* type that originated from the people, and the *false* type, the product of capitalist misuse (i.e., standardized and often sentimentalized adaptations of folk tunes). Eisler encouraged researchers and composers to sort out "the grain from the chaff" and restore the songs' original meanings and functions.[69] Eventually, his ideas proved influential as Seeger began collecting and preserving what he deemed "authentic" versions of folk songs, and Robinson started performing these tunes on tour. However, at least up to June 1935, the Collective's composers were still struggling to define a form or a genre for proletarian music.

To justify Seeger's lack of specificity concerning what constitutes a proletarian musical form or style, Blitzstein remarked:

> A new art has always had more definite ideas about content: form comes gradually to consistency with content . . . the content is given us by literary form (Marxist writers of last century) . . . but [we] must guard against keeping literary form from guiding musical form and processes; be good musicians. Musical expression may be quite surprising to literary expression.[70]

His observation shows a perceptive attention to the autonomous role of the composer as an artist, a position that he later better articulated in his comments about the lecture "The Crisis in Music," which Eisler gave on December 7, 1935, in Town Hall, New York:

> Eisler is first a composer; it is good to remember that his formulation, his theories grow out of, have roots in, music. They are your true "aesthetic," articulated out of the thing, possessed and actual, not cooked-up, not arbitrary, not nursed along to induce the thing, and make it happen. Schönberg once said of the typical theorizer, "Nobody watches more closely over his property than the man who knows that, strictly speaking, it does not belong to him." Eisler's property is his own; he shares it with the working class of the world.[71]

Eisler, whom Blitzstein admired for his theories rooted in music, though, would have disagreed with the American composer's view on instrumental music as the ultimate goal of a proletarian author. For the German, proletarian music, or *Tendenzmusik* as he called it, was meant to be an art that

> the class-conscious worker offered to the non-class-conscious worker with the object of stirring both of them, of arousing class instincts and of drawing him into the class struggle. Music and text, therefore, had to appeal to the non-class-conscious worker and to the emotions of the individual and were actually only the preliminary to a planned propaganda action.[72]

This observation clearly states that for Eisler proletarian music must have words. In fact, in the 1932 essay "Our Revolutionary Music," he considered orchestral music unsuitable to express proletarian aesthetics, because instrumental music without words is a product of capitalism and bourgeois society and as such is not the best choice for a proletarian audience.[73] Blitzstein, however, while he agreed with the revolutionary message, believed in a proletarian idiom that incorporated both vocal and instrumental music showing a wide range of complexities to please both popular and artistic needs. Behind this notion, of course, lies Blitzstein the modernist of the early 1930s, the dreamer who idealized the average worker as a curious mind, eager to experience the "freshness of harmony and rhythm" that only modern music could offer, but most of all the composer who was incapable of accepting artistic leveling and still favored individuality of musical voice.

The choice of musical genres and forms to best match proletarian content became the most heated argument of the symposium and, once again, demonstrated the volatility of these composers' understanding of the revolutionary premises behind this endeavor. At the center of the discussion, of course, there were mass and fighting songs, which everyone recognized as the most effective tool to convey new ideas and establish a broad connection with the workers. Elie Siegmeister (L. E. Swift), highlighting the difficulties that modern composers encountered in adapting their music to the needs of the working class, suggested that it is not enough, as Eisler stated, for the composer

> to sit in his room and write for the working-class movement. He must take an active part in social life and in the struggles of the working class. We must form an alliance between the music intellectuals and the working class. The music intellectual can learn how to think politically and can acquire a revolutionary attitude from the working class.[74]

Indeed, the composers of the Collective appeared to have been only theoretically connected to the working class and, as proven by the two *Workers Song Books*, had yet to develop a style for mass songs that could be musically progressive and at the same time attractive to the masses. The symposium's participants attempted to define the best choice of mass songs for the American workers, but it proved to be an extremely controversial task.

Of course, the easiest solution could have been the use of contrafacta; after all they were at the core of the singing tradition of the International Workers of the World and a proven tool for protest.[75] Still, some members of the Collective, including Siegmeister, argued that they depended too much on the bourgeois musical tradition. They considered no longer suitable for American workers adaptations of old foreign revolutionary tunes, some of which they had already included in the *Workers Song Books*, as their texts were deemed simplistic and uninteresting. The Collective dismissed also new songs with revolutionary lyrics and bombastic music on the grounds that, while they could be appealing to the audiences, they do not always contribute to the actual growth of the working class. Siegmeister argued that even songs from the European proletarian tradition—such as Eisler's "Red Front" and *"Vorwärts und nicht vergessen"* (also known as *"Solidaritätslied"*)—while featuring more refined musical qualities and being appreciated by international workers showcase a spirit and mood foreign to American workers, because they are

46 · CHAPTER 1

sad, monotonous, and "culturally reactionary" (though, of course, politically progressive). Step by step, trying to identify the new proletarian mass song, the composers of the Collective eliminated all types of songs that had successfully accompanied the struggle of the American working class, but were unable to offer a definite alternative. Evidently, this indecision demonstrates how aware—consciously or subconsciously—the participants were of a conflict between ideology and artistry: composers wanted to be socially relevant but could not just accept inconsistency and paradoxical musical behaviors. In the end, Siegmeister solved this conundrum by, once again, relying on Eisler's theory on revolutionary music and his division of choral proletarian music into two categories: "music for practical performance," including songs for struggle, satirical songs, and mass fighting songs, which are vigorous, quickly learned, and easily understood, and "music to be listened to," comprising didactic plays (*Lehrstücke*) and choral pieces with theoretical content, pieces whose music does not need to be immediately graspable and in which the composer must avoid aridity and boredom and the use of the old fashion bourgeois styles.[76] Consequently, Siegmeister preserved artistic integrity by urging the composers of the Collective to write simple songs focusing more on political than on musical values for most of the workers, those who do not have musical background, and—for workers who are musically trained—songs showing musical "intelligence," which avoid outmoded musical conventions and traditional harmony.

Another major area of contention was the discussion of the role of absolute versus program music in the proletarian context, which revealed tensions between composers with different levels of commitment to political ideology. Some, including George Maynard, felt that proletarian composers did not have to limit their creativity and withdraw their efforts from new music to please the working masses. Others, led by Earl Robinson, argued in favor of abandoning the division between absolute and program music, because all art is propaganda, and even when it portrays "pure beauty" it conceals a cultural and social agenda. Not all composers of the Collective, though, truthfully adhered to this underlying principle and willingly expressed revolutionary ideas. In the end, Amnon Balber, an editor of *Music Vanguard*, posed the question "is there revolutionary content in a string quartet by a revolutionary composer?," which crystallized the debate around two major issues reifying the difficulty of composing proletarian music: (a) many of these composers did not have revolutionary roots and were unfamiliar with class consciousness and the workers' struggle, a reality that prevented them from "filling old forms with new revolutionary content"; and (b) music's incapability, as an abstract art, of expressing a political belief.

There are parallels between the dual approach to proletarian music that we witnessed within the microcosm of the Composers' Collective of New York and the ways in which Soviet composers pursued an appropriate music for the revolution during the Lenin period. There, though, composers were adhering to two well-defined and organized groups with opposing strategies and aesthetic views, both aiming at finding the best way to take advantage of the emotional power of music to support the Bolshevik Revolution: the modernist-oriented Association for Contemporary Music (ASM) with its interest in harmonic complexity, formalism, and exploration of new sound sources, and the leftist Russian Association of Proletarian Musicians (RAPM) with its anti-modern and anti-Western stance interested in functional music created by and for the proletariat, that is, amateur performers, which recognized in the mass song its main form of expression.[77] Eventually, the artistic freedom that allowed the coexistence of the two opposing aesthetics ended when Stalin came to power. The government-imposed style of socialist realism signaled the end of the two groups and the promotion of a unified music policy supported by the newly founded Union of Soviet Composers. The new institution opposed formalism and supported tonal music and standard genres featuring clearly defined melodic lines. This music had to be understood by the Soviet people to which it belonged and convey a clear message following the narrative from darkness, to struggle, to triumph. But there was no socialist realism in the United States to ultimately oblige Seeger, Blitzstein, and Robinson to abandon their different approaches to proletarian music for a government-imposed one, and these composers were unable to find a common ground.

Undeniably, musical artistry did not characterize the first steps of proletarian music, as the compositions included in the two *Workers Song Books* prove, and the symposium demonstrated that artistic quality and the preservation of individuality became a major concern in the next and last stage of its development. These issues eventually led to a split within the Composers' Collective. On one side, under the name of the Pierre Degeyter Club, were the composers focused on the power of folk music, including Charles Seeger, Lan Adomian, and Earl Robinson, who promoted it as the true people's art. On the other side, still under the same name but only for at most another year, were Blitzstein and Siegmeister, who hoped to nurture "proletarian art music," a style that would appeal to the masses while allowing composers to express their individuality, to employ modernist techniques selectively, and to serve specific artistic and ideological purposes.

Musical or Political Breakdown?

The goal of establishing a common approach, arguably an identifiable progressive proletarian American style, which animated the discussions of the members of the Collective was at the core of the aims of many young American composers in the 1930s. As Arthur Berger mentioned when discussing the activities of the Young Composers' Group, "many of us started to feel embarrassed at excluding the masses when we wrote music that they found inaccessible or accessible with difficulty."[78] The American Communist Party and other major left-wing organizations seemed indeed to have noticed and taken advantage of the impulse of these composers to be socially relevant and started supporting their activities. Articles and editorials published in the communist media the *Daily Worker* and *New Masses* show how political backing established a strong, albeit very brief link between composers and working-class, or proletarian performers and audiences.[79]

The American Communist Party, at the height of the Great Depression, aimed to educate the proletariat and give workers the means to fight in their class struggle. To reach this objective, starting in the early 1930s, the *Daily Worker* had given culture a prominent role in building a class-conscious proletariat. In May 1933, for the first time, it introduced recurring columns on culture, "Stage and Screen" and "Book Reviews." In June, Michael Gold started his now notorious column "What a World," a daily editorial discussing cultural issues at large. On January 23, 1934, George Maynard, one of the most active members of the Composers' Collective, launched a new section called "Music" with the article "Appreciation among Workers," in which he endorsed the prominent role of music as a weapon in the class struggle. He argued that music could not merely please, it had

> to point a way and be an integral part in the life of the masses availing itself of all technological innovations of our age. [...] The honest Marxist composer of today must ride with the tide of progress. He can't sit down and dream his music in the plushes and satins of yesterday. . . . It must be sturdy, brusque, vigorous and simple. It must have something of the field and factory in it, of strikes and achievements of warm comradeship and bitterness against the ruling class.[80]

To demonstrate that "the proletariat is not the beast and moron that capitalist lies make it out to be," Maynard urged representatives of the working class and composers to cooperate in organizing courses and lecture-recitals and in writing articles to familiarize the masses with the new proletarian idiom.

The editors of the *Daily Worker* accepted the challenge by giving major exposure in their culture pages to music. Most of the articles on proletarian music that appeared in the *Daily Worker* between January and June 1934 were meant to promote the new style among the working class and to create a strong connection between musicians and proletariat. For instance, Adomian's "What Songs Should Workers' Choruses Sing?" addressed issues related to the technical qualities of mass songs as discussed with the other members of the Composers' Collective.[81] Seeger (under his pseudonym Carl Sands) contributed many articles that attempted, alas unsuccessfully, to explain the reasons for the constitution of the Composers' Collective and the meaning of proletarian music. In a series of four articles appearing in consecutive issues, on March 5 through 8, 1934, he set forth guidelines for composers and critics "to help the growth of a new revolutionary style that will support the revolutionary movement."[82] He stated his concepts on proletarian music and called for a reevaluation of the music of the past to define what can still be used to further the proletarian movement.[83]

This interest in proletarian music was called into question on June 11, 1934, when Michael Gold overtly criticized the work of the Composers' Collective. That day Gold's editorial voiced some complaints about the musical settings of workers' songs performed at the Olympiad of the Workers Music League, where "the workers' chorus rendered the association very well, but there was a horrifying gap between the music and the words."[84] According to Gold, the audience felt that the music was too mechanical and angular—too modernist—and he launched his battle against proletarian art music: "I think a new content often demands a new form, but when the new form gets so far ahead of all of us that we can't understand its content, it is time to write letters to the press." From then on only a few articles promoting proletarian music appeared in the *Daily Worker*. A brief surge of interest coincided with the arrival of Hanns Eisler in the United States in spring 1935 and the various activities associated with his presence. But in general, proletarian music, apparently unable to reconcile the weighted message with an art in itself abstract and incapable of taking political sides, failed to have a leading role as a weapon in the class struggle.[85]

Gold's comment on the difficulty of understanding the content of the new proletarian musical style gave voice not only to a concern of the working masses and their quest for a more accessible music, but it also portrayed the new political direction of the Communist Party. As the threat of fascism in Germany, Italy, and Spain became more obvious in the mid-1930s, the Comintern shifted to a politics advocating a united Popular Front against fascism and for peace.

50 · CHAPTER 1

The party stopped supporting proletarian music for propaganda purposes, and the Composers' Collective lost direct connection with its "new" audience. Communists were now encouraged to work with other leftist groups and social democratic organizations supporting anti-fascist causes.[86] Together they created a Popular Front political culture with shared concerns, values, and ideas that combined patriotism and an international sense of solidarity. Instead of discourses on class consciousness, the Popular Front stressed the importance of the common man, the ordinary worker and farmer, the immigrant, the African American, and the Native American and, promoting the slogan "Communism is 20th century Americanism," it triggered a renewed interest in folk songs of protest.

Without political support and the willingness to match the taste of the working class, the dream of an American proletarian musical style, of a musical language that could communicate with wide audiences and give voice to their needs, vanished. With the benefit of hindsight, Seeger recognized that what they produced did not relate to the American political song tradition:

> We tried to [. . .] use ordinary fragments of technique in an unusual way, because we thought that was revolutionary and therefore suitable for the workers to use. We didn't give them those same patterns in the usual way, which was what Broadway did. Broadway just handed out a certain number of formulas in the usual way; but we took those same formulas, simply used them differently, and hoped that we were doing something revolutionary. Eisler does that. Eisler did quite a number of songs for street singing and gave them just a little unusual twist, so that the workers can sing them. The music was in their idiom, but has something in advance of their idiom that brings it up [i.e., to a level of somewhat greater sophistication].[87]

The practice of combining workers' idiom with folk traditions and art music, which had worked in Germany and in the Soviet Union, could not have succeeded in the United States, where the lack of ethnic homogeneity, and in many cases not even a common native language, made the project rather futile. In the name of political propaganda, composers tried to impose a cultural identity on a heterogeneous group of workers with alienating results, and the short-lived concept of an American proletarian music disappeared without leaving behind a single piece of music that could withstand sustained scrutiny or multiple hearings. Seeger concluded many years later with palpable regret:

> We had lost our basic musical vernacular. The only thing with the basic musical vernacular was Broadway, hillbilly, the remaining folk songs of the older people

and finally the old-timey music. Fine art music simply does not have it. That's why we came a cropper, because we didn't have that. [...] Everything we composed was forward-looking, progressive as hell, but completely unconnected with life, just as we were in the Collective.[88]

Seeger highlighted the real problem of the Collective's composers: believing that musical vernacular was not progressive enough, they tried to elevate proletarian music by means of a modernist idiom; instead, they sunk it into a musical aesthetic that was outmoded, overly theoretical, and, at a basic level, unpopular.

The composers of the Collective strived to define a new functional form, one that could "solve the anarchic trend of modern music" and at the same time express different contents, but they were unwilling to see that, ironically, America had already invented precisely such a form or genre: the Broadway musical and the American popular song form.[89] Only Blitzstein proved, with his *The Cradle Will Rock*, that he had the skills to approach the new form.[90] Indeed, as Carol Oja discusses, without his involvement with the Composers' Collective, Blitzstein would have never perfected a style with which he could communicate with the masses.[91] *Cradle*, though, would have most likely resulted in a different work without Blitzstein's period of "apprenticeship" with the Workers' Theater Movement—the topic of the next chapter—and the consequent acceptance of the American musical vernacular as the driving force of his new form.

CHAPTER 2

The Workers' Theater Movement and the Politicization of the Musical Revue

> The leftism of the theatre of the period [1930s] was many things at the same time, if it was not indeed many different things to many different people. Depending upon the way one looked at it, it was Marxist and non-Marxist, foreign to American culture and native, large in compass and small, influential and uninfluential, productive and sterile. It started with the Depression or it started long before. It ended with the end of the Depression and the start of World War II or it never died.
>
> —John Gassner, Foreword to Morgan Y. Himelstein, *Drama Was a Weapon: The Left-Wing Theatre in New York, 1929–1941* (New Brunswick, NJ: Rutgers University Press, 1963), vi

In the 1930s, theater productions became a visible venue for leftist political propaganda. The drive to spread socially and politically relevant messages through the art, though, did not always pair with creative objectives, as finding the subtle balance between experimentation and populism proved to be a difficult task for theater practitioners, too. Moreover, the leftist theater also became the focus of conservative attacks. In particular, the Federal Theater Project (FTP), perceived as the center of this political involvement, became an easy target for the House Un-American Activities Committee (HUAC), which started to investigate communist infiltration within the ranks of the government-sponsored project. Indeed, the FTP, which produced some of the most innovative staging of the 1930s, had attracted many playwrights, actors, and directors affiliated with communist or leftist organizations, and its director, Hallie Flanagan, promoted the creation of a socially relevant theater.[1] Yet, as Gassner argued, this leftism escaped categorizations. It was not necessarily a product of the FTP nor

The Workers' Theater Movement and the Politicization of the Musical Revue • 53

of the 1930s; rather, it had its origins in the theatrical endeavors of the Workers' Theater Movement (WTM), which had expressed the dreams and goals of the American working class, often employing a mixture of serious and comic theatrical devices reinforced by music.

In *New Deal Theater*, Ilka Saal examines the aesthetics and politics of the 1930s leftist theater and focuses on content, script, and performance history of various productions of the decade. Basing her argument on the unsuccessful Theatre Union's production of *The Mother*, a play by Brecht with music by Eisler, she argues that the theater of the New Deal had to rely on vernacular strategies to maximize political engagement, thus abandoning the modernist path of Brecht's epic theater.[2] We will see that the vernacular, and in particular the use of popular musical idioms such as those associated with vaudeville and variety shows, had already proven to be a strong motivator for leftist theater even before the flop of *The Mother*. Indeed, the labor stage played a major role in the development of the theater of the left, and a brief survey of the evolving trajectory of the WTM in the United States—from the skits of the International Workers of the World Union (IWW) to the production of English-language and foreign-language theatrical companies such as the Yiddish theater Artef, the Hungarian Elöre Dramatic Club, and the German Prolet-Bühne, to the first semiprofessional and professional companies, including the Workers' Drama League, the New Playwrights Theatre, and the Workers' Laboratory Theatre—will explain some of the strategic choices of the 1930s. The gravity of the topics and the experimental character of many of the WTM's productions spoke to the revolutionary aspect of the pro-union and anti-capitalist theories of the American organized labor movement. To appeal to a working class that was feeling the hardship and insecurity of the contemporary sociopolitical climate, though, producers needed to find a way to render these topics more familiar to American workers. They found the answer in the musical element, which helped to render the radical propagandistic themes and character of the plays more meaningful to workers who still thought of theater as a leisure-time activity. Music is present in the early twentieth-century labor protest skits of the IWW, in the agit-prop plays of English- and foreign-language theater companies active in New York City in the 1920s, and in particular in the socially relevant plays infused with American vernacular idioms of the New Playwrights Theatre, such as Michael Gold's three-act play *Hoboken Blues* (1928), a portrayal of American racism, and Upton Sinclair's *Singing Jailbirds* (1928) on the persecution of an IWW leader.

Finding a balance between propagandistic message, experimentation, and audience appeal was the major challenge for theater practitioners in the 1930s, too. The task became especially pressing as they turned to the political musical

54 · CHAPTER 2

revue to attract the working-class audience. The Theatre Guild first attempted this new path with Paul Peters and George Sklar's musical revue *Parade* (1935), a satire of the New Deal's failures. The idea of a Labor Day parade consisting of twenty-eight floats/acts with strongly pro-union, anti-fascist, and anti-capitalist sketches could have been appealing from a propagandistic point of view. But the revue failed because the audience found that the strong political message presented with at times crude and even gruesome texts overwhelmed satirical innuendos and rendered the musical component almost ineffective. The perfect realization of this balance between music and content was eventually achieved in *Pins and Needles* (1937–39), arguably the most successful production of the labor theater, which proved that to appeal to a working-class audience, authors had to rely on the combination of serious and humorous strategies that are rooted in the early 1900s theatrical representations of the IWW. "*Pins and Needles* [. . .] can laugh merrily at itself as it can at its foes, and that is a quality that makes it both disarming and persuasive. Here is social propaganda in its most winning fashion."[3] Thus Richard Watts Jr., writing in the *New York Herald Tribune*, greeted the opening of the rather uncustomary musical revue, which was produced by the International Ladies' Garment Workers' Union and featured amateur performers coming from the ranks of the union's workers. Addressing topics such as the growing labor movement, racial equality, rejection of totalitarianism, and anti-war sentiments by means of intelligent political satire and songs rooted in vaudeville skits and Tin Pan Alley's style, *Pins and Needles* delivered the message in a musical language to which the American workers could relate and became the most successful production of the pro-labor theater of the Depression era. By revisiting the development of the American Workers' Theater Movement, this chapter will demonstrate that *Pins and Needles*' success was not the result of chance, but of the many trials and errors that characterized the earlier workers' theater productions.

Staging the Labor Protest: The Wobblies

In the 1920s, workers' social clubs, motivated in part by a strong sense of class consciousness, had established dramatic groups dedicated to the production of agit-prop theater for working-class audiences. On both sides of the ocean, the Workers' Theater Movement drew its actors, playwrights, and directors mainly from the working class, and the support of thousands of these amateur practitioners contributed to the growth of the theatrical movement and secured some success among the intended audiences. From a conceptual point of view, the WTM rejected the illusory nature of mainstream ("bourgeois") theater in favor of theatrical forms capable of involving working-class audiences and awakening their enthusiasm for class struggle. The movement took cues from Soviet agit-prop and German expressionist theaters, which offered valuable formal and ideological models and shared an anti-bourgeois perspective and predilection for montage (sharp juxtapositions of contrasting material). Yet, while European and American branches of the WTM shared many historical, structural, and ideological traits, crucial cultural and sociological differences rendered the movement in the United States a unique experience. In Europe, the labor theater unified ethnically homogeneous groups sharing common political and social foundations. In the United States the proletariat encompassed indigenous workers of European, African, and Native American descent as well as more recent European immigrants from countries such as Italy, Hungary, and Poland. If it lacked ethnic homogeneity, this diverse constituency, though, contributed to greater variety in the productions of the American WTM.

At first, theatrical units, seeking to mobilize and entertain specific communities, performed in their own language and offered plays that reflected their own culture and tradition. But soon, the American WTM comprised mostly English-speaking groups and focused its productions on current events and practical concerns stemming from economic, cultural, and social issues, such as xenophobia and other racial stances (i.e., the Sacco and Vanzetti trial and the Scottsboro case). By portraying events and experiences central to workers' lives, these productions united their audiences in a common class feeling that went beyond ethnic and racial boundaries and empowered their political struggle. Moreover, intentionally simple language helped convey this message and the use of chants heavily relying on simple melodies and steady rhythms promoted audience participation while adding a sense of communal experience. After all, these dramatic groups were at first an occasion for workers to socialize and, even if the WTM later believed in the capacity of theater to change the world, it also valued the communal aspect of its theater making. To reach its goals, the American WTM fully embraced the vernacular component and developed a distinctively national character that incorporated features from such genres as minstrel shows, vaudeville, and musical revues.

The WTM first appeared on the New York scene in mid-1920s, but the use of theatrical performances and music to publicize the needs and aspirations of the working class and to promote socialist ideology enjoyed deep roots in the American labor movement. For instance, beginning in 1905, the Industrial Workers of the World had sponsored "monthly smokers," a combination of staged propaganda and entertainment, as a fundraising initiative. "Smokers" generally comprised four three-round boxing bouts, a volunteer performance

56 · CHAPTER 2

by a professional entertainer (musician, comedian, etc.), a propaganda speech by one of the union's leaders, and a concluding propaganda sketch, which often included ironic and witty songs. A good example of these sketches, which anticipated the one-act agit-prop plays championed by the WTM, is "Their Court and Our Class" (1917) by Walker C. Smith, which mocked the so-called Everett Trial that followed events that happened on November 5, 1916, when 250 Wobblies sailed from Seattle to Everett, Washington, on the steamship *Verona* to make street speeches in support of a shingle weavers' strike. As the ship landed, a crowd of several hundred residents confronted them and a gun battle started. Two townspeople and five Wobblies were killed. Seattle police arrested seventy-four Wobblies upon their return to Seattle and charged Thomas H. Tracy with murder. The IWW launched a national defense fund campaign, and after a two-month trial the jury acquitted Tracy. As this excerpt demonstrates, Smith addressed the trial in a sardonic way:

> *Court Clerk*: Hear ye! Hear ye! The dishonorable Court of Snohomish County is now in secession. (*Turns to Jury, who rise*) Do you solemnly swear to hear no evidence in this case favorable to the accused and to render a verdict of Guilty? (*pause*) Before this dishonorable court comes now the case of the City of Everett, State of Degradation, plaintiff, versus A. Wise Wobbly, defendant. . . . The defendant stands arraigned and accused and is arraigned and accused before the dishonorable Bar of this Court of Injustice in that he did feloniously and with malice afterthought and otherwise with deliberation cause the death of A. Mutt and B. Jeff, to wit, by dodging, twisting, turning, shifting and otherwise evading bullets intended for his person and by so doing in the manner heretofore described did cause said bullets to enter the persons of the said Mutt and Jeff thus slaying, murdering, killing, putting to death, taking the life and otherwise bringing about the decease of the aforesaid Mutt and Jeff.[4]

This type of satirical denunciation of the corrupt American court system found a more mainstream audience in several prominent musical works in the 1930s, such as *Of Thee I Sing!* (George and Ira Gershwin, George S. Kaufman, and Morrie Ryskind, 1931) and Aaron Copland's one-act ballet *Hear Ye! Hear Ye!* (1934). The latter, one of the few compositions in which Copland manifested his interest in leftist activities, satirizes the legal system by enacting a protest against the miscarriage of justice in one of the most discussed issues of the period: the trial of the Scottsboro Boys.[5]

In the hands of the IWW even the pageant, in contrast to the lavishly produced pageants of historical Americana—such as the Kiralfy brothers' spectacles or the Hippodrome extravaganzas—became a bare-bones propaganda tool short on elaborate staging but long on symbolic representation. The "Pageant of the Paterson Strike," performed on June 7, 1913 at New York City's mammoth Madison Square Garden, illustrates this trend.[6] A group of artists and intellectuals led by journalist John Reed, who later became famous for his firsthand report of the Soviet Revolution, decided to help the cause of the Paterson strikers.[7] The pageant portrayed the general strike as the principal weapon of class warfare and allegorized the conflict between the force of labor and the force of capital. Its six episodes reenacted the events of the strike to emphasize how capitalism withers without labor. Some of these tableaux included music: the first, "The Workers Begin to Think," ended with the singing of "The Marseillaise" and the invitation to the entire audience to join in the song. The fourth episode, "Mass Meeting at Haledon," portrayed a mass meeting of strikers singing new songs of protest as well as traditional songs of revolt, such as "The Internationale" and "Red Flag." Episode five, "Sending Away the Children," depicted a May Day parade and presented women and children, dressed in red, waving flags and marching to the beat of an onstage band. Reviewing the pageant, the correspondent for *Current Opinion* considered it an artistic achievement but also recognized it as a dangerous weapon for subversive propaganda.[8] Indeed, the IWW organized this massive public pageant to promote the strike as a weapon in the working-class struggle and raise money for the workers. Most importantly, though, they started a link between working-class and New York intellectuals that proved influential during the period of major activity of the WTM and in general during the years of the Great Depression. Moreover, by carrying economic and social discontent from the "jungles" (as IWW members called the camps close to a town, usually near railroad junctions, where they congregated between jobs) to the stage by means of irony, intelligent wit, and songs, the IWW established a practice that in the next two decades would lead to the politicization of the musical revue.

Organizing the Labor Protest: Workers' Theater Movement

The sporadic and often improvised staged protests of the IWW turned into a more structured organization when, in the second half of the 1920s, a loose coalition of English-language and foreign-language production companies heralded the emergence of the WTM in New York City. The workers' troupes of the WTM considered their principal goal to be agitation, not entertainment. Therefore, to engage the working-class audience, their plays addressed specific issues and events related to their struggle rather than broad themes of social drama. The straightforward plots described local strikes or labor concerns and abounded

58 · CHAPTER 2

with montages of mime and songs, revolutionary slogans, stereotyped images, and allegorical characters portrayed in an almost cartoonish manner.

Among the foreign-language theater groups, the Yiddish theater Artef (Arbeiter Theater Verband), which staged its first play in 1928 and by 1931 had realized five productions, acquired a certain fame.[9] In addition to the primary company, the Artef Players, it included the Artef Club, a group of non-performing members, and the Artef Studio, a training ground for young actors.[10] Two Hungarian-language groups, the Elöre Dramatic Club and the Bronx Hungarian Workers' Club of New York, each attempted to produce a one-act play every month and a full-length play every three or four months. Unlike the Bronx organization, the Elöre Dramatic Club performed in English as well as Hungarian and thus could reach beyond ethnic circles. Elöre specialized in mobile productions and, in 1930, it formed a "shock troupe" that toured industrial towns in New Jersey.[11] No foreign-language group, though, achieved the widespread fame of the German Prolet-Bühne, which operated from 1925 to 1935 and proved to be the most influential in the development of the formal structure of the WTA's plays.

At first, Prolet-Bühne produced standard German-language repertory for the entertainment of immigrant workers; but in 1928, with the arrival of the new director John E. (Hans) Bonn, the company became politically militant and began programming short didactic and "chanted" agit-prop plays, also in English, similar to the mobile propaganda productions of the workers' theater movements in Germany and the USSR. These stylized plays, which generally lasted twenty minutes or less, adopted the theatrical form of a one-act play based on episodes loosely connected by songs and workers' chants. They were performed at labor meetings, rallies, or workers' reunions and were produced with minimal staging (placards, signs, megaphones, and symbolic costumes). The loosely constructed episodes of these works generally featured simple plots loaded with revolutionary slogans and portrayed stereotyped and allegorical characters (the Capitalist, the Worker, etc.) in an almost cartoonish way.[12] The Prolet-Bühne agit-prop plays disregarded the conventional limitations of play-space, as actors would occasionally break the "fourth wall" by calling on the audience to participate both in the show and in political activism.

One of the notable productions of the Prolet-Bühne, the mass recitation with action *Tempo, Tempo!* (1930), which portrays in a propagandistic and dogmatic way the archetypal conflict between labor and capitalism, illustrates the structure of their plays. As the title suggests, the work relies on rhythm and syncopation to depict the perceived evils of the enforced rapidity of production in American industry as opposed to the leisurely tempo of Soviet industry. The loaded dialectical content finds its pace in part in the rhythmic pulsation of the chanted verses:

The Workers' Theater Movement and the Politicization of the Musical Revue · 59

(Characters: Capitalist and seven or ten workers)
Capitalist:
    Tempo, tempo, watch your step
    Hold on tight and show some pep.
    Move your hands and bend your body
    Without end and not so shoddy.
    Faster, faster shake it up.
    No one idles in this shop.
    Time is money, money's power.
    Profits come in every hour.
    Can't stop profits for your sake.
    Tempo, tempo, keep awake.
Worker:
    We are humans, not machines.
    Capitalist:
    You don't like our fast routine?
    Get your pay and get out quick.
    You speak like a Bolshevik.
    Tempo, tempo, watch your step.
    Hold on tight and show some pep.
[. . .]
Worker:
    Soviet tempo—worker's might
    Onward without parasite.
Worker:
    Soviet tempo—worker's power
    Moving, growing, every hour.
Worker:
    Soviet tempo—every man
    Helps complete the five year plan.
Capitalist:
    Insane tempo, absurdity,
    Respect for private property.
Worker:
    Fight the thief and profiteer
    Onward, onward, without fear.
Capitalist:
    Have respect for your tradition
    Honor God and your religion.
Worker:
    Fight the hypocrite and priest

60 • CHAPTER 2

> Who do not work and always feast.
> Capitalist:
> Stop this aimless merriment
> Adopt me for your government.
> Worker:
> Down with all the wealthy classes
> All power to the toiling masses.[13]

The text itself is confusing, because it uses identical meters for the verses about capitalist and Soviet production. But in performance, music differentiated them: contrasting patterns of drumbeats reportedly accompanied the recitation. Unfortunately, the score (if one ever existed) does not survive to precisely indicate the relationship between the percussion and the spoken word. Contemporary accounts, though, suggest that two rhythmic formulas powerfully represented the conflict between the two tempi of industrial growth: the pain of the frantically exploited American workers versus the pride and calm determination of the free Soviet workers.[14]

The first English-language amateur group to impact the labor community significantly, the Workers' Drama League (also known as Workers' Theatre), formed in the spring of 1926. Its founders included some of the most liberal intellectuals of the decade: Jasper Deeter, John Dos Passos, Michael Gold, John Howard Lawson, and Ida Rauh.[15] The first production of the Workers' Drama League was Gold's *Strike*, an agit-prop skit.[16] In a foreword to the published text of the play, Gold explained that he had modeled *Strike* on works he had seen in Europe:

> Immense and dramatic as the revolution itself, Mass Recitation is one of the most powerful and original forms developed in the struggle for proletarian culture. It is an art that has grown out of the workers' life and needs; it is useful art. [. . .] I have tried to write a Mass Recitation here for the needs of American workers, and I hope other proletarian writers will experiment in the form, and workers' dramatic groups produce their experiments.[17]

These words align with the few surviving reports of Workers' Drama League's performances, which relate that the group drew inspiration from Soviet theater but also from Erwin Piscator's revolutionary mass-spectacle productions. The idea of workers' theater, however, was still new in the United States and difficult to define, and eventually after just one more notable production, *The Biggest Boob in the World* (1927, translated by Upton Sinclair from the German play by Karl Wittfogel), the Workers' Drama League dissolved.

From Amateur to Professional Workers' Theater

Although short-lived, the Workers' Drama League had initiated important new developments in American theater and involved, to a previously unmatched degree, many left-leaning intellectuals and professionals from the commercial stage. Three of the Workers' Drama League's founders, Dos Passos, Lawson, and Gold, teamed up in 1927 with Francis Farragoh and EmJo Basshe to establish the New Playwrights Theatre, the first professional theatrical company to reflect the values of the radical left.[18] Aspiring to portray social reality on the American stage, to free the theater from commercialism and sterility, and to restore the creator's right to experiment with form and subject matter, they helped to promote ideas that "would bind them together and give the movement a definite character and direction."[19] The process of gradual engagement of artists and writers in the workers' struggle that the IWW had started with the Paterson pageant was becoming an experience that, by merging innovative forms, use of vernacular, and political message, would eventually typify the leftist American theater of the 1930s.

In three seasons of operation, the New Playwrights Theatre, sponsored by financier and patron of the arts Otto H. Kahn, produced eight plays that employed American vernacular musical idioms on the professional stage. The New Playwrights attracted some of the most radical young actors, directors, and playwrights, including Jasper Deeter, Mordecai Gorelik, and Paul Peters, and experimented with complicated settings, mass groupings, and onstage singing. They staged long and convoluted plays that addressed industrial and economic themes and displayed sympathy for the labor movement, often exploiting the power of music to spread their message. Particularly interesting for its functional use of music is Lawson's *Loud Speaker* (1927), a play that satirized American politics by chronicling the farce of a state election in New York.[20] According to the *New York Times* critic J. Brooks Atkinson who reviewed the premiere, "the story is not substantial enough to piece out the production," but "fortunately the method is more original."[21] The play's "originality" stemmed from Gorelik's constructivist setting with its symmetrical structure of steps and platforms, a clear attempt to emulate the productions of the Russian director Vsevolod Emilyevich Meyerhold, and from the rapidity of action he required from actors and stage personnel.[22]

Music played a major role in this constructivist production, too, as it emphasized movement and action and communicated the author's vision of political corruption and manipulation. Lawson began working on this script in 1924. At first, he opted for the name *A Jazz Tragedy* and only after a series of revisions and changes in title—from the initial to *X Plus Y* to *The Invisible Man*—he eventually decided on *Loud Speaker*. The original title, though, clearly draws attention to the use of jazz to comment on contemporary American society and its paradoxes, and this is certainly one of the play's most striking features, besides its setting.[23] As the plot unfolds in a series of farcical situations involving mistaken identities, disguises, and cross purposes, Lawson introduces gags and comic material borrowed from vaudeville routines, often employing jazz idiom and dance. Staging directions called for a band of Black jazz performers, *The Imperial Serenaders* conducted by Lieutenant Jacob W. Porter, positioned in full view on a high platform on stage.[24] They would direct the audience's attention to the most important stage movements and events, even if at times introducing stereotypes that associate Black people with lazy or corrupt behaviors.[25] In Act 1, for instance, Clare (the daughter of Collins, the main character) who is portrayed as a 1920s flapper only interested in enjoying herself and in extravagant behaviors, encapsulates all these features as she dances a "black bottom" with the family's African American butler to the accompaniment of the jazz band. Lawson also specified "a wild jazz rhythm" to back the dance of the six Black politicians at the end of the act.[26] Ultimately, however, the experimental nature of *Loud Speaker* hastened its failure because actors and audiences, as Atkinson argued, proved unable to cope with the new and still experimental approach to the constructivist techniques.[27]

With Michael Gold's three-act play *Hoboken Blues: or The Black Rip Van Winkle: A Modern Negro Fantasia on an Old American Theme* (1928), the New Playwrights tested more directly the combination of political agitation with satire and jazz to present, at least theoretically, a more pointed critique of American society's treatment of Black people.[28] Gold, who had visited Moscow in 1925, reported his favorable impressions of Meyerhold's theatrical constructivism and praised the way it "broke up the stiffness, the drawing-room stuffiness, the parliamentary talkiness of the old stage. Acrobatic actors race up and down a dozen planes of action. The drawing-room play has been thrown on the junk-pile of history. Things happen—broad, bold, physical things, as in workers' lives."[29] In *Hoboken Blues*, he attempted these same techniques, not only by introducing a constructivist post-Cubist stage full of ladders and scaffolds, but by directly juxtaposing tragedy and "belly-laughter," because, as he argued, "satire and heroism—the silliness of the bourgeois world and the heroism of the proletarian world—these are the basic themes of the new stage."[30]

Hoboken Blues portrayed American racism by utilizing a central aspect of the minstrel tradition, namely blackface. At first, Gold wanted the Provincetown Players to produce the play with Paul Robeson in the role of the main character

Sam Pickins. When Robeson rejected the part on the grounds that he did not want to play the role of a jobless Harlem Black man who spends the day playing banjo, singing, and dancing, Gold turned to the New Playwrights' Theatre.[31] One wonders, though, if Robeson, as eventually did Edward Massey, the stage director of the New Playwrights' production, had misunderstood Gold's activist intentions. In the play, Sam, the lead character, is a man oppressed by society, which constrains him to abandon artistic aspirations to work at manual labor because of the color of his skin. Unable to find a job in Harlem, he goes to Hoboken where, a friend told him, he can find a job as a performer. Once in Hoboken, though, he realizes there is no room for him and his art and, unwilling to accept degrading jobs, he becomes a union activist. However, he realizes it was all a dream and ends up getting a job at Rosewater's Fountain of Youth playing the banjo and dancing, thus stating his failure to overcome stereotypes and denouncing the deleterious effects of American society on Blacks. Gold's stage directions, "No white men appear in this play. Where white men are indicated, they are played by Negroes in white caricature masks," imply that he intended the play as an attack on American racism by exploiting, and often exaggerating, stereotypes associated with blackness in contemporary society.[32] In the actual production, however, Massey decided to cast only white (in blackface for the Black roles) rather than Black actors, thus changing *Hoboken Blues* into a racist production, a real minstrel show filled with cakewalks, circus skits, cabaret scenes, and processionals. He also turned Gold's denunciation of American racism into an unintentionally ironic representation of stereotyped blackness, as some of the ironic lines in the mouths of white blackface performers lost the bite they would have had if uttered by Black actors. The use of minstrelsy might have cast the political message in a more familiar language and allowed the audience to understand the subtle layers of meaning in Gold's play, but Massey's staging denied the play that depth, showing once again that not only the audience but also theater practitioners were unable to abandon stereotypical representations and unprepared to deal with the new theatrical form.

The use of American vernacular becomes even more prominent in the New Playwrights production of Lawson's *The International* (1928), possibly the first American play to attack American imperialism.[33] As with *Loud Speaker*, here too Lawson attempted to emulate Meyerhold's approach to staging, but he combined it with one of the most popular forms of American vernacular, the musical revue, and he exploited the archetype of the Ziegfeld Girls, a chorus of showgirls sharing visual appearance who were dancing in simple synchronized choreographies and portrayed the image of women as beautiful objects lacking agency. As Brooks Atkinson observed, "There is a vague background of expressionism, a constructivistic stage setting, and jazz interludes in which the theme of the moment is reduced to lyric and sung by eight stenographers, or communists, or

64 · CHAPTER 2

whatever they happen to be at the time."[34] Indeed, the incidental music, which included original material by Edward A. Ziman with some popular tunes such as "The Internationale" and "The Birth of the Blues," plays a major role in this play. In his production notes, Lawson states that the play should be considered a musical throughout and that "it requires full musical score along modernistic lines with special emphasis on broken rhythms, machine noises, and chanting blues."[35] The chanting he refers to is "a weaving of jazz rhythms with orchestral background," and therefore, various roles are meant for singing actors. Lawson also gives specific instructions for the chorus of sixteen women divided into two groups: eight musical-comedy-type girls of average height who dance and perform jazz and blues songs "stand against" eight taller women who narrate in the dignified manner of the Greek drama.

In this play, the jazz idiom is often used to represent freedom and revolutionary changes in societal matters. For instance, in the third act, the chorus of stenographers in a New York office sings the blues while equating sexual freedom with revolutionary causes as they dance off to a brothel, thus legitimizing their right to free sex. Jonathan Chambers, though, suggests that "the chorus of stenographers, a group that idealistically connects their rebellion for sexual liberty with the triumph of the people's revolution, are situated as figures who lack the proper material and mental resources and are thus doomed to fail."[36] This observation becomes relevant when paired with Lawson's indication that the stenographers' "dancing is also adapted from simple revue formation," a clarification that links them to the Ziegfeld Girls. The paradoxical pairing of revolutionary ideas with these revue girls added another layer of meaning to the play. While the two choruses, playing on the dichotomy between high- and lowbrow entertainment, mark symbolically the significant moments of the work and offer a critique of American imperialism, one could also argue that in this play Lawson problematized contemporary approaches to the musical revue and its portrayal of female performers as consumable objects.

An even more prominent use of music, specifically workers' songs, characterizes Upton Sinclair's *Singing Jailbirds* (1928), an account of the persecution of an IWW leader named Red Adams who was arrested with other union members while organizing a strike of marine transport workers in Southern California.[37] The play, introducing labor songs, especially those of Joe Hill, to the professional stage took advantage of the value of music to spread messages of solidarity and equality, a feature that is at the core of the IWW rhetoric. In the play strikers were imprisoned without criminal charges and were compelled to stop singing their Wobbly songs. Yet, inciting each other with the line "Sing, you Jailbirds, sing!," the jailed workers, defying orders, demonstrated with their communal singing the union's strength. While *Singing Jailbirds* failed at the box office, it became

The Workers' Theater Movement and the Politicization of the Musical Revue • 65

the New Playwrights' most appreciated production among politically militant workers. Its success spread also in Great Britain among groups belonging to the Plebs League and the National Council of Labour Colleges, with actors recalling the efficacy of the use of Wobbly songs to heighten the drama.[38]

The New Playwrights understood the importance of speaking directly to the average American worker by addressing complex sociopolitical messages in a vernacular idiom. As such, this group of playwrights was promoting revolutionary art using innovative constructivist techniques, but also experimenting with jazz and popular musical idioms, which acted as the glue that connected revolutionary content and the proletariat. Taking advantage of the American vernacular, though, did not suffice to lessen the difficulties that the New Playwrights encountered in spreading their political message through innovative theatrical forms. In fact, not only did these authors often have to fight against stage directors' and/or actors' failure to understand the new forms and content, but their efforts to encourage activism by employing American musical practices did not yet create a sea of change in attitudes toward theater attendance, as none of their productions ran for more than fifty performances. As Virginia Hagelstein Marquardt states, their experiments became a site for major debates concerning artistic form versus political content, a truth that raised questions on the actual value of this pairing.[39] Kenneth Fearing, reviewing Gold's *Hoboken Blues*, claimed that the New Playwrights' message was confused and encouraged them to clarify their intentions in regard to their "ulterior motives" if they really wanted to use theater as a weapon in a political propaganda that did not sound patronizing or boring. Fearing addressed this predicament in the most candid way:

> The New Playwrights cannot go on pretending that revolution and modernist technique and good plays are, by some curious magic, a Holy Trinity of which the members are One and the Same. It is probable that the most effective play, from the standpoint of winning new converts, would be an old-fashioned heart-breaker couched in stale language and stale form. And on the other hand, it seems likely that a play of which the directors of the theatre themselves approve immensely would be absolutely valueless from a revolutionary view.[40]

Arguably, in his honest remarks Fearing stressed the major issue affecting the success of the New Playwrights: the radical propagandistic topics and experimental character of their plays overlooked the needs of average American workers, who seemingly still preferred to be entertained rather than educated. Lawson himself later recognized the missed opportunities of the New Playwrights:

> We of the New Playwrights were trying to educate a "mass audience," before we ourselves were educated—and the audiences was conspicuously absent. [. . .]

66 · CHAPTER 2

Only a few unions could be persuaded to come en masse and there was no massive enthusiasm in their response.[41]

The New Playwrights assumed that if their topics featured enough substance, workers would go to the theater. But this audience proved largely unprepared to understand and negotiate the subtexts of expressionist drama even when rendered more palatable with the use of the vernacular. As Malcolm Goldstein acutely observed, "a theater established for such a purpose could not use densely plotted, allusive material of the sort staged by the New Playwrights, for the audience from shops and lofts would have neither the patience to sit through prolonged action nor the learning necessary for grasping the allusions."[42] Nevertheless, the New Playwrights understood the importance of music, and specifically of American vernacular musical idioms such as jazz, vaudeville, and labor songs, to break through the wall that still existed between the needs of the working class and the socio-artistic aspirations of the professional theater.

The Turn of the Workers' Laboratory Theatre

Developing an awareness of and appreciation for the dramatic arts among participants of the labor movement became the task of the Workers' Laboratory Theatre (WLT, later called the Theatre of Action), which, founded in 1929, received sponsorship from the Workers International Relief of the Communist Party. Like other units of the WTM, it followed the example of European agit-prop workers' troupes. Blake describes their portable productions as short, topical plays featuring rhythmically chanted dialogue delivered by actors in stock costume (high hat for the Capitalist, hatless and open-throated shirt for the Worker, etc.).[43] The most valuable contribution of the WLT, though, consisted in the support for greater collaboration among the diverse branches of the American WTM, an effort that, at the end of 1929, contributed to the foundation of the Workers' Dramatic Council of New York, which united twelve groups performing in English and in foreign languages. The Council eventually reached out to similar dramatic groups in other major industrial cities nationwide, such as Los Angeles, Chicago, and Boston. This unionizing effort prompted, in April 1931, the first publication of *Workers Theater*, a magazine for discussion, guidance, and exchange of experiences for workers' dramatic groups. The WTM had thus become a nationally organized entity and its magazine functioned not only as a speculative mouthpiece but also a forum for the dissemination of workers' drama. In April 1932, New York hosted the First National Workers' Theatre Conference where the WTM established its first nationwide organization, the

League of Workers' Theatres (LoWT) of the USA, a national federation of producing groups with headquarters in New York. The League took over publication of *Workers Theater* (renamed *New Theatre* in 1933) and promoted on a national level the concept of labor theater. It organized dramatic training schools, and it supplied groups with new short plays.[44]

The LoWT supported cooperation between workers' and professional theaters with the goal of revitalizing the national stage to the advantages of both. Blake noted:

> A mighty idea took shape—the idea of a theatre, including amateur and professional, far broader than the labor movement yet drawing sustenance from this great force, a theatre whose repertory would reflect the important social questions of the times, would mirror the clash of social forces, would side with the masses of American people against the forces of reaction and repression.[45]

Blake's insider observations portray the zeal of a group of enthusiastic radical minds as the workers' theater began to increasingly recruit skilled professionals and liberal intellectuals committed to firsthand involvement with the workers' struggle. Morgan Y. Himelstein noted that, at the height of the Great Depression, this interest might have stemmed more from the crisis of the Broadway bourgeois theater than from an increased devotion to leftist principles.[46] Yet, with even middle-class families (to which most of these professionals belonged) suffering the hardships of a disintegrating economic system, communist ideology surely seemed to certain segments of the population a viable solution. Some theater professionals keenly felt the appeal of Soviet culture, especially the revolutionary dramatic theories of Stanislavsky and Meyerhold; they idealized Soviet theater as a product of Communism and dreamt of a country where society and culture appeared to serve the common good.

Undeniably, though, thanks to the current economic and political circumstances, the LoWT succeeded, albeit for only a short time, in building a link between amateur and professional theater. To achieve this goal, it attempted to transfer the concept of labor theater from workers' dramatic groups to mainstream stages, and it promoted the principle that theater must connect to real life and attract people who believed in the responsibility of artists to engage social issues. Championing the most suitable genres and styles for a successful workers' theater, these practitioners considered expressionism and realism, but, quite interesting, also vaudeville, which was deemed the only native popular form acceptable in this context.[47] Blake reported that, while some authors advocated a uniform recognizable technique employed by all international workers' groups, others emphasized the necessity of creating an American workers' theater as a corrective to a tradition that privileged bourgeois forms addressing

68 · CHAPTER 2

upper-middle-class audiences, and vaudeville—that is, the American musical vernacular—seemed to offer them a possible solution.

The Challenge: Balancing Aesthetic and Political Goals

The discussions among practitioners of the WTM mirror the debates within the Composers' Collective about form and content in proletarian music (see Chapter 1), and they display how, in the early 1930s, the quest for a proletarian aesthetic to counterattack the perceived degeneration of the bourgeois aesthetic engaged all arts. Unsurprisingly then, when, in 1932, a group of professional artists guided by the author Jack Shapiro, the designer Mordecai Gorelik, and the playwright-director Philip Barber founded the Theatre Collective as a branch of the LoWT, we come across the same issue for the workers' theater that we examined for proletarian music: the dichotomy between aesthetic and political goals prevented the radical theater from reaching its intended audience.[48]

The Theatre Collective aimed to move beyond agit-prop Marxist skits featuring workers' chants of protest characterized by strong and steady rhythms. Instead they presented full-length plays with semiprofessional casts drawn from its membership. The group promoted the trend toward realism, aspired to abandon the strictly propagandistic formula (workers suffer, workers pass out leaflets, workers go on strike) and, to appeal to a middle class suffering the hardship of the Great Depression, they adopted a style deriving from the American tradition of vaudeville and staged in a more humoristic way real characters and their everyday issues. However, while conceptually they understood the importance of the American vernacular, the Collective's members were still equating professionalism with traditional bourgeois theater. Among the professional practitioners who collaborated with the Theatre Collective there were members of the Group Theatre, including Joe Bromberg and Clifford Odets, who shared the idea of the stage as a mirror of real life.[49] They found in the Collective an outlet for their work and an organized company moving toward professionalism that could potentially reach a wider audience interested in contemporary issues.[50] The enthusiasm for professionalism and full-length plays, however, did not spread to the base of the WTM, as an editorial postscript by Shapiro demonstrates:

> Although we heartily endorse the Theatre Collective's program to establish a permanent company on a high technical and artistic plane, we do not feel that any revolutionary theatre group can at this critical hour plan to withdraw from actual work on the revolutionary theatre front. [...] We urge that the Studio work of the Collective include short revolutionary plays and skits for public performance.[51]

Ultimately, the reluctance to address workers' concerns in a more accessible way caused the demise of the Theatre Collective, which operated only until the 1935—36 season. This defeat evinces, once again, the difficulties that the WTM encountered in combining a more popular approach to theater with the artistic demands of the professional theater, a struggle that in those years, as we have seen, also compromised the existence of the Composers' Collective.

A similar trajectory, even if on a larger scale, accompanied also the activities of the Theatre Union, founded in 1932 by Charles Walker, the only professional workers' theater active at the time in New York. The company, which did not belong to the League of Workers' Theatres and was not directly associated with the Communist Party (although it benefited from party support and from that of numerous left-wing and liberal organizations and trade unions), attracted the usual cadre of left-leaning artists and authors interested in revolutionary theater, including John Dos Passos, John Howard Lawson, Joseph Freeman, Paul Peters, and Elmer Rice.[52] These playwrights envisioned a new theater intended for a new audience and identified some key elements for a revolutionary play—a theme of class struggle, clear action, and a militant solution to the struggle—but did not argue that the American vernacular, including music, would have helped spread their message.[53] Following the lead of the Theatre Collective, they abandoned the agit-prop movable one-act skits and their stylized characters in favor of full-length plays for proscenium theaters, and they staged plays based on issues and themes connected with the working class, such as social conflicts and economic turmoil. Between 1933 and 1937, the company produced seven plays, which were essentially professional productions of leftist dramas.[54] None of these plays, however, garnered major critical approbation (except from members of the left-wing press).

Lawson, who contributed the last play staged by the Theatre Union, *Marching Song* (1937), while applauding certain features of the previous productions, lamented that they were not successful because the authors lacked actual engagement with the working class and were more interested in the idea of art for art's sake than in the workers' needs.[55] Advocating for a split between "the theatre of the workers and the theatre of the reactionary bourgeoisie" to promote the growth of the revolutionary theater, Lawson recognized that the work he started with the New Playwrights Theatre in the 1920s was the first step toward this change and stated:

> There is only one direction in which the drama can move forward: it must join the march of the advancing working class; it must keep pace with the quickening momentum of the revolution.[56]

70 · CHAPTER 2

This political revolution, according to Lawson, could not have happened if writers had not abandoned artistic pretentions and had consciously focused on the message. His answer to this problem was the aforementioned contribution to the 1937 season, *Marching Song*, a play in which he sought to express the workers' needs in a "lyrical poetic form."[57] It is indeed quite revealing that the play with which he wanted to address this needed change relied on music, most specifically labor songs, as a unifying element. Communal singing is in fact the tool that Lawson used to give voice to the workers' struggle—for instance, at the end of Act 2, when workers sing in solidarity marching out of the factory to support Pete, their former colleague who has been unjustly fired. But not even Lawson's political engagement and the unions' massive supporting web for ticket sales could save the Theatre Union. Professionalism, artistic productions, militant struggles, and affordable tickets did not help the company to survive, and the dream of a professional workers' theater ended in 1937.

Evidently, the writers of the Theatre Union could not convey their sociopolitical messages in an easily graspable and perhaps even an enjoyable way. After all, even if aware of their struggle, workers preferred to address their issues with humor and irony rather than be presented with doomed real-life conditions. What then was missing? In her analysis of the Theatre Union's conflicted production of Brecht's *The Mother*, Saal addresses the problematic definition of political theater in the United States. Should it be the European modernist theater influenced by the Frankfurt-School and Brecht's theories of epic theater based on *Vermfrendungstechnik* and absence of empathy, or a more popular and traditional theater based on a compassionate and emotional approach?[58] What is more relevant, that the message effectively reaches the audience and actually promotes social change, or that the plays fulfill the artistic objectives of playwrights and stage directors no matter what? The answer to these questions was the conundrum that the WTM had to solve, and it proved to be a difficult and often contradictory task.

As demonstrated above, a pro-amateur, anti-bourgeois stance characterized the first stages of the American WTM, when the dogmatic and overtly propagandistic message was delivered with the help of American vernacular, often in vaudeville-like forms. Music had constituted a fundamental element in the parodies and pageants of the Wobblies, the agit-prop plays of the earlier WTM groups, and the productions of the New Playwrights Theatre, where American minstrelsy, vaudeville, jazz, and revue often abutted agit-prop skits of European social drama and Marxist doctrine. However, a diverse attitude emerged over time as the movement increasingly embraced professional actors, directors, and playwrights who frequently neglected the power of the vernacular. Arguably, then, one of the problems affecting the success of the Theatre Union was its inability to understand that to appeal to a wider audience it had to accept the vernacular while, in the name of professionalism, it abandoned the tradition of vaudeville, which the LoWT and the Collective Theater had identified as essential to engage a working- and middle-class American audience. At the height of the Great Depression, average Americans wanted anything but a reminder of their precarious economic and living conditions; they wanted to forget their anxieties or, at least, have them addressed in a lighter way filled with self-irony and laughter. This issue became especially critical after 1934, when the professional theater turned to the political musical revue to keep afloat.

Parade: Broadway's Attempt to Move Left

Social critique was not a novelty on Broadway, which, by the early 1930s, had already witnessed notable musical revues dealing with topical issues. For instance, *Americana* (1932), produced by the Shubert Brothers, exhorted audiences with humor, music, and dance to face hardships of the Depression, and made a hit of Yip Harburg and Jay Gorney's "Brother, Can You Spare a Dime?" Another example was Moss Hart and Irving Berlin's *As Thousands Cheer* (1933), which featured musical numbers connected by means of newspaper headlines. Captions painted on a curtain, replicating the newspaper format, introduced the various satirical sketches, which poked fun at current events and people in the news. Several of the show's numbers became standards, including "Heat Wave," "Easter Parade," and "Harlem on My Mind."

Both *Americana* and *As Thousands Cheer*, however, wore their topicality lightly, and lacked the controversial implications that characterized Paul Peters and George Sklar's *Parade* (1935), the first attempt to approach political issues in the format of a non-book musical. A satire of the New Deal and its failure to live up to its promises, *Parade* originated as an attempt to save the sinking Theatre Union by presenting lighter works, such as comedies about working-class life, vaudeville, and revue, to a working-class audience.[59] But, as Robert Garland stated, the revue "was found to exceed the ambitions of that ambitious organization," and, when the Theatre Union turned down *Parade*, the work became part of the 1934–35 season of the Theatre Guild.[60] Significantly, the Guild had neither a history of leftist involvement nor a mandate to reach a working-class audience. It had begun in 1918 as a private, commercial organization geared toward the production of full-length, contemporary art-theater.[61] To ensure financial stability, the Guild's governing board developed a subscription network that, by the end of the 1920s, had reached more than 60,000 in New York and the other cities of the Eastern theater circuit.[62] But even the robust Guild suffered during the Depression as subscriptions fell and financial burdens increased. To help limit losses and reach

72 · CHAPTER 2

a wider audience, it turned to two propagandistic works with social significance: *They Shall Not Die* by John Wexley (1934), a play dealing with the Scottsboro case, and the musical revue *Parade* (1935). The Theatre Guild was not new to the musical revue, as it had already produced three versions of the *Garrick Gaieties* in 1925, 1926, and 1930. The 1925 edition, with music and lyrics primarily by Richard Rodgers and Lorenz Hart, had opened on May 17 as a two-performance benefit for the Theatre Guild, but rave reviews prompted a reopening and a subsequent run of 211 performances. Rodgers and Hart contributed to the 1926 sequel as well, and the 1930 version included numbers by Blitzstein, Vernon Duke, Ira Gershwin, and Johnny Mercer. The *Garrick Gaieties*, which became a critical and popular success, parodied and satirized current subjects, such as the New York City subway system, President and Mrs. Calvin Coolidge, and even the Theatre Guild itself: the opening number of the 1925 show, "Soliciting Subscriptions," spoofed the Guild's "serious pretensions." In this light, the Guild's decision to present *Parade* as its final offering of the 1934–35 season appears less surprising, albeit not the most fitting choice for its subscribers.

Parade featured an illegal Labor Day parade, which the police attempted to stop. The story behind each float became a satirical sketch about issues related to unions and the workers' struggle. Sklar and Peters, among the most prolific writers of the Theatre Union, wrote the basic material of the show. As stated in *New Theatre*, which reprinted three of the sketches from *Parade* hoping to encourage workers' theater groups to include the musical revue form in their repertory, the two authors had come to the realization that popular songs, vaudeville, and revue sketches could reach larger audiences and be more effective in spreading the sociopolitical message.[63] In their effort, they were joined by comedy writers Frank Gabrielson, David Lesan, and Kyle Crichton, who provided some sketches, and Jerome Moross, who composed most of the music, with several other authors contributing material. Blitzstein, for example, supplied words and music for "Send for the Militia," a sketch that, as Jay Williams reports, had originally been intended for the Theatre of Action (which grew out of the Workers' Laboratory Theatre).[64]

Before opening night, the show went through many cuts and changes. While this is customary for musical revues, in this case many of the afterthoughts and modifications were the result of frictions between the authors, who wanted the revue to be a powerful leftist statement, and the producers, who feared that some numbers were too politically dangerous. Eventually, the Theatre Guild opened a tryout of *Parade* at the Colonial Theater in Boston on May 6, 1935. The twenty-eight original acts of the show included musical numbers sympathetic to the working class, such as sketches satirizing capitalism, fascism, and other perceived enemies of the proletariat. The program notes left no doubt about the authors' expectations:

Parade is 1935 set to music. We are living in unusual times. We are inclined to take some of the foibles of the day too seriously. Others we pass by too lightly. *Parade* is designed to give you a perspective. It is bright, witty and nimble—and yet it has a sting. It is, in fact, a revue with a definite idea and not just a potpourri of songs and sketches about sex and love and the moon above.[65]

The result, though, failed to match the producers' enthusiasm, as apparently no one took the Theatre Guild seriously as a promoter of left-wing politics. The extreme propagandistic issues in *Parade* might have appealed to the militant audience of the Theatre Union, but they frightened the Guild's heavily middle-class subscriber base. For instance, Peter and Sklar's gruesome attempt to ridicule the red scare and stereotypical conservative views in "The Tabloid Reds" came off as a dull form of theatrical suicide. Moross's setting follows the strophic structure of the lyrics and features a simple martial melody in C minor over a steady repetitive rhythm in the accompaniment (see the first stanza in figure 2.1). Even if the theme could be catchy, though, how could any production expect to succeed with anonymous actors chanting from a darkened stage the following text?

1st Red
Destruction is our chief delight
We plot in cellars in the dead of night
Our diet is buckshot and dynamite
We are the tabloid reds

2nd Red
We eat little children with gunpowder sauce
We make little bombs which we love to toss
And if we miss we're very cross
We're the tabloid reds

3rd Red
We're those monstrous ghoulish creatures
That populate the Sunday features
Scare the kindergarten teachers
We're the tabloid reds

4th Red
We butcher, slaughter, lust for gore
Blood's our drink and we thirst for more
When we can't get it we're very sore
We're the tabloid reds.[66]

Indeed, the force of the political message threatened to obscure the sound dramatic construction of some of the sketches, and negative reviews greeted opening night at the Colonial. Helen Eager of the *Boston Traveler* wrote:

> *Parade*, the Theatre Guild's newly born offspring, might be listed on its pedigree "By 'As Thousands Cheer,' out of 'Waiting for Lefty.'" For there was no one at the Colonial last evening at 11:45 who had not been thoroughly reminded that there was a depression bowing down these United States, that starvation was

Figure 2.1. Jerome Moross, "The Tabloid Reds," mm. 1–9. "Jerome Moross Papers, 1924–2018," Series III: Works by Jerome Moross; Subseries III. 62, Box 49: *Parade*, Rare Book and Manuscript Library, Butler Library, Columbia University

The Workers' Theater Movement and the Politicization of the Musical Revue • 75

stalking the land. Between these often grim reminders there was beauty of dance, there were costumes strikingly bizarre and exquisitely lovely, there were tunes hauntingly melodic, lyrics amusingly pointed. And there was Jimmy Savo with his pantomimic comedy. [. . .] "A satirical revue" it is termed. But realism, often too stark for comfort, much less amusement, frequently overwhelms the satire.[67]

An even harsher verdict came from Elinor Hughes of the *Boston Herald*:

The audience came with the evident intention of being pleased: it is a safe guess that by the time *Parade* was over it was either bewildered, alarmed or annoyed. . . .

A superabundance of energy characterized the beginning of the evening, together with such an amplitude of material that it was impossible for us to see all the scheduled numbers. The authors of the sketches [. . .] poke fun at capitalism, communism, college education, politics, the AAA General, Hugh Johnson, Huey Long, Fr. Coughlin, Hitler, and the ladies who take up socialism and then call out the police to protect them. [. . .] As the evening wore on, matters grew more and more serious until entertainment became propaganda and those members of the audience who had come to be amused wondered whether they had not made a mistake. [. . .] New York may like it later on, but before it leaves Boston it will need some drastic cutting and reviewing. At the present time it wavers midway between entertainment and propaganda and succeeds in neither.[68]

News of the controversial opening and consequent decisions to cut some numbers arrived in New York too, as the *New York Post* reported:

According to reports from Boston, where the Theatre Guild's final offering of the season opened a tryout engagement last Monday evening, *Parade* is just a bit too vigorous to please the more solid Back Bayites. A satirical revue with plenty of sting and bite, it is declared by some reporters to be definitely Communistic in tone. Others say it is merely satirical. Hardly anybody in present-day affairs is spared, apparently, and the show is now being pruned and tightened up for its Broadway bow a week from Monday at the Guild Theatre.[69]

But cutting and polishing could not mitigate the overt propagandistic tone of the sketches, and the "socially conscious" musical revue ran in New York for only forty performances at a loss to the Theatre Guild of approximately $100,000.[70]

Only a few sketches won praise for wit and fine craftsmanship. Hughes commended "College Daze," "The Free Clinic," and mostly "The Dead Cow," "The Last Jackass," and Blitzstein's "Send for the Militia" largely on the strength of Eve Arden's performance, stating that "[i]t is not especially barbed fun, suggesting that the authors were writing with one eye on the Theatre Guild subscribers rather than with all their attention on their satirical purposes."[71] Arden seemed to have been the star of the show, as George Holland

76 · CHAPTER 2

in the Bostonian *Evening American* praised Blitzstein's number, too (but failed to acknowledge the composer) and focused on her charismatic presence: "In this song Miss Arden finds perfection in material. The quality of this song manages to strike the exact mood that would make 'Parade,' if it could be sustained throughout the show, swell entertainment."[72] Elliot Norton in the *Boston Post* wrote: "The sketch entitled 'Call for the Militia' [*sic*] (beautifully done by Miss Eve Arden) is excellent."[73] And Garland, in the *New York World-Telegram*, suggested that the communistic aspect of the revue had been exaggerated: "Frequently *Parade* turns satiric at the expense of the red scare propaganda. [. . .] It comes up again—and artfully—in 'Send for the Militia' an interpolated song with words and music by Marc Blitzstein. Eve Arden sings this with a subdued gusto that wins the audience."[74]

The critical positive response to Blitzstein's one-woman number warrants attention, as it foreshadows the success of the composer's subsequent leftist musical plays. The sketch satirizes American liberal thought about socialism, anti-war sentiments, labor strikes, and poverty in a four verse-refrain format.[75] A fifth verse, penciled in an unknown hand on the verso of the typewritten script, addresses contraception.[76] The central figure of this satire is a wealthy clubwoman who, on being asked to put her liberal theories into practice, calls loudly for help to prevent an uprising:

> Last club meeting, we ladies took up Socialism,
> And you know it's quite nice.
> We all sit around the fire drinking tea.
> Last year it was Art,—No, Technocracy.
> But this Socialism is so much more exciting, it's so daring,
> With its equal rights and economic love and sharing,—
> What's that you say? Did we ever stop one day and decide
> That the time had come to really try it?
> You mean Socialism? Sounds like Communism.
>
> Send for the Militia, the Army, the Navy,
> Quick, bring out the Boy Scouts, ev'ry Captain, ev'ry Ace,
> The country's on the brink of disaster,
> We better have the troops around us in case.
>
> [. . .]

The musical accompaniment, scored for alto and baritone saxophones, clarinet, drums, piano, and string quintet, follows the style that characterizes Blitzstein's agit-prop theater.[77] The clear verse-refrain structure and the use of a simple

The Workers' Theater Movement and the Politicization of the Musical Revue • 77

melody rendered the song more palatable to the theater audience than the rhythmic workers' chants or mass songs that characterized other numbers of the revue, such as the previously mentioned Peter and Sklar's "The Tabloid Reds." But Blitzstein's harmonic treatment did not lose its characteristic complexity and unmistakably shows features that will define his more mature agit-prop works: dissonant harmonization of diatonic melodies and modal ambiguity, in this case between C major and C minor.[78] The critical approbation for "Send for the Militia" brought Blitzstein good exposure, as the Theatre Union invited him and Arden to perform the sketch at a benefit. Moreover, he began to network with some major personalities of the American social theater, including Elmer Rice, thus opening possibilities for his achievements with *The Cradle Will Rock*.[79]

Blitzstein's sketch aside, though, critical reception apparently agreed that the Guild had no credentials as a promoter of left-wing politics, and the show treated its material too realistically to be received as merely entertaining satire. Percy Hammond commented in the *New York Herald Tribune*:

> "Parade," a leftish musical show, is on view at the Guild Theatre, hitherto a citadel of advanced conventionalities. Aided by the hostile forces of song, dance and fun, the young rebels continue their demand for Change, and defy the axiom that "Revolutions are not made: they come." In a somewhat monotonous procession of bitter little burlesques they tweak the noses of established things. They are not good-natured satirists. Beneath their beetling brows they glare rather than twinkle. [. . .] The U.S.A., one gathers from "Parade," is the land of the heel and the home of the knave. The bird of freedom is a buzzard, and the Star-Spangled Banner with its candy-stick colors is a tawdry rag, emblematic of oppression.[80]

Parade evidently suffered an identity crisis. It met the expectations of neither a leftist propaganda piece nor a mainstream satirical revue. It lost its bite as a consequence of the Theatre Guild's concerns for its own audience, which led to the many changes that undermined the original conception.

But there were also artistic concerns. In 1935, Jerome Moross, who had written most of the music for *Parade*, claimed that the show's attempt to rise "to the formal level of the professional revue" failed because it adhered too closely to the principles of the commercial musical theater rather than formulating new rules peculiar to the revolutionary theater. Based on his critical analysis of *Parade's* failure, Moross theorized guidelines for the successful leftist writer seeking to convey sociopolitical content:

> The revolutionary revue should, if possible, combine both musical comedy and revue forms, telling an important story in swift-moving five-minute blackouts, revue fashion. The function of the music and dance would be to carry the

78 · CHAPTER 2

audience over wide emotional leaps, and passages of time and space. Very often the two could be integrated in the form of swift mass choruses and chants or any other imaginative device, which uses the music against the action. The settings, instead of being very elaborate (so that final production depends on the number of "acts" possible of performance in front of the curtain while shifts are in progress), should be skeletal. Possibly an almost bare construction or an impression would be sufficient, if heightened by exciting lighting. Any number of possibilities exists depending upon the ingenuity of a clever scene designer working on a low budget. Aesthetically, there is another reason for dispensing with elaborate sets in a class-conscious musical: the speed of the form requires constant attention to achieve its maximum effect. By the time the audience has inspected the setting, the sketch or song is well on its way. Broadway producers may not mind this, but for the revolutionary stage it is disastrous.

I envision a new revue in America, a swift and vital form rising above flippancies, the music being more than the banalities of Tin Pan Alley, the lyrics achieving the worth of a Gilbert or a Brecht, the sketches using the blackout technic [sic] not for bathroom humor, but for terse dramatic punches. [. . .] It is one of the most important types of native culture yet to be developed and it should be restored to the working class, from whose vaudeville and minstrel show entertainment it came.[81]

Indeed, when it followed Moross's advice and addressed the target audience with intelligent satire and wit in a simple and direct musical idiom, the political musical revue became a stunning success, as *Pins and Needles*, the runaway hit of the workers' theater movement, and Blitzstein's *The Cradle Will Rock* proved.[82]

Pins and Needles: The Workers' Lesson for the Theatre Guild

With *Parade*, the professional theater failed to convincingly deliver a strong political message in a musical revue form, a task that *Pins and Needles*, produced by an amateur cast and initially addressing an audience of workers, achieved by nimbly combining political satire, vaudeville skits, and Tin Pan Alley songs. Its production history reads, to some extent, like a fairy tale. In 1935, the American Federation of Labor voted at its annual convention to sponsor labor drama as an educational tool for the cultural enhancement of workers. In response to this resolution, the International Ladies' Garment Workers' Union (ILGWU) acquired the Princess Theatre on 39th Street, renamed it "Labor Stage," and organized classes in the performing arts for its workers.[83] Louis Schaefer, the ILGWU executive director, formed the amateur company ILGWU Players (which included only members of New York City ILGWU's locals) and arranged for

The Workers' Theater Movement and the Politicization of the Musical Revue • 79

instruction from the Theatre Union's Victor Wolfson and other prominent professionals.[84] The ILGWU Players produced only one other show besides *Pins and Needles*: a fifty-performance revival starting in January 1937 of John Wexley's spoken drama *Steel*, which, in collaboration with the New Theatre League, the Theatre Union, Artef, and the United Mine Workers, toured Chicago, Youngstown (Ohio), and Pittsford (New York), after closing in New York City.[85] Thereafter, *Pins and Needles* became the primary focus of ILGWU dramatists, who wrote new material for incorporation in various editions of the show.

Harold Rome wrote the bulk of the revue's lyrics and music, but other writers and composers prominent in the workers' movement—including Arthur Arent, Charles Friedman, and Marc Blitzstein—contributed to the show as well.[86] Schaefer first hired the semiprofessional Contemporary Players directed by Philip Loeb to present the show on June 23, 1936 in a small studio above the main auditorium of the Labor Stage for an invited audience and members of the union; Rome and Earl Robinson accompanied at the piano. Ben Irwin, critic of the *Daily Worker*, praised that production for its revolutionary approach to the genre:

> *Pins and Needles* is certainly a heroic and ambitious enterprise. Heroic in a definite sense, because with terrifically limited facilities, a small stage and two pianos its producers have attempted a form of entertainment that is usually accompanied by a full-fledged orchestra, revolving stage, enormous cast and a full staff of high paid technicians.[87]

Thus, to some extent, *Pins and Needles* hewed closely to Moross's prescription for successful workers' theater and demonstrated that elaborate costumes and choreography, so central to Broadway productions, were unnecessary in a revue with "something to say."[88] The success of the showcase convinced Schaefer and the ILGWU to move ahead with performances by the union's amateur forces. From that private run of the show Rome retained only five sketches: "Lesson in Etiquette"; "Dear Beatrice Fairfax"; "Mother" (which later became "The Little Red Schoolhouse"); "Mussolini Handicap"; and "Peace Quartet" (renamed "Four Little Angels of Peace").[89] He and his collaborators spent a year revising the show and planning for studio tryouts during the summer of 1937. This process took so long in part because of Schaefer's decision to schedule the concurrent revival of *Steel*, a production that involved many of the amateur garment workers and prevented them from devoting more time to rehearsals for the revue. Eventually, *Pins and Needles* moved to the main auditorium on November 27, 1937, for a regular run. It became the news of the day and attracted theater critics from major newspapers and magazines.

80 · CHAPTER 2

The fifty-five original cast members (male and female) represented ten of the thirty-eight metropolitan branches of the ILGWU, from the Corset and Brassière Workers' Local to the Dressmakers' Local and the Bonnaz Embroiderers' Local. At first, they performed only on weekends, but after a month, box office receipts encouraged Schaefer to commence nightly performances. He obtained leaves of absence for the actors from their regular factory jobs and enrolled them in Chorus Equity or as junior members of Actors Equity.[90] Still, they gained no economic advantage over other members of the ILGWU:

> With the exception of two or three players with minor parts, the entire cast will take a leave of absence from their jobs during the run of "Pins and Needles." The ILGWU will pay them strictly according to garment union scales. This being a slack season in the garment industry, the girls are receiving $23 a week, the men $45. If the run extends to February, when business always picks up, the pay will be raised to $45 and $80 respectively. The production, which cost $10,000, will be out of the red if it runs until March. Any profit will be turned back to the union for future productions.[91]

A second company directed by Robert Gordon performed five o'clock matinees; in the spring of 1937, *Pins and Needles* played as many as fifteen performances a week.[92] Eventually, the ILGWU Players left the 299-seat auditorium of the Labor Stage and in June 1939 moved to the Windsor Theatre, a slightly bigger house (about 400 seats), but still smaller than most theaters devoted to musical plays. At a time when most hit plays lasted an average of six months, *Pins and Needles* ran for 1,108 performances—nearly three full years—before closing on June 22, 1940.[93] The company also presented, on February 3, 1938, a command performance at the White House for President Franklin D. Roosevelt and his wife Eleanor. When garment workers and general audience alike clamored for a nationwide road tour, ILGWU officials created a third company, and the original cast went on the road.[94]

The sensational run of *Pins and Needles* took everyone by surprise, as Strauss remarked in the *New York Times*:

> But who, last year, would have suspected that "Pins and Needles" would soon be hailed as the entrance of the "left wing" theatre into the field of the musical revue—a field which Broadway thought, and reasonably, that it had all to itself; or that it would become the forerunner of such later productions as "Sing Out the News," Cabaret TAC and other Leftist extravaganzas. It is safe to say that no one was more surprised by the attention given to this lusty contender on the doorstep of Broadway than the ILGWU, i. e., the parent, itself.[95]

The Workers' Theater Movement and the Politicization of the Musical Revue • 81

Moreover, the show received many positive reviews, which demonstrate that it became a successful tool for pro-union propaganda. A brief survey of these commentaries, though, also emphasizes how *Pins and Needles* was considered the ultimate achievement of the workers' theater. Critics stressed that a combination of meaning and musical revue defined its essence, and the gaiety and freshness of the show accounted for its success, especially if compared with the earlier productions of the WTM. In the same article, Strauss argued:

> In New York the drama study groups of the various locals had for a long time been staging the usual sort of "agit-prop" sketches—grim little items which for the most part were soliloquies on to strike or not to strike, or depicted the drab and colorless lives of the workers until they joined the union, after which everybody lived happily ever after. Many of them ended with the fist and a strident rendition of "Solidarity Forever." Even the workers were bored.[96]

Even the correspondent for the *New York Times* considered the ILGWU Players "a new addition to the growing list of imaginative and youthful theatrical groups which are making monkeys of the folks who think it is fashionable to say the theatre is dead," and continued, "accepted in the good-natured spirit in which it is offered, *Pins and Needles* is certainly a revue out of the ordinary and one which only occasionally droops to the level of the things which it is satirizing."[97]

Unsurprisingly, the failure of *Parade* appears to have lingered in some critics' minds: the *Times* reviewer concluded "all in all, the left-wing theater may take pride in this delayed descent from the usual soap box"—surely a veiled reference to *Parade*. Robert Reinhart of *Variety* unambiguously stated: "Since 1934 he [Rome] has been trying to sell a Broadway producer the idea of a leftist revue, but he's found that, since the Theatre Guild produced *Parade*, that idea is poison along the big street."[98] And Richard Lockridge of the *New York Sun* wrote:

> You may be surprised, considering and no doubt deprecating all this, to hear that the boys and girls of the ILGWU are often pretty funny; that at their best their songs and sketches have the enlivening sting that wit has, whatever side it comes from. They have their moments of heavy-handedness and dead-pan propagandizing, but they can also laugh. And, probably for the first time in labor stage history, they can laugh at themselves as well as at their antagonists.[99]

Initially, the left-wing press hailed the show's innovations. Eric Englander of the *Daily Worker* wrote: "Here is an entertainment which may very well become the norm of brightness and freshness in left-satirical material and of the skill with which non-professional performers can be coached into giving really

82 · CHAPTER 2

adequate accounts of themselves."[100] But even the non-political press recognized that the revue, employing genres and forms peculiar to the American tradition, became an effective propaganda tool. Burns Mantle made a particularly pointed remark linking *Pins and Needles* to the earliest Wobblies' use of music on stage: "I suspect it is also the nearest approach to a revival of the old labor guild spirit of self-expression that labor groups have achieved in our day."[101] Richard Watts Jr., in the *New York Herald Tribune*, compared *Pins and Needles* to other successful American revues:

> The customary charge that the Left Wing boys and girls lack a sense of humor is most effectually refuted in the bright, tuneful and vastly entertaining revue called "Pins and Needles." [. . .] A gaily satirical revue that possesses much of the fresh and unspoiled quality of "The Garrick Gaieties" and "The Grand Street Follies," the new work not only makes cheerful and contemptuous fun of such class enemies as Mussolini, Hitler, the Japanese militarists, the professional patriots and the local reactionaries, but turns with high good humor on the excessive seriousness of some of its own graver partisans. It can laugh merrily at itself as it can at its foes, and that is a quality that makes it both disarming and persuasive. Here is social propaganda in its most winning fashion.[102]

John Mason Brown, summarizing the most salient features of the revue, emphasized the propaganda potential of this type of entertainment:

> "Pins and Needles" is a gay show, and an intelligent one. It widens the theatre's horizons, as they stand in desperate need of being widened, to include the interests and the problems of those who do not belong to what was once known as the carriage trade. It is class-conscious enough to satisfy the most avid propagandist. Yet it manages to say serious things lightly and to indict with a song and a smile. By so doing it makes its points twice as effectively as it would have done had it followed the sober routine-methods of agit-prop drama in this country. [. . .] Indeed the whole production eloquently justified the claims of its sponsors that the labor theatre in this country has found its sense of humor. "Pins and Needles" is related at once to life and to joy. By turning its propaganda into good entertainment, its message is doubly insured, and doubly telling as propaganda.[103]

As Saal noted, though, the success of the show on Broadway led some leftist reviewers to criticize its overt emphasis on entertainment values.[104] The production, using Mary McCarthy's words, was accused of turning dictators into comedians and indictment of capitalism into spoofing of commodification, militarism, and Americanism.[105] And even the *Daily Worker*, in November 1939, withdrew support for the *New Pins and Needles* production, accusing the writers of modifying the political content to the point where it had lost its bite.[106] Saal herself challenges the sociopolitical relevance of a show that seemed to have lost its labor identity and replaced it with "a commercially produced image of labor," and asks: "Can we still speak of a propagation of working-class culture if this very culture is turned into a luxury item to be consumed by the upper middle class only?"[107] Indeed, when it moved to the Windsor Theater after an almost two-year run at the Labor Stage and it substituted some amateur with professional actors, *Pins and Needles'* freshness and novelty had vanished, as partially did its politically conscious message, and many of its skits lost relevance. Yet, by embracing the American vernacular in a straightforward way, without embroidering it with pretentious constructivist staging, sophisticated theatrical ideas, and overt radical seriousness, the ILGWU turned the musical revue into a winning political endeavor. And, while it lasted, it was indeed its topicality that partly conditioned its success.

Sketches toed Popular Front lines regarding racial equality, justice and commitment to freedom, rejection of fascism and oppression, and concern for the worker. Yet they also skewered broader issues ranging from world politics and anti-war sentiment to high taxes and the growing labor movement in the United States and abroad.[108] To appeal to its working-class audience and address typical pro-union topics, the ILGWU production embraced some of the most salient features of the Broadway musical revue, including romance songs, comic skits, and satirical takes on topical issues. While the show offers a critical approach to the musical revue as an example of capitalist consumption, it also criticizes the traditional role of female performers as consumable objects; after all, women constituted most of the garment union workers. As Michael Denning emphasized, the central character in *Pins and Needles* is the working girl—not the Ziegfeld Girl in her sumptuous statuary stage aura, rather a smart woman who is aware of her place in society and capable of dealing with current sociopolitical situations.[109]

The program for the original production, directed by Charles Friedman and produced by Louis Schaffer, included the following numbers:

1. "First Impression"
   Lyrics by Harold Rome and Charles Friedman
   Music by Harold Rome
2. "Why Sing of Skies Above!"
   Music and lyrics by Harold Rome
3. "Mussolini Handicap"
   Sketch by Arthur Arent
4. "Public Enemy Number One"
   Music and lyrics by Harold Rome

84 · CHAPTER 2

5. "The General Is Unveiled"
Staged by Benjamin Zemach
Ballet music by Harold Rome
6. "We'd Better Be Right"
Sketch by David Gregory, lyrics by Arthur Kraemer
Music by Harold Rome
7. "The Little Red Schoolhouse"
Sketch by Emanuel Eisenberg
8. "Sunday in the Park"
Music and lyrics by Harold Rome
9. "Dear Beatrice Fairfax"
Music and lyrics by Harold Rome
10. "Economics I"
Sketch by Charles Friedman
Music and lyrics by Harold Rome
11. "Men Awake"
Music and lyrics by Harold Rome
Conceived and staged by B. Zemach
12. "Lesson in Etiquette"
Music and lyrics by Harold Rome
13. "Vassar Girl Finds a Job"
Music and lyrics by Harold Rome
14. "FTP Plowed Under"
Sketch by Marc Blitzstein
15. "What Good Is Love?"
Music and lyrics by Harold Rome
16. "One Big Union for Two"
Music and lyrics by Harold Rome
Dance routine by Gluck Sandor
17. "Four Little Angels of Peace"
Music and lyrics by Harold Rome
18. "Slumming Party" (containing the song "Doing the Reactionary")
Music and lyrics by Harold Rome
Dance by Gluck Sandor
19. "We've Just Begun"
Lyrics by Harold Rome and Charles Friedman
Music by Harold Rome [110]

Topics ranged from satires of wealth and reactionary attitudes at home ("Slumming Party," "Lesson in Etiquette") to anti-fascist satire ("Mussolini Handicap," "Public Enemy Number One," "Four Little Angels of Peace").[111] *Pins and Needles* even upheld the long-standing revue hallmark of self-reflexivity with "Give Me the Good Old Days," a sketch added in 1939 about a member of its cast who sings of the simple days back in the shop without rehearsal problems and having to sing two songs a night. The show also cleverly mocked the radical theater. Eisenberg's "The Little Red Schoolhouse" (originally titled "Mother, or Let Freedom Ring") satirized the unsuccessful Theatre Union production of Brecht's *Mother* that the workers' theater audience had treated with hostility because of its condescending didacticism. Eisenberg's sketch mocked Brecht's symbolism and mimicked *Mother*'s presentational style, the *Verfremdungseffekt* of epic theater. In one scene of "The Little Red Schoolhouse," characters spoke directly to the spectators while holding placards for them to see, as one actor said, "We're not taking any chances on your intelligence" and others chanted meaningless slogans: "Now that we have found out about a strike / Now that we have found out about a union / . . . Maybe we can give up chanting. . . . "[112] Joseph Schrank's "Paradise Mislaid," a sketch added to the third edition, *New Pins and Needles*, presented "all of Odets in six minutes" and mocked the playwright's unsuccessful *Paradise Lost*.

Blitzstein's contribution to the show, "FTP Plowed Under," became, as did his "Call for the Militia" for *Parade*, one of the most controversial and discussed sketches of *Pins and Needles*. The composer wrote it to attack the Federal Theater Project and its censorship and the shutting down of his own *The Cradle Will Rock* earlier that year, in June 1937, by satirizing events that had prevented the official opening of the play (on *Cradle*, see Chapter 5).[113] The title parodies "Triple A Plowed Under," written in 1936 by the editorial staff of the FTP Living Newspaper Unit under Arthur Arent's supervision.[114] The living newspaper dramatized the story of the Agricultural Adjustment Act and the plight of the Dust Bowl farmers and suggested that farmers and workers join to cut out the "middlemen" dealers and other commercial interests. In Blitzstein's sketch, the FTP officials become censors and unite to excise any social meaning from his play. The main character, Hippity Bloomberg (Blitzstein), meets with officials from the FTP, including Mrs. Clubhouse (Hallie Flanagan, the head of the FTP), to discuss the production of his play, *Workers Also Love*. Out of concern for a preponderance of sexual innuendo in the play, they ask Bloomberg to change the title, to cut some of the overtly romantic aspects of the plot (such as a barefoot walk in a brook), to avoid dances because the members of the FTP dance company are troublemakers, and to delete any reference to strikes or leftist activities. Bloomberg follows their directions, resulting in the virtual decimation of his play, but Mrs. Clubhouse approves and remarks: "No actors, no stagehands, no musicians, and next to no play. . . . We will simply have a

86 · CHAPTER 2

very intimate production of—practically nothing." At this point Bloomberg, commenting that he thought the FTP did not practice censorship, mordantly suggests that the play, now consisting only of the words "The Curtain Rises," should be performed for no audience. The FTP officials agree, but ask: "Now why can't our play open SMACK like that? Do we have to have a curtain?"[115]

The full score of "FTP Plowed Under" has been lost, but some musical fragments are available in the Marc Blitzstein Papers at the Wisconsin Historical Society in a folder labeled "The Cradle Will Rock: Ten Sketches to Music." Trudi Wright has offered a detailed analysis of the sketches, and she has emphasized how some typical features of the agit-prop skits of the WTM, such as simple rhythms, homophonic hymn-like texture and melodic lines, are at times accompanied with percussive and dissonant sounds more typical of Blitzstein's musical language, for instance in the opening fanfare.[116] The difference between this musical idiom and that of the predictable harmonic structure of the 32-bar chorus form of most of the other songs of *Pins and Needles* is quite striking. One could argue that Blitzstein was still under the influence of his experience with the Composers' Collective of New York and their mass songs, but, as Wright claims, there is indeed a pungent irony in the use of clashing dissonant chords to highlight the presence of the FTP officials, in particular its director Hallie Flanagan, in light of the censorship of *Cradle*.[117]

Blitzstein's satire did not go unnoticed, even if some reviewers reacted negatively. Richard Watts Jr., who praised the whole revue as winning propaganda, could not hide his dissatisfaction with this particular sketch: "It is disappointing to find so wise a satirist as Marc Blitzstein, the composer of *The Cradle Will Rock*, snarling at the Federal Theater Project and its bureaucracy in such feeble fashion."[118] His view did not change several months later:

> Last week the reviewers were invited back to "Pins and Needles," to see a new edition, with new people, new costumes, new scenery, and presumably a new number or two. It was a bit disappointing when we got there to find that at least one number in the engaging show put on by members of the International Ladies' Garment Workers' Union had not been changed. Marc Blitzstein's sketch assaulting the management of the Federal Theater Project seemed pretty bad when the revue opened, and it certainly hasn't improved with the months. [. . .] In fact, only Mr. Blitzstein's sketch is an utter botch, and I think it should be done away with as soon as possible. It is not so much that it supplies the one outstandingly bad item in the show, for "Pins and Needles" is good enough entertainment to stand one such left-down. But Mr. Blitzstein's reputation is too good, after his "The Cradle Will Rock," and it should not be marred by something he apparently wrote in a moment of excessive pique.[119]

The Workers' Theater Movement and the Politicization of the Musical Revue • 87

Others, such as Sidney B. Wriffle of the *New York World-Telegram*, praised the sketch: "The wallop taken at the Federal Theater Project and bureaucracy under the title 'FTP Plowed Under' was excellent."[120] Heywood Broun singled out Blitzstein's satire as the only biting moment of the whole revue:

> I am disturbed to discover that the critics are right in saying that Pins and Needles ... is the best revue Broadway has seen in several seasons. This fact worries me. And I am not kidding. The show is too funny. I wish it had less entertainment and more bite as propaganda. Pins and Needles has attracted the carriage trade, but the carriage trade just eats it up. [...] The only really savage satire is directed against the Federal Theater, a movement which worker groups ought to support in spite of its present limitations.[121]

In a later editorial about the FTP, Broun pressed his point:

> Indeed, the most savage satire on the government's activities in the theater is a sketch in *Pins and Needles*. That is impressed into my mind, because I was so much excited by *The Cradle Will Rock* when I first saw it that I ran around backstage and introduced myself to Marc Blitzstein, the author. We sat down and talked about the theater in general, and I expressed the opinion that *Cradle* had much more bite than *Pins and Needles*. "The only really mean thing in *Pins and Needles*," I said, "is the slap at the Federal Theater, and I think that a labor group should not attack government pioneering in theatrical production. I thought that sketch was terrible." "You may be right," said Mr. Blitzstein, "I wrote it." Just the same I was right.[122]

The sardonic sourness of the sketch may appear self-indulgent, but, as Gordon argues, staging his own troubles with the FTP served also as promotion for the Mercury Theatre revival of *The Cradle Will Rock* whose first performance (December 5, 1937) followed after a few days the opening night of *Pins and Needles* (November 27, 1937).[123]

The emphasis on self-irony and the power to be politically convincing while being able to make fun at the daring circumstances of a working class still suffering the hardships of the Great Depression was indeed *Pins and Needles'* winning card. As Harry Goldman noted, the recovering economic conditions helped, too:

> Had *Pins and Needles* appeared in 1935, perhaps it would have been a failure, too. America was still in the throes of a severe depression and the time seemed to call not for laughter and song, but for anger and action. By 1937, however, this mood had abated somewhat. President Roosevelt's New Deal had reduced unemployment and the country began to see an end to its misery. [...] It appears, therefore, that *Pins and Needles* was well-timed. America was more receptive to

88 · CHAPTER 2

humor and satire, and the Labor Stage production was fortunate enough to take advantage of that mood.[124]

It can be argued, though, that the financial and sociopolitical success of the revue derived also from other concurrent circumstances associated with the peculiar American musical and theatrical workers' traditions and innovations. As Denning claims, the revue's unique fusion of proletarian drama and vaudeville results from the experience of Charles Friedman, its director.[125] Before turning to the professional stage of the Theatre Union, Friedman had cut his theatrical teeth with agit-prop skits modeled on European workers' theater and with the Shock Troupe of the Workers' Laboratory Theatre. But, having learned the lesson from the lukewarm reception of his previous productions, he gave American audiences a show built on a form of entertainment they could understand:

> I directed in the music hall tradition where you sing directly to the people in the audience. I did not direct it as an illusionistic play. I broke down the fourth wall for them. I gave them the analogy of Al Jolson. He had a gang plank built that went way out into the audience and when he sang he went out there.[126]

Moreover, an idiosyncratically American quality, reminiscent of the Wobblies' irreverent songs and skits from two decades earlier, permeates the satire and comedy of *Pins and Needles*. These genuine, and somewhat naïve, attributes appealed to the audience more than the dark and angry features of the agit-prop street dramas of the Workers' League Theater and even the bitter propagandistic sketches of *Parade*. American audiences found it difficult to accept the rigid stereotypical images used in agit-prop plays, because they portrayed a world they did not belong to. Rome's competent and lighter, yet still prickly, sketches depicted real people and situations to which the audience could easily relate: the New York family planning a Sunday in the park as the only affordable entertainment, the Vassar girl unable to find a job anywhere but behind the counter at Macy's, or a consumption-oriented woman who avidly follows advertising's suggestions in the hope of finding a man.

Pins and Needles not only offered satire of current political and economic events, its entertainment values and intelligent humor also spiced up songs about working-class romance, as in "One Big Union For Two," a song that compared a love story to a union contract:

> I've decided the only way I can woo you,
> Is to take a hint from the A.F. of L. and the C.I.O.
> [...]
> I'm on a campaign to make you mine,
> I'll picket you until you sign

In One Big Union For Two,
No court's injunction can make me stop,
Until your love is all closed
In One Big Union For Two
Seven days a week I want the right,
To call you mine both day and night,
The hours may be long,
But! Fifty million union members can't be wrong!
When we have joined up perhaps there'll be,
A new recruit or two or three,
For that's what teamwork can do
In One Big Union For Two

Rome's witty and biting lyrics in "Doing the Reactionary" (a song included in the skit "Slumming Party") made the audience laugh while ridiculing the red scare and stereotypical conservative views. By turning right-wing stance into a fashionable dance (equivalent to "Doing the Foxtrot"), Rome satirized the same conservative behaviors that Peter and Sklar described with gruesome lyrics in *Parade*'s "The Tabloid Reds":

Verse
    It's darker than the dark bottom,
    It rumbles more than the rumba,
    If you think that the two-step got 'em,

    Just take a look at this number.
    It's got that certain swing,
    That makes you want to sing!

Chorus
    Don't go left but be polite
    Move to the right
    Doing the reactionary.

    Close your eyes to where you're bound
    And you'll be found
    Doing the reactionary.

    All the best dictators do it
    Millionaires keep stepping to it
    The four hundred love to sing it
    Ford and Morgan swing it

90 · CHAPTER 2

Hand up high and shake your head
You'll soon see red
Doing the reactionary.

Coda
So get in it, begin it,
It's smart oh so very
To do the reactionary!

Friedman's innovative direction and Rome's intelligent satire, however, might not have succeeded if *Pins and Needles* had failed to give American workers a familiar musical idiom: not the mass songs and propagandistic choruses of the Composers' Collective, but Tin Pan Alley (TPA) tunes. Not only that, the familiarity with the popular form allowed Rome to imbue his songs with subtle layers of meanings, which would have been understood by the average American audience.

"Doing the Reactionary," for instance, follows the standardized TPA structure: the 4-measure introduction establishes the tonic (C minor) and concludes on a half cadence; the 12-measure verse divided into three 4-measure phrases sets the joke: being a reactionary is but a dance; the 32-measure lyric binary chorus (AABA), with refrain and a 9-measure coda as second ending, lampoons the ease with which politicians and tycoons move from left to right with closed eyes to avoid acknowledging what they leave behind. The conventionality of the musical structure helps Rome stress the social meaning of the lyrics, as he subtly undermines the norm to bring out the political satire. One example occurs at the end of the second phrase of the A section of the chorus (see figure 2.2), where the words "doing the reactionary" are sung on a bluesy A♭ major with flattened seventh, and the awkward subdivision of "re-ac-tion-a-ry" forces the melodic line to stumble inelegantly and end on a weak fourth beat. The unusual phrase ending goes against the conventions and seems to stress humorously the "irregularity" (at least for the workers!) of being a reactionary. In a commercially available recording of this song, a young Barbra Streisand responds well to the tension in the vocal line with her mocking nasal inflection, perhaps preserving a performance tradition that she had learned from Harold Rome himself.[127] With its two-beat feel (half notes on 1 and 3 are the pervasive rhythm), Rome's swinging and upbeat foxtrot in C minor does not just play with the conventions of popular songs. To get the message across, Rome also specifically refers to and capitalizes on a category of popular songs about fashionable dances of the day by mimicking their titles: "Doing the Apache" from *Topics of 1923*, "Doing the New York" from the *Ziegfeld Follies* (1931), and "Doin' the Waltz" from *The*

Figure 2.2. "Doing the Reactionary," words and music by Harold J. Rome, chorus mm. 1–10. Mills Music, Inc., 1937

Fireman's Flame (1937).[128] Indeed, Rome showed that a skillful composer could be socially significant by manipulating the conventions of popular song.

The use of popular idioms in *Pins and Needles* even prompted a reaction from T. W. Adorno in his essay "On Popular Music," written after he had fled Nazi Germany in 1938 and joined his colleagues of the Frankfurter School at the Princeton Radio Research Project:

> It may be noted that a moderate leftist theater production such as "Pins and Needles" uses ordinary jazz as its musical medium [....] Those who ask for a song of social significance ask for it through a medium which deprives it of social significance. The use of inexorable popular musical media is repressive *per se*. Such inconsistencies indicate that political conviction and socio-psychological structure by no means coincide.[129]

For Adorno, American popular songs lacked social significance because of their standardized 32-bar form. Workers, he argued, seek novelty in their leisure time, an alternative to the boredom of their mechanized jobs. But they are ironically exposed to, and compelled to like, a music that is based on repetition and imitation and spoils their only chance for a real change.[130] Promoters of commercialized entertainment, he claimed, aim at these standard reactions, and seek

92 • CHAPTER 2

to render the musical experience a mere automatism to control the market. But to support his criticism of popular music Adorno cited *Pins and Needles* and disregarded Rome's idiosyncratic and pointed use of the 32-bar song form to emphasize the satirical text and call attention to the social significance of his song.

In fact, the political and social impact of the sketches included in *Pins and Needles* did not go unnoticed.[131] Even though Schaefer wanted to avoid communist allusions in the show, many of the ILGWU men and women, as well as the professionals who joined the second and third casts, were left-leaning or directly involved with the Communist Party. They knew exactly which jokes Rome and his collaborators intended to make and what the lyrics implied. For Sylvia Cahn, one of the original ILGWU members of *Pins and Needles*, "It was a labor show, political to an extent."[132] And Joe Alfasa, also an original cast member, recalls, "I know that they did not want us to be known as Communists. There were a lot of left-wing kids there, as I remember."[133] Gene Barry, a professional who joined the show once it moved to Broadway, stated:

> The point of view that the show took was very courageous for that time. It took courage to lampoon the establishment and power figures. These were points of view that might have differed from the general population. I liked "Doing the Reactionary" the best, it was a very clever, political travesty.[134]

The revue became such a powerful image of an emerging American working class that, as "ringer" Lee Morrison recalled, it turned into a catalyst for politicians in search of public exposure: "Because of the political importance of the show, many politicians felt it was significant to be seen with members of the *Pins and Needles* cast." But she also emphasized the degree of political involvement of cast members: "The actors were very socialistically minded. They knew what it was like to be a worker. They weren't like the intellectual Communist sympathizers who had no idea what it was like to be a worker."[135]

In the end, because of these political overtones, Rome reported that censorship became an issue:

> All the songs were banned from the radio. The only one played on the air was "Sunday in the Park." It got to be a Hit Parade song. The songs were too controversial for the air. "One Big Union for Two," "Doing the Reactionary," "Mene, Mene, Tekel"—all were too controversial, so radio scrubbed them. I was politically suspect of being of the Left. I've always had that problem more or less. I write songs that concern themselves with people and their problems.
>
> [...] There was strong government criticism and strong criticism from the Left. It got so any piece had to be reviewed before it could be done. You have to

The Workers' Theater Movement and the Politicization of the Musical Revue • 93

know the history of the period before you can understand why things like that were so controversial.[136]

Censorship followed the show as well, especially when it left the liberal-minded stage of New York City and went on tour. In some cities, certain skits had to be deleted to avoid repercussions. Nettie Harary remembers:

> In Des Moines, at intermission, people lined up to get their money back. They didn't know what was happening. They probably didn't read the papers and our show was topical and so we bombed in Des Moines.
>
> In St. Louis they called us Bolsheviks. At that time there was a fashion craze in New York, girls wore kerchiefs on their heads, much like Eastern European women. That added to our troubles. There was also a lot of anti-Semitism. They saw us as a bunch of Jews from New York.[137]

Political implications aside, many of the revue's songs became entrenched in the national musical consciousness. They became the soundtrack to workers' everyday life and, as Denning argues, "though their forms were taken from Tin Pan Alley, they became as much the 'folk songs' of New York's garment workers as were the southern mill songs of Gastonia's Ella May Wiggins or the mining ballads of Harlan County's Aunt Molly Jackson and Sarah Ogan Gunning."[138]

Show business and labor theater nevertheless made for strange bedfellows, and no other production of the WTM ever equaled the success of *Pins and Needles*. But were the workers' productions really conceived to be box-office hits? In a movement born of the necessity to address the concerns of a rising American working class, theater became a leftist propaganda tool. Thus a play's success was better measured by the number of people it could convert to the cause than its economic profitability. The WTM, in truth, while addressing pressing sociocultural concerns also failed in its political purpose—communism never threatened capitalism in the United States. Prescient contemporary commentators such as Ben Blake and Barrett H. Clark focused more on the avant-garde aspect of the movement than on the motives that led many small labor theaters to spread the "gospel of radicalism to a public already sold on that commodity."[139] Unlike later scholars who pigeonholed the entire movement as propagandistic and denied the existence of any artistic or dramatic merit in its productions, these critics recognized that a class-conscious theater could embrace a wide range of contributions, from the moderate works of a liberal mind like Rice to the militant plays of an activist like Lawson. The Workers' Theater had broadened the field for writers to choose their material and encouraged them to investigate unfamiliar problems. Odets's *Waiting for Lefty* and Blitzstein's *The Cradle Will Rock*

94 • CHAPTER 2

are telling examples: neither author grew up in a proletarian environment or was familiar with union and working-class struggle, yet they allowed themselves to get in touch with the "real" world and show their concern with issues that until the 1930s had been all but absent from the American mainstream theater. In the end, though, it matters less whether the labor theater helped the communist cause than that it contributed to the development of one of the features of American spoken and musical theater in the 1930s: the need to address contemporary life with the hope of persuading the audience to engage in social change. This was a goal, as we will see in the next chapters, that many of these writers and composers attempted also to pursue, more or less successfully and deliberately, with their contributions to the Federal Project One of the WPA under the aegis of the federal government.

CHAPTER 3

Keeping Politics at Bay

Composers' Forum Laboratory

> See, that was a great time. At that time the left wing move-
> ment, because of the Depression, had a face on the political
> scene.... Every New Yorker in the Depression was a left wing
> person; they had to be, there is nothing special [in that].
>
> —Mordecai Baumann (interview, November 20, 2007, Manhattan)

The activities of the Composers' Collective of New York and of the Workers' Theater Movement, although at times naïve and not always successful, accomplished something of a rapprochement between political activism and artistic innovation. Artists who aimed to communicate in pioneering ways with new audiences—especially those comprised of members of the lower and middle classes—found an outlet for experimentation in these and other left-wing institutions and movements. However, the devastating economic conditions of the 1930s left many young intellectuals trapped between idealism and reality because, besides having to deal with the challenge of balancing social commitment and avant-garde art, they realized that these activities did not always help to make ends meet. A temporary answer to their needs came from the Federal Project Number One (hereafter "Federal One") of the WPA, which not only offered meaningful financial relief to unemployed workers in the arts and entertainment industry but also encouraged experimentation in artistic content and form.

Federal One, which primarily nurtured local and grass-roots development, approximated the initial missions and achievements of the Workers' Theater Movement and Composers' Collective. Ironically, communist-leaning artists

96 · CHAPTER 3

who had earlier fought against the government now became its partners. The New York branches of the Federal Theater and Federal Music Projects, for instance, offered a particularly fertile soil for composers, performers, playwrights, and actors who had been engaged with the working-class struggle. Like the Workers' Theater Movement, the New York Office of the Federal Theater Project promoted and preserved minority cultural activities by establishing foreign-language and ethnic theatrical companies, including the Yiddish Theatre, the Negro Theatre, and the German Theater.[1] At the same time, the Federal Music Project with its twenty-two instrumental units and countless freelance opportunities ensured not only a concert season, but also the musical accompaniment for many social and political events organized in the city.[2] Federal One created much-needed work, but, as Mordecai Bauman recalled, in New York City it also transformed many unemployed musicians and workers of the theater into de facto left-leaning liberals by supporting the importance of the social and educational value of art.

Given the activist background of many of the artists involved in Federal One, ongoing sociopolitical engagement could have been perhaps inevitable; yet a closer look at reception history shows us how expectations did not always match reality. In this chapter, rather than just looking in an abstract way at the activities of the Composers' Forum Laboratory organized by the Federal Music Project in New York, we are invited to think about these endeavors from the point of view of those who created and those who received them. This approach shows how the subtle balance between personal political commitment, experimentation, and adherence to the terms of governmental programs at times transformed initial expectations. The Forum Laboratory could have offered a venue for a more political engagement with music, yet the elitist musical activities it presented rarely intersected with political activism; on the contrary, most composers avoided overt declaration of their affiliations or leanings. Matching artistic aspirations and sociopolitical content proved to be a hard task for the composers who presented their work to the inquisitive audience of the concert series. Still, the fluid creative experience that typified the Forum Laboratory reflected the kaleidoscopic and socially relevant artistic nature of the 1930s, and situates the project as part of that turn to the left that, citing Michael Denning, "was not simply a shift in political opinion, nor was it a retreat from modernism to a Victorian realism," rather an attempt to reconstruct modernism by connecting experimentation to a "new social and historical vision, to invent a social modernism."[3]

The Composers' Forum Laboratory of New York, one of the many endeavors of the Federal Music Project, began its activities on October 30, 1935 at the

Midtown Community Music Center on 93 Park Avenue with a concert of the music of Roy Harris.[4] This event established a precedent for a concert series that continued for the next five years, effectively presenting American composers and introducing New York audiences to contemporary music. The format of the concerts remained constant throughout the years: a pre-concert talk introduced the composer and the pieces on the program, and a post-concert Q&A session engaged composer and audience in a discussion of the music performed, which often also attempted to define the composer's role in society. The weekly concerts, which initially were free to the public, had a twofold aim: to build new, educated audiences and to provide a venue for composers to hear their works performed and receive feedback from colleagues and audience alike. The Forum evolved into a showcase for American-born and American naturalized professional composers and for composition students of the major schools of the East Coast.[5] Initially, each forum session presented a single composer, but by the end of the first season, the gatherings featured the work of two or more composers. In 1937, federal funding cuts compelled the FMP to curtail some of its activities; consequently, in its third season the Forum turned into a biweekly event that alternated chamber and orchestral concerts and charged a nominal admission fee. Despite such vicissitudes, the Forum functioned as one of the most successful platforms for new American music: in five seasons, 141 concerts introduced 244 American-born and American naturalized professional composers and more than 500 compositions.

Scholars, including Melissa de Graaf, who discussed the nature of the transcripts of the Q&A sessions, have emphasized the relationship between modernist music and politics that, together with issues of national identity, is at the core of the activities of the Forum.[6] Moreover, accounts of some participating composers draw attention to what appears to be a strong connection between music and the contemporary political climate. For instance, Ross Lee Finney argued in a later interview:

> At all those concerts, they would always talk about the work, and even branch out into the other arts. Composers' Forum was rather progressive, too, in both aesthetic and political ideas. In the discussions, it would be surprising if there hadn't been some political reference.[7]

Yet, behind these rather astonishing numbers and the de facto promotion of American music, one wonders if a narrative on the Composers' Forum that emphasizes a clear link between politics, Americanness, and experimentation is more the consequence of an accepted assumption than a conscious effort by composers to address the politics of music. An analysis of contemporary

98 · CHAPTER 3

commentaries and transcripts of the Q&A sessions that followed the Forum concerts can help to answer this question.

If the Composers' Forum Laboratory seems, in some ways, to parallel the Soviet composers' forums (meetings between composers and audience to test their music against the tenets of the doctrine of socialist realism), one reason may be that Ashley Pettis, its founder and passionate advocate, had built his reputation in New York as a supporter of communist causes while serving on the editorial board of the two major New York City communist print media: the *Daily Worker* and *New Masses*.[8] Pettis had visited Moscow in 1932 to observe musical conditions under the Soviet regime, and he admired how the government sponsored the "technical preparation of those possessing creative talent" and how the "determination and hope of the people [found] outlets not only in work but in many forms of expression, the most vital of which seems to be music."[9] His interest in working-class musical activities and in promoting cooperation between workers and intellectuals surfaces in an article written in 1934 for *New Masses*.[10] In this review of a series of concerts by the Moscow Philharmonic Orchestra organized by the Soviet government, he praised the use of pre-concert lectures to "prepare the auditors for an intelligent approach to this great experience." He condemned the lack of such educational initiatives in the United States, where the government, through the Civil Works Administration, attempted "to allay distress, fears and cries of a pitifully small group of the unemployed by the presentation of hastily organized ensembles of destitute musicians, in concerts[,] in museums, school buildings, etc."[11] However, he allowed that other nongovernmental organizations, such as the Workers Music League and the Pierre Degeyter Club, "[had] been working indefatigably in the technical preparation of their various ensembles, as well as the creation of new music through the Composers' Collective." Pettis drew particular attention to the educational purpose of the events organized by the two groups and looked forward to the moment in which audiences would have the opportunity of hearing and judging their accomplishments:

> The reaction of the auditors should be of the greatest value and inspiration to these musical workers, and it is to be hoped that all those interested in extraordinary new musical developments, of the utmost cultural value to the masses, capable of inspiring them with fresh vigor and unity, will take advantage of these significant events.[12]

Pettis was so excited by this possibility, that, less than two years later, the ideology behind the Soviet approach, filtered through the activities of Workers Music League and Composers' Collective, had permeated his concept for the New York forums:

The purpose of the Composers' Forum Laboratory is manifold in its nature. Not only are we interested in the composer and his work, *per se*, but in the development of a more definite understanding and relationship between the composer and the public.

We are hoping that, through these evenings in intimate contact with composers, we may do our part in removing the barrier, which has always existed between the composer and the people who are or should be the consumers of his goods.[13]

The Forums as he described them, though, sounded more like a venue for artistic exchange than a propaganda tool in the hands of the Communist Party. A change in Pettis's approach had already begun in the spring of 1934, when he had witnessed the Composers' Collective's failure to provide a venue for successful artist-audience interaction and, in his review of the songs that some of the Collective's members submitted for the *New Masses* May Day Song contest. Although he appreciated their efforts to reach out to the workers, he also underlined the impracticality of most of their experimental songs.[14] This failure—combined with the perception that a governmental-sponsored event in the United States could succeed only if dissociated from political, ideological, and aesthetical bonds—encouraged him to avoid overt political associations and unilateral directions and to emphasize the importance of the creative aspect of the forums:

Here in the Composers' Forum-Laboratory will be offered an opportunity to observe the composer at work, producing for us—his audience. We will observe every type of music written by competent musicians—music expressive of every shade of thought and feeling peculiar to this moment in history. A panoramic view will be had of what is happening, in a musical way, about us.[15]

Pettis's colleagues likewise counseled broad perspectives. In a brief note dated September 17, 1935, Daniel Gregory Mason, an avowedly anti-modernist voice, endorsed Pettis's proposal for the Composers' Collective but cautioned him that "much, indeed all, would depend on how it was done. I should suppose it would be necessary to avoid favoritism or cliquism of any kind."[16] Mason also suggested:

Keep the publicity element out of it as much as possible—have it an affair for the composers themselves and those of their friends who were spontaneously interested. The curse of all such undertakings in America is propagandism and publicity.[17]

Mason's advice to restrict the concerts to composers unequivocally promoted the modernist art for art's sake stance by avoiding any concern with a possible audience. One could also argue that Mason, known for his extremely conservative views, worried about the Forum becoming another venue for communist propaganda. Pettis, who needed Mason's support because of his position in the New York musical academic community, wrote a diplomatic but pointed reply addressing the issue without blatantly dismissing his suggestions:

> In order to enlist your continued interest in our project we wish you to be informed concerning our plans for procedure.
>
> There is to be no favoritism or "cliquism" whatsoever. Composers of competency, irrespective of affiliations with groups or organizations, are being invited to participate, and many have already expressed their willingness to work with us.
>
> But you must understand that our foundation must rest upon a very broad base. We are not interested in the development of the composer in a vacuum nor yet in an "ivory tower," and our antipathy to cliques is so great that we would not willingly see him restricted in his creative efforts to the narrowing influence of his "friends." Rather would we save him from his friends!
>
> As for "propaganda": our only propaganda is for music; not music for propaganda![18]

His words strongly objected to the political affiliation and highlighted his desire to offer a site where composers and audience could interact and bridge the gap that had estranged the creator from his public. Moreover, in his response to Mason, Pettis also emphasized the importance of introducing a broader audience to contemporary music and that "it is inconceivable that we could operate freely without publicity of the right kind." To mitigate Mason's fear of "cliquism," Pettis also assured him of the diversity of the participating composers:

> We are receiving a large number of responses from composers, assuring us of their eagerness to cooperate. In the near future we shall supply you with a list of those responding, and you will be able to see for yourself that our activities are in no way under the influence of narrow cliques.[19]

Undeniably, the list of leading composers and music educators who initially supported the Forums and/or agreed to participate represented an astonishingly broad spectrum of American contemporary music: George Antheil, Amy Beach, Aaron Copland, Roy Harris, Howard Hanson, Frederick Jacobi, Wallingford Riegger, Bernard Rogers, Carlos Salzedo, William Grant Still, and Edgard Varese, among others. Mason, reassured by the roster of interested individuals, quickly endorsed Pettis's project: "From what you say it seems to me that you and I look at these matters from much the same angle. I certainly heartily agree with what you say about the necessity of saving the composer from his friends—there are too many mutual admiration societies about."[20]

Still, Pettis's known communist affiliations had most likely triggered initial misgivings about the Composers' Forum and may explain why the series started almost on the sly, in a small venue and lacking the full collaboration of musicians on the FMP's payroll. The first night, only one of Harris's compositions, the Piano Trio, received a live performance; the rest of the programmed pieces were presented in preexisting recordings. These reservations, though, vanished in a letter that Chalmers Clifton, the regional music director of the FMP for the City of New York, wrote to Nikolai Sokoloff for immediate attention on October 31, the day after the first Forum:

> The first of the Forums Laboratory evenings for composers was entirely dignified and effective. Roy Harris's comments were quick-witted and technically sound, and the public gathered in the small auditorium keen and appreciative. Pettis had arranged [it] very well indeed.[21]

The absence of any political commentary and the focus on artistic quality convinced the federal authorities, and Pettis's forums not only attracted the attention and full support of the higher ranks of the FMP, but, as Sokoloff proudly stated, they also served as an example to be emulated:

> I want to commend you for the splendid way in which you are directing the Forum. I think it is one of the most successful of our activities and it is one, which I am hoping to put into operation in other large centers.[22]

Eventually, the New York forums received nationwide attention and, in the spring of 1936, just a few months after the opening event, the WPA began promoting similar programs in other major American cities. In some venues the initiative was not welcome. For instance, in San Francisco, where Ernst Bacon, who was the supervisor of the local FMP, characterized the forums as an "eastern inquisition" and "another attempt of the big octopus city to throw its tentacles over the rest of this country and, under the guise of protection, strangulate local enterprise."[23] However, Harry Hewes, the assistant project supervisor of the FMP, reported that in Philadelphia the Civic Orchestra devoted an entire program to the works of Otto Mueller on March 18, and the Symphony Orchestra organized a forum performance of George F. Boyle's Concerto in D minor on April 5.[24] In Milwaukee, the Symphony dedicated two programs to the music of Thomas Calrow Carver and Carl Eppert, respectively on April 15 and May 21, whereas in Detroit, Boston, Cincinnati, Los Angeles, and Oakland forums modeled on Pettis's were already being planned.[25] Hewes distributed Composers' Forum materials to venues in Jacksonville, Cleveland, New Orleans, Chicago, Portland, and several other cities, all of which had expressed interest in the activities that Pettis directed in New York.[26]

102 · CHAPTER 3

A growing public justified, after the eighth forum, relocation of the New York meetings to larger halls. After the first eight events, the Forums moved to the Federal Music Building on 110 West 48th Street, in a larger hall that could host more than five hundred people. The high numbers would suggest that Pettis accomplished his goal of interesting a new audience, but quantity did not always go hand in hand with quality, as the Forums attracted an extremely heterogeneous, and not always interested audience. The free concerts provided temporary warm shelter for poor and homeless people who, in most cases, as reported by Ross Lee Finney, fell asleep during the performances and following discussions. Still, the composer argued, the committed portion of the audience, "the one-third that was awake—the young composers, the people who were already interested in new music—they had a very lively discussion afterward."[27]

The question, though, remains unanswered: were composers really interested in the social contextualization of music promoted by Pettis or were they just eager to hear their music performed? Was Finney's remark about the Forum's progressiveness in both aesthetic and political ideas tainted by the subsequent politicization of the musical activities of the 1930s or were the post-concert discussions truly rich with political references? The transcripts of the Q&A questions, which are available at the National Archives in College Park, Maryland, prove that the actual relationship between Americanness, politics, and experimentation is in fact as complicated as the scenarios just rendered.

Pettis did not keep records of the post-concert discussions until near the end of the first season, when Hewes encouraged him to consider this possibility:

> It strikes me that it would be a valuable record if we could have the questions and answers taken verbatim by a stenographer at a Composers' Forum Laboratory. In transcribing notes I made at the Hunter Johnson program on March 25, I gained a new insight into the composer's method and intention.
>
> It occurs to me also that some of the questions might have to be contrived, but out of the many queries put to composers in the past, there ought to be plenty of them. How does the idea strike you?[28]

Pettis agreed with the idea and a stenographer began transcribing the Forums starting with Edwin Gerschefski's concert on April 29, 1936.[29] In general, the transcripts document that musically literate listeners, who wrote their questions on slips provided at the beginning of the forum, asked pertinent questions challenging composers and their work, often in a very colorful and aggressive yet competent way.

The first available transcript shows that Gerschefski had to face an almost belligerent audience. Questions contested every aspect of his compositional technique, from his unclear use of dissonance ("I found your treatment of dissonance confusing; in some instances you resolve in the classical manner, in other instances you seem to consider it on a par with the consonance") to his structural ambiguity ("Do you think you convey anything in your music? To me it is not even abstract. Don't you think your music lacks pulse and construction?"), and his ability to communicate emotions ("Please, advise how does one develop a taste for such strange combinations of tones? Could one hear and feel such music and be happy?").[30] Indeed, some people in attendance had issues with modernist approaches while others wanted to understand the processes behind the music. For instance, when Aurelio Giorni, on May 13, 1936, presented consonant music, the audience criticized his lack of modernist dissonance treatment: "Very beautiful writing but not in modern idiom. Do you feel antagonist to modern trends in music?"[31] The Q&A sessions clearly show the tension that audiences perceived between traditional and modern musical idioms, but they also disclose many preconceptions and stereotypical attitudes toward music and its creators.

As de Graaf noted, the audience treated even more harshly female composers who ventured to employ a modernist idiom.[32] For instance, at the end of Johanna M. Beyer's concert on May 20, 1936, some audience members unleashed their rage at her experiments with tone clusters: "Really Miss Beyer, is there any beauty in your pathological sounds and noises? Or does it appeal to some other sense?"[33] "What are these weird sounds? Perhaps your wild genius or what have you is far above the immortals?" They accused her of copying Henry Cowell, and she became an object of misogynist scorn: "Miss Beyer, you seem to have gone your male preceptors one better in search for strange and ineffective tonal combinations. Have you consciously adopted Rudyard Kipling's statement 'The female of the species is deadlier than the male,' as a guiding principle in your composition?"[34] These unkind comments demonstrate how contemporary perceptions about gender and sexuality prevented women from having a prominent role as composers in a decade absorbed in defining American national identity in music. Already in the early 1920s, Deems Taylor had claimed that women were responsible for the weakness of American music.[35] This was a comment that certainly influenced modernist composers, who found it hard to write music that was largely educational and edifying, attributes associated with the marginalized female presence in American music. Consequently, as Ellie Hisama argues, female composers struggled to find their way in the post-tonal music individualistic world of the early twentieth century.[36] Women also had to face this reality when they were promoting the social value of music. Male hostility against female composers within the leftist musical movement of the 1930s,

104 • CHAPTER 3

as we have seen with the Composers' Collective of New York, could indeed be linked to the stereotyped role of women in American music and a desire to preserve the manliness of the political engagement.

The Forums' transcripts also offer many other illuminating perspectives on music making in 1930s New York City. For example, the audience, apart from technical questions on compositional processes, seemed particularly interested in finding ways to distance American modernism from its European equivalent and to define "Americanism" in music. Almost every composer had to field a loaded question on the current state and the future of American music and its relevance. Even Pettis addressed this issue in his opening speech of the second series when he emphasized that the Composers' Forum Laboratory aspired to address the role of music in contemporary society and cited a passage from Lazare Samimsky's (the featured composer) book *Music of Our Day*:

> My aim is the definition of our esthetic longitude and latitude—of our place in history. Its exact position we have long since lost. My questions run as follows:—Where do we find ourselves, aesthetically and historically?—What is the present waterway of our musical thought?—To which type of spirituality belongs the musical culture created today and what is its destiny?[37]

Sokoloff likewise tackled the issue in his pre-opening concert speech, but with an even stronger nationalistic tone:

> I didn't intend to make much of a speech, but when we begin to talk about the importance of what we have done and what I hope will be the result to the whole national music life of America, this is one of the important events, and we hope to present more composers and to get to know them and their personalities. I believe that the more the composers will mingle with the people and the more the people will mingle with the artists—that is the real life in any community.[38]

Of course, Sokoloff's words reflect aims at the core of Federal One's activities, such as the emphasis on the educational purpose of art and its ability to recreate that sense of community and belonging that the hardships of the Great Depression had weakened. Nevertheless, this is exactly what the audience of the Forums was looking for, as it frequently demonstrated a desire to attach a functional role to music and inquired about the relevance of artistic endeavors in relation to the contemporary socioeconomic context.

In most cases, though, composers felt uneasy with these questions. For instance, when the audience confronted Aurelio Giorni's lack of connection with the real world:

How do you account for the fact that your music has so little been influenced by contemporary music or life? . . . Do you feel your sort of romanticism to be sufficient for the expression of your composition? Are you not inspired with the present age and its developments—the so-called modernism?[39]

The uncomfortable composer answered evasively:

Well, in the first place I do not think that all contemporary music is in the slightest modern. I think that in one respect I am very much influenced by the present day and have been adversely criticized because of my restlessness.[40]

A young William Schuman sounded more decisive in his answer; when asked if composers write music for specific events or reasons, he commented that composers rarely find inspiration in contemporary events and just let the music flow from them, as what music says cannot be translated into words.[41] But not even the directness of answers such as Schuman's seems to have appeased the listeners, who did not show any signs of relenting and kept pressing composers with questions about music and its relation to contemporary life. On October 23, the audience gave Werner Josten the third degree:

Do you not feel that your compositions would be more significant and meaningful if their inspiration came from events of our time? Do you not think your age should have an art-form indigenous to it? Does your contribution lie in that direction? . . . Do you consider the social upheaval, unrest and general turmoil which is so much a part of our generation to have influenced the direction and shape of modern music (as exemplified in your works) or do you think that the change in music is due only to the enlarged palette given to the composer by the tremendous mechanical improvements in instruments and by the relatively high level of performance among musicians?[42]

The overwhelmed and unfortunate composer could do nothing more than mutter, "I think the two go hand in hand in this case" and reclaim his right to compose absolute music. The audience became almost insulting with Frederick Woltman:

Frost, the poet, lives gopher-like, secluded in his New England farm, writing again of Autumn while in the outside world there are winter floods and whole seasons of bloody war. And you sing sweet and sensuous sounds. Wake up, Mr. Woltman. This is not the world of Debussy—this is 1937. (laughter)[43]

This comment, prompted by the piece *Introduction and Two Songs*, two selections from Frances Frost's "Songs of Autumn," caught Woltman off guard. Unable to address the actual issue, he muttered, "Well, if the writer would prefer to have

106 · CHAPTER 3

floods and disaster, he is welcome to them." Evidently, while Pettis and Sokoloff aimed to create a space to share artistic choices and beliefs, and the audience called for answers that would have justified the artistic product within the challenging contemporary social context, composers appeared almost reluctant to openly discuss these issues. Ironically, the first season of the Forums did not exactly help to bridge the gap between composer and audience, as Pettis envisioned, but emphasized even more the elitist attitudes of some of the showcased artists.

This tension did not change in the following seasons, as the social contextualization of music remained an animated topic; still, the audience often received half-mumbled or irrelevant answers. As, for instance, from Lazare Saminsky on October 26, 1938:

> QUESTION: Does music reflect the social and economic forces of a period? If so, how is it evident in your compositions? Could both you and Mr. Haubiel discuss this question?
>
> ANSWER: (Saminsky) Well, music certainly reflects all of that, but it is not always evident. Some music is definitely of a certain class, music of a certain clique, like the music of the 18th century. For instance, folk songs definitely reflect the mood of the people. They express needs and privations and strain and struggle, but it does it through an emotional channel.[44]

Even Roger Sessions, when asked about the function of the artist in contemporary society, merely recited the modernist credo that Paul Hindemith had put in the mouth of Mathis the painter (*Mathis der Maler*):

> Well, that also is a very difficult question. The trouble is, in so many things one either has to say about five words or else one can take several hours. I think the clearest answer is—"To produce works of art." I am sorry I seem to make obvious replies sometimes. That is because the answers seem to me obvious.[45]

Only a handful of composers dealt with these topics in a more discerning manner, often reclaiming their right to be part of the country's present crucial historical moment, as did Arthur Cohn on May 26, 1937:

> QUESTION: Do you believe that a creative artist should be identified in spirit with the social movements of his day to be able to organize his work effectively?
>
> ANSWER: Absolutely. A composer who decides that he is a little genius and goes to his studio and works, knowing nothing of what is going on around him, will not write a true music report of the day in which he lives. He must be tied up with the conditions under which he lives.[46]

Similar exchanges were often also charged with questions related to the definition of American national musical identity, a concept that had occupied composers and historians alike at least since the turn of the twentieth century and that proved to still be a debated and controversial one. As Charles Hiroshi Garrett argues, both composers and historians encountered many difficulties trying to define a national identity in music because of the United States' fluctuating population, which impeded them in finding a homogeneous characterization of American music.[47]

The following exchange between a member of the audience and Saminsky on October 26, 1938, speaks volumes about the issue of national identity and the role of race and ethnicity in its definition:

> QUESTION: Is there such a thing as American music—of course excluding Broadway jazz? If so, what are its characteristics and who are some of the composers?
>
> ANSWER: (Saminsky) I am really amazed that someone in NYC in 1938 would ask such a question. It is quite astonishing. I think certainly there is no question that America has outgrown the Negro and Indian songs. There is in American music clear characteristics, the same as the characteristics of the American people—a certain snappiness, a clear-cut quality of speed and the direct grappling with any problem with every fact of life; a certain sense of humor; a certain rash vivacity and verve; a certain snap, everything which is careless, perhaps I should say a certain gayness. In its broad, epic qualities all of this is characteristic of the best American music. Among the best? That is a matter of opinion. I would say, to my mind the most gifted, the strongest creative, is Roy Harris. I think he is the most original, the most American. Inasmuch as the main characteristics of the true American race, the basic American race, has the Anglo-Celtic strain, the source of American music, as such I see the quality in Harris, as I see it in the great American writers, Eugene O'Neill or Robert Frost. You want natives. All right. Roy Harris is one, Roger Sessions is another.[48]

The audience member admitted that "Broadway jazz" was indeed recognizably American music, but this person purposefully distinguished it from what he or she considered art music. Arguably, this almost appears to be an attempt to "cleanse" art music from certain ethnic influences, that is, Jewish and Black, which had already left a major imprint in American sound. Indeed, the tone of the question prompted an answer that leaves no doubts on where Saminsky stood in this debate; after quickly dismissing any Native or Black influence in contemporary American art music, he proclaimed the musical experience of what he called the "basic American race," the Anglo-Celtic, to be at the core of American national music. This is a rather conservative view, of course, which many contemporary composers had challenged. Among them was a young

108 • CHAPTER 3

Leonard Bernstein, who, in his 1939 senior thesis at Harvard, "The Absorption of Race Elements into American Music," argued that American national musical identity is the result of the combination of an organic process of assimilation of different racial characteristics and the strong prominence of Black music rhythms.[49]

While the Forums' Q&A exchanges confirm Ross Lee Finney's account of the post-concert sessions as being rather politically progressive and lively, the transcripts seem also to contradict him in that they lack animated political debates. Given the radical background of Pettis and many of the composers it showcased, one wonders why politics did not echo within the Composers' Forum Laboratory. Perhaps records of some of the first season forums, which had been stocked with the music of such leftist top names in the Composers' Collective as Marc Blitzstein, Henry Cowell, Herbert Haufrecht, and Wallingford Riegger, would have borne witness to more highly politicized discussions. In view of what transpired in all other recorded forums, though, it looks plausible to assume that politics, if at all present, emerge in passing and appear an unrelated and often laughable issue, as though organizers, composers, and listeners alike had checked their political affiliations along with their coats at the door. The first hint of contemporary politics appears in the transcripts in a question addressed to Pettis after Josten's concert of October 23, 1936:

> QUESTION: Mr. Pettis, could you please tell me, will this beautiful music, free to the public and a savior to the contemporary composer, continue if Mr. Landon is elected? (laughter and amusement)[50]
> ANSWER: I don't think it is politic to answer this, but it is a great temptation to [be] unpolitic. (laughter) I am sorry I can't answer this by "Yes" or "No." I can say that neither Mr. Landon nor the Republican National Committee have taken me into their confidence and I am not a prophet. (amusement)[51]

The exchange could have turned into an interesting dogmatic discussion, yet the ironic tone of both inquirer and addressee was intended more to solicit laughter in the audience than to address a tangible political issue. The same sardonic approach to politics appears again on November 18 in an exchange between a member of the audience and composer Rosalie Housman:

> QUESTION: Do you try to express communistic feeling in your music?
> ANSWER: No! I'm only wearing a red dress because I happen to like red. I'm not a communist—either musically or politically.[52]

Housman's answer could be the simple truth, she likes the color; however, in light of the aggressive Q&A exchanges reserved for other women in the Forums, one wonders if her sarcastic rebuttal could have been an attempt to anticipate

Keeping Politics at Bay • 109

a possible attack on her role as a woman composer and her position in contemporary society.

The cynical approach to politics dissipated when the audience queried established composers about their potential political involvement. Nonetheless, the transcripts highlight an almost ubiquitous desire to bypass the topic. Roy Harris's Q&A session on October 6, 1937 (the Forum organized a full concert of Harris's music also in its second season) evinces this strategy:

> *QUESTION:* Do you believe in composing with a conscious motive (political, portrayal, etc.) or should composing be purely an intuitive process? Can really great music come from using the former procedure?
> *ANSWER:* I think music is abstract and will not gain anything by trying to illustrate concrete literary ideas. (applause)[53]

In another Forum, Aaron Copland's vague or monosyllabic answers show that he was very uncomfortable, almost reluctant to respond or to turn the discussion from musical to political:

> *QUESTION:* Do you think it is necessary for a composer to actively participate in political activity?
> *ANSWER:* No! (emphatically)
> *QUESTION:* Do you think that a composer has to be a political partisan in order to be able to compose?
> *ANSWER:* No!
> *QUESTION:* Does your music have any social significance?
> *ANSWER:* All music that is any good has social significance.
> *QUESTION:* Have the recent depression and economic upheaval and consequent changes in social thinking had any effect on your music in your opinion?
> *ANSWER:* Yes! It affected it very much.[54]

This rather dry and detached exchange sounds surprising, especially coming from a composer who had already made some strong political allegations with his music, including the song "Into the Streets May First," with which he won the contest for a May Day song promoted by *New Masses* in 1934, and *Statements for Orchestra* (1935), in which, possibly influenced by the proletarian music aesthetic promoted by the Composers' Collective of New York, he addressed in a modernist style leftist political content.[55] Yet, in 1937, the year of this Forum, Copland had already lost the modernist and political bite that characterized those earlier works and had entered, with the premiere of *El Salón México* (1937), the more populist aesthetic that typifies his later works. It would thus seem plausible that Copland, in his attempt to reach a wider audience, did not want to be associated with a political subgroup.[56]

110 • CHAPTER 3

Not all composers, though, were so eager to dismiss loaded questions about politics, and in some instances, firm answers left the audience no room for sarcasm or confrontation, as in the case of Quinto Maganini:

> *QUESTION:* Do you think the creator of music builds out of his emotional life, his intellectual life, his attitudes and interests in his social environments and his conception of what society is?
>
> *ANSWER:* To the man who asked that question: Do you think Art is necessarily connected with man's position in society or to his social or political concepts? If you do, I think you are entirely wrong. As I understand it, art is a purifier of man's thoughts. At least it should be. It relaxes the strain brought on by the stresses of daily existence. It is something that takes man away from the consciousness of everyday things. Why mix it up with all the ideology of politics and social envies and desires. Art should be a form of hypnotism, something that pulls a man out of himself and away from those very things that your question refers to. I am bored with all these things that are dragged in at every discussion of Art. Art is in itself a complete self-explanatory language and need not to be occupied with either the "left" or the "right."[57]

Maganini's answer, in the form of an attack on the questioner, shows that by the end of the decade, when the leftist impulses that characterized the first years of the Great Depression were giving way to more positive prospects, composers were again more interested in the concept of art for art's sake than as a socially relevant tool. But, when accused of elitism, as in the case of Howard Hanson, the answers took different directions. Hanson arrogantly, yet diplomatically, counterattacked the accusation coming from a member of the audience that his music is politically and socially irrelevant. The exchange is eye opening and deserves to be reported at length:

> *QUESTION:* I want to thank you for your splendid speech—encouraging the work of music education. In a united spirit can we work for the attainment of a music-conscious America. However, I should like to discuss a point with you. Our purpose as you state is not only to make music serve economic and political ideals, but beauty in itself. As a composer you are educating the emotions of people, you are also molding their thoughts and habits of life. If then, as educators, we are to elevate the cultural level of our people, we must not speak of economic ideals in music in abstract, but the composer must, physically and organically, align himself with the forces of democracy and progress so that beauty in music will function to achieve the beautiful pattern of social phenomena. Beauty in music means beauty for our people, music to awaken them, to make possible greater participation

in the making of music. Your compositions are romantic in nature and do not reflect adequately the needs of our people. You are very gifted and have the material to bring about such music. Let the events of the world and our country throb in every fibre [*sic*] of your great musical talent. Make your music serve our people in this period of transition and cultural need. If you break with romanticism and mysticism, you will be more of a servant to humanity, highly appreciated by the forces of progress. How about it?

ANSWER: Well, how about it? I appreciate the compliment, both positive and negative. I am, of course, absolutely old hat in this matter. I am 16th century. Oh, way back—maybe the 15th or 14th. I would like to be; and I hope I am not thrown out for saying this, but I don't think music has very much to do with economics or politics. Shostakovich tried to express a certain political thought in his music and the music becomes uninteresting music. Music is much more worthwhile when it stands on its own feet, than when it is made a slave of something else. We are always justifying music: because it is good for our health. We justify it for physical therapy, etc. I think these reasons are fine, but I think the greatest thing about music *is music*! I would not, however, want to be misconstrued, or have these few words imply anything I do not mean. I think music should minister to people and to the lives of living human beings, but when you monkey with the creative arts you are tampering with a strange force we do not understand. I have been and will always be a mystic, and if I wouldn't continue to be I would be a poor sham and counterfeit. . . . [58]

The anonymous question from the audience, especially when stating that "beauty in music means beauty for our people, music to awaken them," addressed some of the most pressing concerns that, as we have seen, were at the core of the rhetoric of the Composers' Collective. It also seems to support Denning's idea of "social modernism," of music that in its progressive and revolutionary qualities can talk to the need of contemporary society. Yet, while Hanson's answer reclaims the *super partes* role of music and criticizes those, like Shostakovich, who used it to make political statements, he apparently could not address this question nor another one from an audience member who asked him to define political music with specific examples:

QUESTION: I would like to know what prompts you to define political music, especially when you speak of Shostakovich as composer.

ANSWER: Well, I don't know. I would really like to talk with him about that. You never know, "except," as Will Rogers said, "what you read in the newspapers." I have been told that he was attempting a political philosophy at one time or was supposed to. I suppose that is true of other countries which have been mentioned in New York City.[59]

112 · CHAPTER 3

Hanson answered evasively, thus showing how even the most experienced composer struggled with such questions and preferred to stick to the artistic and apolitical value and significance of music.

As a matter of fact, post-concert discussions never directly addressed politics for politics' sake, not even when the forums hosted composers known for strong political views or involvement. For instance, the second forum of the third season presented music by Elie Siegmeister, a musician who more than anyone else had epitomized the idealistic political aims of the Composers' Collective of New York. Siegmeister, announced by Pettis as a composer of work songs, introduced selections from his book *Negro Songs of Protest* published in 1936 ("Sistern and Brethren," "I Went to Atlanta," and "John Henry") and his dissonant and modernist musical setting of Michael Gold's workers' chant "The Strange Funeral in Braddock" sung by Mordecai Baumann.[60] Curiously, though, none of the members of the audience asked questions about the use of music as weapon in the class struggle; rather, they addressed the effectiveness of modern music as an expression of distinct social strata:

> QUESTION: Do you think the Southern Negro or Pennsylvania steel worker would recognize the idiom of your music as their own? Explain.
>
> ANSWER: I think they would if given a sufficient opportunity to hear it and get to know it. Although since I am a composer and not a steelworker, my music is composed music, and not folk music. I have played my compositions to many audiences of plain working people, and they have told me that my music expresses their way of looking at things. Many Southern Negroes have taken up and sung these songs; as for the Pennsylvania workers, I have never been in Pennsylvania, but other workers' groups have claimed this music as their own, if one can judge by applause.[61]

Siegmeister, apparently unconcerned by the collapse of the proletarian music project, still believed in 1937 that workers could learn to appreciate and understand the modernist musical language, a position that he articulated in an exchange with the audience:

> QUESTION: Do you write songs for workers and such compositions as the *Lento* for "musical sophisticates"? Which do you consider your most typical style?
>
> ANSWER: I consider them both my most typical style. I also think it possible that many whom you call "musical sophisticates" really liked the songs better than the quartet, and it may be quite true that people who have been denied the opportunity to a musical education, which is their right, may find quartet music hard to listen to. When the common people are given a chance, they rapidly develop an interest and a taste for all forms of music

from the simplest to the most complex. I know a country where the workers go in for string quartets in a big way.[62]

Although Siegmeister mentioned no specific country, one may infer the Soviet Union; if so, this veiled remark constitutes the only allusion to music as a tool for political edification to be found in the transcripts of his post-concert discussion.

While the Forums were essentially a vehicle to promote the music of American composers, they occasionally also hosted guest foreign composers such as, on April 6, 1938, Hanns Eisler. The audience members were aware of the political commitment of the German composer, whose lecture "The Crisis in Music" (given on December 7, 1935 in Town Hall, New York and published by the Downtown Music School in 1936) had become a quasi-manifesto for proletarian music in the United States.[63] Eisler's ideas and music inflamed the spirit of the most progressive members of the Composer's Collective; yet, as Marc Blitzstein acutely observed:

> Eisler is first a composer; it is good to remember that his formulation, his theories grow out of, have roots in, music. They are your true "aesthetic," articulated out of the thing, possessed and actual, not cooked-up, not arbitrary, not nursed along to induce the thing, and make it happen. Schönberg once said of the typical theorizer, "Nobody watches more closely over his property than the man who knows that, strictly speaking, it does not belong to him." Eisler's property is his own; he shares it with the working class of the world.[64]

And it was indeed Eisler the composer whom the Forum's attendees greeted, as his militancy, which could have potentially triggered an atypical politicization of the post-concert Q&A session, gave way to questions focused on the compositional mechanics of his works:

> *QUESTION*: Why introduce propaganda as a recitative and call it a cantata? Can we not have art for art's sake?
>
> *ANSWER*: In these cantatas I did not intend to introduce, nor do I think I did introduce, what you refer to as "propaganda." For that matter you might well ask why Schubert wrote "propaganda" for a trout in a river ("Forellen"), or why Beethoven "propagandized" for "Joy" (choral symphony). These times give composers new ideas for his art.
>
> *QUESTION*: What difference is there between proletarian music and bourgeois music—also, how is one to differentiate?
>
> *ANSWER*: Such a difference doesn't exist. There is only a difference between progressive music and conventional music: there is only a difference between music for thinking persons and music for non-thinking persons.

114 · CHAPTER 3

QUESTION: Do you think that the subject matter in the varied Cantatas loses some of the militant significance, because of a solo voice instead of a chorus? Also, the small instrumental set-up?

ANSWER: The subject matter of the cantatas is actually light, lyrical and sometimes satirical. That is why I chose a mezzo-soprano and the small instrumentation. If every piece of music, which the questioner refers to as "militant," were to have the same form and manner of presentation music would be useless for any purpose.

QUESTION: Inasmuch as your work is addressed to the masses, why do you couch it in such strange melodic terms?

ANSWER: The melodies are strange only at first hearing. If you were to hear them again, I am sure you would not find them so strange.[65]

In particular, even when loaded questions ventured near contemporary politics or the social relevance of music, Eisler—the quintessential sociopolitically involved composer—refrained from expressing his personal beliefs, as though even he felt it inappropriate to engage in political discussions in such a venue:

QUESTION: What in your opinion will be the effect upon music in America of the growth of Fascism in Europe?

ANSWER: I am sorry, but I believe this question to be too involved to answer in so brief a manner.

QUESTION: Do you think that the revolutionary word content of your work makes it better musically than if you were, for example, a religious enthusiast?

ANSWER: No.[66]

The questions could have led Eisler to answer in more political terms, yet, like the American composers, he strayed away from pure propaganda.

A recorded decidedly political turn of events occurred only in the first season of the Forum, when Blitzstein, at the time secretary of the Composers' Collective, had vainly tried to boycott Pettis's attempt to omit Siegmeister's "Biography," a choral setting of a text by the communist writer A. B. Magil, from a program presenting multiple composers on February 26, 1936. The poem, which tells the story of a man shot during a protest, symbolically portrays the fate of many working-class leaders who lost their lives in similar circumstances. The text blames the police, government officials, and business tycoons for his death:

Remember this, you who killed him:
  Deputy thug, sheriff, chief of police, mayor, governor,
  President, Ford, Mellon, Rockefeller—
  All you who fired the shot:
He is not one, but many.

He is a thousand, a million, a hundred million.
His name is written in factory smoke,
His life in strike leaflets,
His face marches on picket lines from coast to coast, from the
Great Lakes to the Gulf.[67]

Pettis felt that such a direct attack on government and wealthy families known for their patronage of the arts could jeopardize his successful initiative, but Siegmeister appealed to the First Amendment and refused to change the piece. Blitzstein immediately sided with Siegmeister and circulated letters to encourage composers to sign a petition to Lee Pattison, head of the New York division of the WPA Music Project, in favor of freedom of speech:

> . . . We have examined the poem, and find that it is a sincere and artistically valid example of indignation at social persecution; a legitimate subject, one very familiar throughout the history of poetry.
>
> As American composers we feel you will agree that the W.P.A. is heartily in favor of freedom of expression, and would not willingly subject itself to the charge of censoring works on its program for other than artistic reasons. We therefore protest the suppression of Mr. Siegmeister's work, and urge the reinstatement of the entire program.[68]

Blitzstein found a handful of people willing to co-sign the letter, among them Aaron Copland and Wallingford Riegger, but others refused because the case was political and not musical and exhorted Blitzstein to abandon this crusade. Among them was Colin McPhee, who wrote to Blitzstein:

> . . . I do not believe in propaganda of any sort in art, and furthermore I am surprised that you should resent the exception taken to this text (with its music), which so bitterly criticizes and threatens the very government which in this case is expected to sponsor its music.
>
> . . . You know I feel as you do that I would like to see music have a closer contact with daily life, and become an easily accessible pleasure for the worker. But I cannot see music as a festoon for political opinions, and I cannot see how the text which you enclosed, which is *not* poetry in any sense, can gain by a musical setting.
>
> . . . And say what you like, you cannot convince me that the present case is not a question of politics rather than music.[69]

Virgil Thomson was even more outspoken:

> . . . I can't really sign that manifesto because it doesn't make sense.
>
> It accuses Pettis of using the WPA for political purposes, when the most he has done is to refuse to let somebody else use it for political purposes. If even that.

116 • CHAPTER 3

It turns out that the poem is quite normal politically, anyway, it could be published or performed practically anywhere. It is the use of names and titles in an accusatory manner that makes it a *case*. It is less incendiary than it is libelous. Hence, although there may be small chance of Mellon or Ford making trouble, one cannot seriously object to the director of the concerts wishing to keep within the letter of the law. It may be foolish of him but it is his right. . . .

I suspect, considering the weakness of the case, that Siegmeister may not be entirely pure in his motivation. Framing up situations to get oneself persecuted in, however entertaining it may be as a private amusement or as a source of annoyance to a personal enemy, does not justify marshaling the phalanxes of the solid professional front.

No, Marc, the case stinks. I hope you let it drop.[70]

Blitzstein's attempt to "politicize" the Composers' Forum Laboratory fizzled out, and the only other connection the composer had with the institution, besides writing press reviews for some of the concerts, was an evening dedicated to his music on April 15, 1936. The concert highlighted some of his modernist works: the Piano Sonata of 1927; a movement of the Serenade for String Quartet; the String Quartet of 1930; and the Piano Concerto (with Norman Cazden as the soloist and Blitzstein performing the orchestral reduction). The program also included three songs sung by Mordecai Baumann: "Jimmi's got a goil" on a text by E. E. Cummings, an excerpt of the Dialogue from the ballet *Cain*, and only one piece associated with proletarian music and the Composers' Collective, "A Child Writes a Letter" from the *Children's Cantata*. The dense proletarian rhetoric of this propaganda composition, in light of the turmoil instigated by Blitzstein two months earlier, might have solicited interesting questions from the audience, but we will never know, as Pettis began keeping record of the Q&A sessions only later that month.

De Graaf maintains that the Forum "had its birth in the midst of a hotbed of leftist musical activity" and that only "Pettis's inclusionary music policies . . . reflecting a Populist ideology of appealing to a broad public" saved it from those anti-leftist attacks that preoccupied the Federal Theater Project.[71] Yet the transcripts, as well as the correspondence among composers, show a slightly different narrative. In the Q&A sessions, the audience often pushed composers to discuss basic aspects of the sociopolitical implications of music in Depression-era America. Pettis alone, therefore, would have never been able to stop the Forum from becoming a site of political propaganda if composers, pressed by these questions on the social and political role of music, had not kept musical and militant activities separated, thus giving the Forum its surprisingly apolitical bearing.

Absent political allegations, the Forums became the ideal site for experimentation, and as such earned praise from major critics, including Olin Downes:

> It has long been recognized that a great need of the American composer was a practical laboratory for experimental scoring and for hearing his works.... Until very recently they [American composers] had few opportunities of hearing their music, discovering their weaknesses, and profiting by the experience. But the situation is rapidly changing for the better. One of the most promising of these developments has taken place under the auspices of the music division of WPA, a development which goes by the name of Composers' Forum Laboratory.[72]

After praising the format of the Forums and the quality of contemporary American composers, Downes focused on the experimental aspect that the Forums favored:

> The compositions played are by American composers of all kinds, grades and ages. Composers of reputation already established are called upon to furnish material for the programs. Young experimenters, who may not even have found their feet, technically speaking, are given opportunity to know themselves in the thorough practice of their art.

Indeed, the Forums provided the first government-funded venue where composers could test, using Downes's words, "the actual value and actual weaknesses, if such exist, of their music," subjecting their works to fiercely critical discussion not only from their peers, but also from an audience for which, generally, "the American composer is an unknown quantity." Downes hoped that the Forums could indeed help remove the barrier existing between composers and the consumers of their goods, and stated:

> Our attitude with relation to these forums must not be a narrow one. It is not intended that they be "sufficient unto themselves." They should prove a focal point for the presentation of works of vitality in concerts of greater scope. But, above all, they are designed for the stimulation, in direct contact with an intimate public of disinterested participants, of a strong, indigenous culture—far removed from the vitiated atmosphere which has been the realm of many composers of the day.[73]

Downes's assessment and belief in the long-ranging benefits of the Forums was matched by the comments of many of the composers who had embraced Pettis's proposal. For instance, Roy Harris thus affirmed the initiative's viability:

> Two years ago you asked me to begin the Composers' Forum Laboratory in a small hall with an impromptu lecture-concert of which most of the music was provided by phonograph recordings of my music.

118 • CHAPTER 3

Last night the Composers' Forum Laboratory presented an entire evening of my orchestral works in a fine theatre centrally located. Mr. Schenkman conducted brilliantly, the orchestra played with precision and vitality; the audience was attentive and enthusiastic.

Such circumstances indicate a cultural development of which both you as Director of the Composers' Forum Laboratory, and I, as an American Composer, can only feel proud and happy.

Please accept my congratulations for what you have accomplished for Contemporary American Music in New York City.[74]

This enthusiasm, however, was not unconditional, and some criticized the effectiveness of the format and of the Forums at large. Elliott Carter, for instance, questioned their usefulness in bridging the gap between composer and audience; he argued that "the concepts appear to have done nothing more than to give a small group of friends and others a chance to hear their works" while leaving American contemporary music out of the mainstream concert halls.[75] Carter's assessment addressed the fact that the Forums did not encourage American audiences to ask for more frequent performances of contemporary American music; but, as Pettis rebutted, he did not take into consideration the wider direct and indirect benefits of the Composers' Forum Laboratory:

The record of the Composers' Forum Laboratory contains numerous eloquent tributes, both from individuals and educational institutions, acclaiming the value of appearances and performances, and its stimulating and inspiring influence upon creative activity. The accent in these written statements is upon the incentive hitherto unknown to the native composer.[76]

Pettis also claimed that works presented at the Forums were often programmed by the League of Composers, the National Association of American Composers and Conductors, various nationwide units of the Federal Music Project, and events sponsored by "the recently formed National Committee for American Music, which includes twenty-four leading musical organizations of national importance." There is no doubt that the Composers' Forum Laboratory, like other musical institutions active in the 1930s, provided a venue to showcase, more or less successfully, the broad range of American contemporary music. However, like the Composers' Collective of New York, it never really succeeded in bridging the gap between composer and general audience, and for the most part, as Carter argued, American contemporary music was still not present in the mainstream concert halls.[77]

The tension between experimentation and populism that we found at the core of the activities of the Composers' Collective and the Workers' Theater

Movement, which could have also been a driving force of the Forum, dissolved in the face of the reality that these composers, after all, did not want to give up their artistic integrity. While the transcripts show that many questions aimed to connect new musical compositions to societal issues, they would also challenge the image of the politically conscious American composer of the 1930s. Avoiding engagement with pressing questions on the role of the composer in contemporary society, or else engaging in a very tentative and elusive way, even musicians known for their interest in socially relevant music indicated that more than for political inclinations, even more than for issues of national identity, they were participating in the series to hear their own music. In the end, the Composers' Forum Laboratory provided American composers with a "safe" site under the patronage of the WPA where they promoted their more or less progressive and experimental music in front of engaging and challenging, even if at times insolent, audiences. Only a handful of the 244 American-born and American naturalized composers who appeared in the series had successful musical careers and survived the dissolution of the WPA and the pressing concerns that engaged the United States in the second world conflict. However, it would be wrong to judge the importance of the activity of the Forum on the grounds of this outcome. As the transcripts of the Q&A discussions prove, its relevance goes beyond the fate of contemporary American music to portray how art, politics, and society intersected during one of the most devastating decades of American history.

CHAPTER 4

The Living Newspaper Unit and Innovative Musical Approaches

> Fragments, flung off from the rapid revolutions of the Broadway seasons were our inheritance: good, bad, beautiful, ugly, the faker and the genius, the young man waiting for his chance, the old man who had passed his. Federal Theatre got them all. Thus the New York City project became the best and the worst of Federal Theatre. It presented the widest range of productions, talents, attitudes, races, religious and political faiths. It was everything in excess. In short, it reflected its city.
>
> —Hallie Flanagan, *Arena: The History of the Federal Theatre* (New York: Benjamin Blom, 1940), 51

In the excerpt above, Hallie Flanagan vividly captured the frenetic cultural life of New York City in the 1930s when artists aiming to communicate in pioneering ways with new audiences—especially the working class—found an outlet for experimentation not only in left-wing groups such as the Composers' Collective and the Workers' Theater Movement, but also in the activities promoted by Federal One. Particularly significant toward these goals was the Living Newspaper Unit of the Federal Theater Project (FTP), which started its pursuits in September 1935 and became one of the most prominent sites where experimentation, sociopolitical objectives, and popular accessibility combined to deliver powerful messages. As Stuart Cosgrove documented, the theatrical genre of the living newspaper originated in the Soviet Union when, after the Bolshevik Revolution, the Central Committee of the Communist Party not only promoted public readings of the news but also encouraged dramatization of events to ensure the dissemination of revolutionary propaganda, especially to the illiterate population.[1] This theoretical approach found its ideal form in this new dynamic and creative genre, which featured propagandistic dramatization of current events delivered in an agile way through a sequence of short, stylized scenes, often enhanced by music, especially rhymed and rhythmic songs, and other multimedia elements. In the United States, pruned of its overtly propagandistic connotation but still politically inflaming, the living newspaper became one of the most successful staged endeavors of the Federal Theater Project and, eventually, the ostensible cause of its demise as, according to its director Flanagan, "Enemies made by the living newspaper were . . . powerful enemies, instrumental in the final closing of the project."[2]

While scholars have addressed the theatrical significance of the Living Newspaper Unit productions, their musical components have drawn very little attention, possibly because this genre, in essence a topical revue, failed to attract composers already involved in the experimental activities of the Workers' Theater Movement, or composers working in mainstream Broadway shows. Most of the enlisted composers lacked either the skills or the interest to match the innovative achievements of dramatists and stage directors. However, the experimental nature of the genre still offered a potential forum for testing original musical approaches. This feature is evident in the living newspapers' musical connection with two new contemporary trends: a growing interest in exploring music outside the Western tradition and the emergence of percussion music. This chapter positions these two musical peculiarities at the center of musical experimentalism, especially thanks to the music and activities of Henry Cowell. Thereafter, drawing primarily on archival materials, it considers the Living Newspaper Unit's establishment and the role of politics in the shaping of its future as a consequence of the events surrounding *Ethiopia*, its first planned production. The chapter then connects contemporary interests in non-Western and percussion music to the incidental music of *Ethiopia*, which avoided the stereotypical portrayal of ethnicity that typified Broadway conventions, and *Injunction Granted*, for which Virgil Thomson wrote a percussive score that, albeit in the end unconvincing, could be seen as one of the earliest examples of musical modernism on the theatrical stage. These two examples are also the proof that the Living Newspaper Unit, if it had continued its activities, could have succeeded in loosening the tensions between experimentation and populism that affected much of the leftist musical and theatrical efforts of the 1930s.

The Modernist Appeal of Percussion Instruments and Non-Western Sounds

Henry Cowell (1897–1965) was one of the most radical and progressive composers of the 1930s when, with his piano pieces, he experimented with new

122 • CHAPTER 4

ways to approach pitch and timbre. He was an early advocate for many of the main developments in twentieth-century music—including the systematization of musical parameters, the exploration of timbral resources, and transculturalism—and his influence pervades American modernism. In providing incidental music for their productions, even the composers and music teams of the Living Newspaper Unit expanded on Cowell's approaches to non-Western musical cultures and advocacy for percussion music.

Cowell drew attention to non-Western music and musical instruments as early as 1931, when, after returning from a trip to Berlin where he worked with the German comparative musicologist Erich von Hornbostel, he introduced courses in non-Western music at the New School for Social Research in New York, including one titled "Newly Discovered Oriental Principles."[3] He believed that indigenous music had enormous potential for further developments in experimental music, and it was, as Sally Bick argues, "part of his creative exploration" together with his modernist music.[4] Particularly relevant to the spreading of interest in non-Western music—considering that ethnomusicology was not yet an independent field in the early 1930s—was another course that he taught at the New School in the fall of 1934 titled "Primitive and Folk Origins of Music." Cowell presented in twelve lectures the concept that contemporary music is the result of the combination of Western and Eastern art music as they slowly developed through folk music. Leta Miller provides excerpts from the course description taken from the New School catalog for fall 1934, which show not only the breath of topics Cowell addressed, but also sustained his theory for the development of music.[5] In the unit "Primitive Music," he included musics of the Native Americans, South Sea Islanders, Bushmen, and other African ethnicities; in "Oriental Music" he included ancient Indian and Chinese musics, as well as traditional Japanese, Siamese, Balinese, and Javanese musics. He also incorporated a unit titled "Folk Music," which he considered to be the result of the union of primitive and cultivated systems and finally, one on "European Cultivated Music," to show its connection with East Asian and folk sources. Cowell illustrated these lectures with live performances of world musics, as well as field work recordings he had acquired in Germany during his studies at the Berlin Phonogramm-Archiv in fall 1931 and fall 1932. Miller argues, "One is struck by Cowell's almost postmodern linkage of what H. Wiley Hitchcock called the cultivated and vernacular traditions, as well as his concern with commonalities among the world's musical cultures."[6] Indeed, Cowell's conceptualization of the origins and development of contemporary musical systems was very progressive for the time, and his lectures must have attracted the attention of many music practitioners in New York. After all, among the students enrolled in this class appears a certain John M. Cage, and the influence that Cowell had on this composer has been well documented.[7]

Percussion music was at the forefront of the attention of American modernist circles in the 1930s, not only because of Varèse's *Ionisation*—whose premiere in New York (1933) and further performances on the East and West Coasts benefited from Cowell's contribution as performer, facilitator, organizer, and/or conductor—but also because of the interest Cowell himself, together with Varèse and Chavez, showed for this medium from the foundation of the Pan-American Association of Composers in 1928.[8] In particular, as Haley Jo Nutt contends, percussion music allowed modernist composers to be experimental while testing a new musical idiom influenced by Latin American rhythms and percussion instruments and not ruled by the harmonic and melodic constraints of the European Western tradition.[9] Cowell's *New Music Quarterly* and *New Music Orchestra* series became fundamental tools to publish and promote percussion music starting with William Russell's *Fugue for Eight Percussion Instruments* in March 1933 followed a year later by Varèse's piece. At the same time, in early 1934, Cowell began composing his own percussion ensemble work, *Ostinato Pianissimo*.[10] Even the rhythmic structure of his *United Quartet* (1936), as David Nicholls argues, bears parallels with his percussion music and is very similar to that of *Pulse*, a 1939 percussion piece, which Cowell wrote for the Cage-Harrison ensemble.[11] Quite predictably, in *Pulse*, besides more traditional percussion instruments, such as drums and woodblocks, Cowell also calls for trans-ethnic non-pitched instruments including Korean dragon's mouths, Chinese tom-toms, Japanese temple gongs, and rice bowls.

Cowell's interest in non-Western music, in particular the sounds of non-Western instruments, is combined in *Pulse* with his experimentation with the new medium, the percussion ensemble, demonstrating that the two new trends in American music really had in this composer a true initiator and that they held a prominent role in contemporary musical circles. It shouldn't then come as a surprise that the genre of the living newspaper provided an often-unacknowledged medium for progressive music experimentation, as Cowell's innovative approaches were also at the core of the musical content of the productions of *Ethiopia* and *Injunction Granted*.

Ethiopia: A Difficult and Controversial Start

In the spring of 1935, during a preliminary meeting with Harry Hopkins and Jacob Baker (director and assistant director respectively of the WPA) to discuss the prospect of a Federal Theater Project, Hallie Flanagan suggested the

124 • CHAPTER 4

dramatization of contemporary socioeconomic topics in a series of living newspapers on the grounds that "a theater which had its roots in economic need should be concerned in some of its plays with economic conditions."[12] While her goal was to give work to a larger number of people rather than to a handful of leading actors, she was also trying to demonstrate that the project had higher aspirations and would not only be caring for the unemployed but also recreating a national theater and building a national culture.[13] After all, her activities as director of the Vassar College theater, a position she held intermittently from 1925 to 1942, exemplify her activism through drama and her interest in progressive theatrical genres to promote socially relevant meanings. For instance, Flanagan, who penned one of the first articles referring to the Workers' Theater Movement in the United States, had co-written with Margaret Ellen Clifford and staged for performance at Vassar an agit-prop piece, *Can You Hear Their Voices?*, adapted from a story by Whittaker Chambers. The play portrayed the social conflict between a rich congressman and the poor rural class by using a mixture of German agit-prop and Soviet living newspaper formats.[14] Indeed, the exploratory nature of this play, more suitable for the workers' theater than for a college theater, shows how left-leaning professionals were beginning to find in the labor stage a source of innovation and experimentation and establishes a strong connection between the living newspapers and the agit-prop skits of the American Workers' Theater Movement.

Flanagan's idea to stage living newspapers took shape in September of the same year in the hands of Elmer Rice, who accepted leadership of the New York branch of the FTP and started the New York Living Newspaper Unit that employed, as predicted, a host of jobless journalists and theater professionals. Rice immediately secured the support of the Newspaper Guild and appointed Morris Watson, a former Associated Press reporter who had been fired for his union-organizing activities, as editor-in-chief and Arthur Arent as managing editor. The Biltmore Theatre on 117 West 46th Street became the official showplace of the Living Newspaper Unit of New York. *Ethiopia*, an account of the Italian invasion of the African country, was the first scheduled piece of the Unit readied for production in January 1936. The genesis of *Ethiopia*, which was assembled but never publicly performed, chronicles the difficulties the Unit had to endure to succeed as its leadership navigated the tricky line between political propaganda and populism. From an organizational point of view, *Ethiopia* follows the structure of the subsequent productions, which are essentially staged representations that present a problem, discuss its causes, and offer solutions. By choosing the Italian invasion of Ethiopia in October 1935 as the subject of the first living newspaper, the editorial staff wanted to take advantage of the

The Living Newspaper Unit and Innovative Musical Approaches • 125

prominence of the topic, as Mussolini's colonizing aspiration to win Italy "a place in the African sun" had led to vociferous international indignation and aroused the interest of the American people to become the most discussed issue in the news.

Among the most notable traits of the Unit were the impulse to adhere to the facts as much as possible and the reportage-like way of assembling information. The materials related to the production of *Ethiopia* available at the National Archives already confirm that the staff of the Living Newspaper Unit meticulously prepared by studying political and social contexts concerning the invasion.[15] The working folder contains data on Mussolini and Haile Selassie, war tactics, native and Italian troops in Ethiopia, but also press articles, maps, and sources about Italian and Ethiopian history and the role of international diplomacy in this conflict. The staff also gathered plenty of information about costumes, cultural customs, language, Ethiopian architecture and geography, the Church of Abyssinia, and the role of women in Ethiopian society. The Unit's staff displayed the same accuracy as they were preparing the musical accompaniment for the various episodes of *Ethiopia*.

The musical selection was evidently dictated by the venues where the events took place. When the action took place in Italy at the presence of Mussolini, for instance, it relied on fascist songs, such as "Giovinezza," performed by a band on stage and sung by soldiers. However, most of the instances of incidental music happened on Ethiopian soil and local music is present beginning in Scene 1:

> Ethiopian encampment at Walwal, flat terrain. It is the mid-day rest, and soldiers in their white shammas are sprawled on the ground, eating, drinking, etc. A few musical instruments are seen on the ground.
>
> Soon the first few notes of a native song are heard, vague at first, then growing clearer as one instrument after another takes it up. It is a sad, keening sort of air. The song mounts and soon a single plaintive voice is heard. The harmony is picked up by all, pianissimo. Sharply the song ends, and without pause the players start a livelier tune. A soldier starts to dance. The song rises, the tumult increases.[16]

Thereafter, drum rolls and rhythmic beats of a tom-tom mark changes of scenes and dramatic situations. A remarkable example is the beginning of the elaborate Scene 5 at the court of Haile Selassie, where music acquires both a ritualistic meaning and a menacing tone:

> In a position of great prominence stand three huge war drums, covered with lion skins. Above is the balcony used for state occasions. On it is a thronelike chair. A

126 • CHAPTER 4

gigantic warrior stands beside a smaller tom-tom used to signal the approach of the Emperor. In the courtyard, the warriors wait, all wearing their native white shammas, some accompanied by their wives and families. They carry guns and spears. There is a group of native musicians carrying biblical harps (*herars*). In each group there sits a tribal chief in bright uniform and lion's mane headdress. Each tribe has its drummer beating a small tom-tom which has taken the beat right through from the previous scene. As the curtain rises, there is an intense, electric atmosphere. Suddenly, a single clear voice rings out, singing one of the psalms of David. The melody is taken up by the musicians, and then the entire multitude. At the topmost note, the melody suddenly stops dead. There is a pause, and then a witch doctor steps forward, fantastically dressed. She emits weird, blasting cries, starting a dance of incantation. The tom-toms beat more furiously, the voices become hysterical. The entire scene becomes a saturnalia. . . . At this point the warrior on the balcony pounds his tom-tom, signalling [*sic*] the entrance of the Emperor![17]

It would have been easy for the musical team to have just incorporated stereo-typical Broadway representations of African music; instead they strove for authenticity and the archival papers show a desire to genuinely portray Ethiopian music and dances. The staff meticulously prepared not only by studying political and social contexts concerning the Italian invasion of the African country, but also by gathering plenty of information about Ethiopian musical practices. One wonders if someone on the music team was familiar with Cowell's lectures at the New School in New York, or with his demonstrations with traditional non-Western instruments, and felt compelled to aspire to authenticity in the musical choices for *Ethiopia*.

An accidental circumstance also provided the production with a troupe of African performers, as, to meet its obligation as a relief office the Federal Theater had to give work also to the artists of an African operatic company whose contract had fallen through and had found themselves stranded in New York (at the beginning, the WPA did not discriminate on the grounds of nationality). As Flanagan recalled:

Since few of them could speak English we had had some hectic conferences as to just what we would do with them; now they were to beat drums, sing, and shout in the courtyard of Haile Selassie. There was no caricature; the characterizations and quotations were as literal as we could make them.[18]

Flanagan's remark suggests that she was aware that there could have been the potential for stereotyping, but also aligns with the Unit's plea for authenticity and shows her desire to distance herself and the living newspapers from the stereotypical representations of African music that were familiar to Broadway audiences. Theatrical depictions of African characters often presented the trite image of either the ignorant or the cruel savage and musical conventions largely indebted to minstrelsy and late nineteenth-century variety shows. Indeed, this practice was so rooted on musical stages that even African American performers and producers could not escape it. For instance, as Kristen Turner argues, in William McClain's *Before and After Africa* (1894), the Missionary is a veritable Zip-Coon character, and native Africans are portrayed as uncivilized cannibals who throw the white man in the hot-pot to the tune of minstrel plantation songs.[19] Even Black authors such as Bert William, George Walker, and Will Marion Cook, while infusing their works with political and cultural meanings connected with the "back to Africa" movement, ideas that would have resonated with Black audiences, spread this powerful message through a stereotypical musical language that was familiar to both white and Black Americans but that erased the complex and rich African traditional musical culture.[20]

Descriptions of traditional instruments and influences from nearby African countries on Ethiopian music abound in the archival material to support an authentic depiction of African culture:

Influence of other Nations:
Ethiopian music bears a marked resemblance in construction to that of the ancient Assyrians, Egyptians, Armenians, and Hebrews, and to that of the present day Copta (of Egypt) and Nubians. Also replicas of the Hebrew "sistra" (rattle) are found in Ethiopia today, and the Nubian "kissar" (harp) has its duplicate in Ethiopia. The music of all these peoples is based on the same scale, the pentatonic.[21]

The collected data contain fragments of Ethiopian melodies and refer to their structure, arguing that they usually begin with a short phrase, which is reiterated at different levels and with increasing ornamentation (see figure 4.1).

The analysis details differences of chant and performance practices, which disclose the identity of different Ethiopian tribes (possibly for the music performed at the beginning of Scene 5). These remarks are supported by transcriptions of Ethiopian music (see figure 4.2).

The records do not mention if the musicians of the stranded African company contributed to the research. Still, even if this musical study does not bear the markers of a genuine ethnomusicological investigation, it nonetheless underscores the commitment of the Living Newspapers' staff to authenticity in musical matters. As Flanagan envisioned, the stranded African performers would have introduced American audiences to a rather different image of African

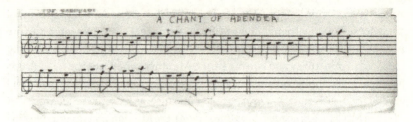

Figure 4.1. Transcription of an Ethiopian chant of Adendea. NARA II, Record Group 69—Records of the Work Projects Administration—Records of the Federal Theater Project. Living newspaper research materials ca. 1936–39, Box 552, Folder: "Ethiopia—No. 1"

Figure 4.2. Transcription of Ethiopian chants. NARA II, Record 69—Records of the Work Projects Administration—Records of the Federal Theater Project. Living newspaper research materials ca. 1936–39, Box 552, Folder: "Ethiopia—No. 1"

music and culture than the exoticized clichés or the Americanized portrayal that Broadway and the entertainment industry had until then promoted, thus demonstrating the progressiveness of the FTP.

Unfortunately, though, audiences had still to wait before they were exposed to this authenticity, because *Ethiopia* generated such a turmoil around the Living Newspaper Unit of New York that eventually it not only prevented its performance but also precipitated Rice's withdrawal from his FTP role in protest. The determination to adhere as much as possible to real facts, ironically, caused a political kerfuffle. The dramatic action of *Ethiopia* involved the presence on stage of impersonators of Mussolini and Haile Selassie. For the final scene, the writers thought that adding an excerpt from one of President Roosevelt's speeches about this international issue would render the production even more realistic.

The Living Newspaper Unit and Innovative Musical Approaches • 129

Watson tried in vain to get a recording of the presidential address. Not only did the government refuse permission to use the speech, but, for fear that a too strict adherence to reality could compromise international relations with Italy and Europe, it also issued a slap on the wrist to Flanagan in the form of a directive forbidding the impersonation of any foreign minister or head of state in this and subsequent living newspapers.[22] Rice reacted to this order with a telegram, worth reproducing in full, which left no doubt about his intention to defend his right to free speech:

> I am disturbed to learn that Mr. Baker has ordered modification of the first production of the living newspaper unit which effectually prevents presentation. This unit promises to be most novel and interesting one of the federal theatre project here. Opening has been given great publicity and is being awaited by press and public with eager anticipation. Its factual representation of actual news events contains no criticism or satire of any foreign power or official. I took this job on your assurance that we should have a free hand and that there would be no censorship. This seems to me a direct and arbitrary act of censorship and if you support Baker's decision there is nothing for me to do except regretfully tender my resignation as regional director giving my reasons for such resignation to the press.
>
> Elmer Rice[23]

The telegram, instead of winning the Unit the right to proceed, triggered another memorandum from Baker to Flanagan with even more restrictions and the hope that "the script is susceptible of such modifications as to enable you to present it."[24] Rice, however, remained faithful to his initial statements and eventually resigned from the project. On January 24 he distributed a press statement to explain his action and accused Baker of trying "to raise a smoke-screen to conceal the real issue. That issue clearly is free speech."[25] In the release he reminded the press that in his first interview upon accepting the job, he had vowed that "any attempt at censorship would be followed by immediate resignation. Washington has broken its word; I have kept mine." After *Ethiopia*, Rice had planned two other productions, one called *Class of '29* dealing with unemployment and the handling of relief, and the other on the Southern states' treatment of racial issues such as lynching and discrimination against Blacks and the plight of the sharecroppers. Apparently, Baker found these topics too politically dangerous, and Rice claimed:

> The issue of free speech and the preservation of the bill of rights seem to me of greater moment today than they have ever been in the history of America. I cannot conscientiously remain the servant of a government which plays the shabby game of partisan politics at the expense of freedom and the principles of democracy.[26]

130 • CHAPTER 4

Rice, though, was not ready to leave without showing the fruit of his first and only living newspaper production and organized a private representation of *Ethiopia*, mainly for journalists and critics, where he illustrated even more eloquently his reasons for leaving.[27] The press gave the event and controversy ample exposure. Members of the Living Newspaper's staff considered Rice's a splendid stand against censorship but felt that the FTP deserved a second chance before leaving en masse. Morris Watson, in a press release that followed on the heels of Rice's resignation, summarized the feelings of those who decided to stay:

> Because nearly 400 jobs are involved, and because I believe that the Living Newspaper could be a very valuable contribution to the community, I have decided to stay with it and fight the best I can against interferences with its announced intent to present unbiased, objective news reports on the stage.[28]

In the end, the activities of the FTP New York Living Newspaper Unit continued along the line of the original plan under the leadership of Philip Barber, Rice's assistant.

Success and Experimentation

After such a rough start, the Living Newspaper Unit of New York abandoned international politics and effectively produced, not without political tensions, a series of five issues dealing with domestic news: *Triple A Plowed Under* (1936), a dramatization of the Agricultural Adjustment Act and the plight of the farmers against middlemen, dealers, and commercial interests; *Events of 1935* (1936), a collage of sociopolitical gossip and facts of the year and, possibly because of the lack of in-depth analysis, the least appreciated of the living newspapers; *Injunction Granted* (1936), a chronicle of the American labor movement and its struggles with the court system, which provided an inflamed and ironic lampooning of capitalism in support of workers' organizations and attracted further criticism from the government; *Power* (two productions, in 1937 and 1938), a clever play on the double meaning of its title that presented a story of the development of electricity as well as the struggles to control and own electric utilities; and *One-Third of a Nation* (1938), a realistic account of the housing problem in big American cities that, citing President Roosevelt's second inaugural speech, presented the origins and causes of the increasing number of filthy and dangerous slums in American cities.[29]

The success of these living newspapers cannot be compared with that of contemporary commercial Broadway shows, as not even the low ticket prices generated long-lasting productions. But attendance of the New York productions, as shown in figure 4.3, places the living newspapers among the most popular endeavors of the FTP, especially considering that they were merely experimental documentaries, which offered substantive analysis of contemporary American social issues. The New York Living Newspaper Unit's productions traveled also beyond the metropolitan area with performances in other major American venues hosting branches of the FTP. Often shows were even produced in several cities at once, sometimes with the introduction of local variations. For instance, the FTP encouraged regional productions of *One-Third of a Nation*, the living newspaper on slum housing, because every major city had its own areas affected by this problem. As a result, companies in Detroit, Cincinnati, Portland, Philadelphia, Hartford, New Orleans, Seattle, and San Francisco simultaneously staged the "saga of the slums."[30]

TRIPLE A PLOWED UNDER	Opened 3/14/36	Closed 5/3/36 (Biltmore)
	Performances	45
	Paid Attendance	29,066
	Free Attendance	3,851
	Total Attendance	32,917
	Gross Receipts	$ 7,731.95
	Net Receipts	$ 7,731.95
	Tax	————
HIGHLIGHTS OF 1935	Opened 5/12/36	Closed 5/30/36 (Biltmore)
	Performances	35
	Paid Attendance	5,261
	Free Attendance	1,540
	Total Attendance	6,801
	Gross Receipts	$ 1,415.00
	Net Receipts	$ 1,415.00
	Tax	————
INJUNCTION GRANTED	Opened 7/24/36	Closed 10/20/36 (Biltmore)
	Performances	76
	Paid Attendance	26,106
	Free Attendance	10,115
	Total Attendance	36,221
	Gross Receipts	$ 7,288.90
	Net Receipts	$ 7,288.90
	Tax	————

Figure 4.3. Analysis of Attendance and Receipts at the Six Productions of the Living Newspaper. Federal Theater Project, NYC. NARA II, Record 69—Records of the Work Projects Administration—Records of the Federal Theater Project. Living newspaper research materials ca. 1936–39, Box 537, Folder "Publicity."

132 • CHAPTER 4

POWER First Production	Opened 2/25/37	Closed 7/10/37 (Ritz)
	Performances	118
	Paid Attendance	66,286
	Free Attendance	11,109
	Total Attendance	77,395
	Gross Receipts	$ 17,216.63
	Net Receipts	$ 17,216.63
	Tax	————
POWER Second Production	Opened 2/12/38	(49th Street Theatre and Spot Booking)
	Performances	26
	Paid Attendance	6,363
	Free Attendance	2,931
	Total Attendance	9,294
	Gross Receipts	$ 1,678.98
	Net Receipts	$ 1,672.33
	Tax	$ 6.65
ONE-THIRD OF A NATION	Opened 1/17/38	Closed 10/22/38 (Adelphi)
	Performances	237
	Paid Attendance	183,253
	Free Attendance	28,205
	Total Attendance	211,458
	Gross Receipts	$ 76,131.50
	Net Receipts	$ 70,342.02
	Tax	$ 5,489.48
TOTALS FOR THE SIX PRODUCTIONS		
	Performances	533
	Paid Attendance	316,335
	Free Attendance	57,751
	Total Attendance	374,086
	Gross Receipt	$ 111,462.96
	Net Receipts	$ 105,966.83
	Tax	$5,496.13

Figure 4.3. *continued*

The Living Newspaper Unit's technique of superimposing layers of visual and aural information in short and dynamic discrete numbers caught the attention of the press. Burns Mantle in the *Daily News* claimed the living newspaper was "the most vital idea which has entered the American Theatre in years."[31] The supposed novelty of this format, though, needs some reconsideration, as the living newspapers had their roots in the agit-prop skits of the American Workers' Theater Movement, and, as Ilka Saal argues, their format borrows also

The Living Newspaper Unit and Innovative Musical Approaches • 133

from epic theater, especially in didactic goals, use of episodic plot structure, and non-illusory staging.[32] But Arthur Arent, who in his role of the Unit's managing editor oversaw all productions, maintained that he never even read a script of a Soviet living newspaper and other forms of agit-prop and political theater that everyone had associated with his productions:

> What are the sources of this technique? As far as I know, there aren't any. At least if there are, we didn't know about them. Among those immediately concerned—author, director, producer, designer, technician and composer—each had ideas as to what could be done in his particular orbit, and we all had a healthy respect for the opportunity of experimentation that the Federal Theatre offered. Best of all, there was apparent all along the line a happy distaste for repeating ourselves and as we went on only certain features, gradually evolved, were retained as the hallmark of the medium.[33]

Yet some of the personnel of the Unit came from the experience of the Workers' Theater Movement's agit-prop productions; thus, episodic structure and epic elements were already part of their artistic tools and of a tradition that, as we have seen in Chapter 2, developed in the United States in the late 1920s. In his claim to uniqueness, Arent argued that the living newspaper is a dramatization of a problem:

> composed in greater or lesser extent of many news events, all bearing on the one subject and interlarded with typical but non-factual representations of the effect of these news events on the people to whom the *problem* is of great importance.... Let me explain: a news item will carry information concerning a Congressional debate on a Housing Bill. We produce this debate, let's say, including the statement from one of the Bill's partisans that one-third of the nation is ill-housed. So far we are literal, transposing a front page story to the stage, using only the direct quote. But the human element is missing. The statements and statistics are flat. We have made no use of the theatre. The next step, then, is the creative scene, based on slum conditions as we know them to exist, where instead of one-dimensional characters, speaking the unattractive patois of the politicians, we have a man expressing himself in the warm speech and theatric idiom of a humanity undeterred by the hopelessness of being immortalized in the Congressional Record. This character represents the one-third of the nation. He is the audience's identification, the bridge that leads to an understanding in human terms of the subject of the debate. And the proof of his being is the debate itself.[34]

These statements, though, draw a connection with the experimental agit-prop plays that Flanagan had produced at Vassar College and those staged by the

134 • CHAPTER 4

Workers' Theater Movement in the late 1920s and early 1930s. The "technique of dramatizing an abstraction," as Arent defined it, using an episodic approach enhanced by songs, projections, montage, loudspeakers as commentator, and generically labeled characters (such as *first farmer* or *first city man*), conform to the canons of agit-prop theater, a form that mainstream critics had often undervalued and dismissed as propaganda.[35] Ultimately, by dramatizing reality through direct experience the Unit adapted the politically saturated mechanisms of Soviet and German revolutionary experimental theater and, indeed, the living newspapers readily crossed the subtle line between informative and political aims when the staff, in collaborative efforts to dramatize a problem, added layers of interpretation to factual information.

Why then, did the living newspapers capture the attention of wide audiences and become the most successful endeavor of the FTP? The answer lays in Arent's claim that Americans can recognize themselves in the stereotypical characters of the living newspapers. As Saal contends:

> In choosing a common-man protagonist who is just like the average spectator, in developing a dramatic structure that emulates his commonsensical understanding of problems of immediate daily relevance, and in enhancing the basic documentary style of their issues with fictional, yet highly realistic vignettes, the Living Newspaper turns the analysis of a current problem into an individual dramatic adventure, providing its audience with a comprehensive factual and yet entirely personal and sentimental (and therefore vernacular) education on current political issues.[36]

In her discussion of the vernacular aspect of the living newspapers, Saal maintains that some of their epic techniques, which were more the result of economic necessities than artistic choices, "remained firmly embedded in a native concept of realism, one that privileged fact and experience over theory and abstraction."[37] Indeed, the realistic aspect of the theatrical genre turned what could have been a heavily political exercise into an experience that average Americans dealing with the hardships of the Great Depression could recognize as their own. But the combination of experimentation and vernacular elements of the living newspapers extended also to their musical component, which combined modernist approaches and incidental music selections drawn from the vernacular tradition.

The Living Newspaper and Music's Strategic Role

If the incidental music for *Ethiopia* would have introduced audiences to rather authentic representations of the African country's traditions, the music that Lee

Wainer (1904–79) oversaw for *Triple A Plowed Under, Highlights of 1935, Power,* and *One-Third of a Nation* meant to underscore dramatized news events by matching the directness and quick pace of the delivery with incisive musical commentary, often inspired by popular musical styles. Wainer, who had also composed for the FTP the music for the musical *Sing for Your Supper* (1939), was a composer, performer, writer, and director without having achieved prominence in any of these activities. Yet Wainer's problem-solving ability was exactly what the Living Newspaper Unit needed, as archival material supports the claim that music had a prominent role in these productions. As reported by Ethel Aaron in an interdepartmental memorandum, preparing the incidental music for *Triple A Plowed Under,* Wainer "had to keep in mind the necessity for integrating the scenes through the musical score as well as making the music responsible for change of mood and for effect."[38] It is unclear from the archival material at NARA if Wainer wrote also original music or if he only arranged already existing pieces. For instance, the "Sound Cues" section of the script of *Triple A Plowed Under* only gives instructions on when to turn on microphones during music performances but does not indicate which music was used for the overture or any of the scenes.[39] The only clear mention refers to the piece "Blue Danube," which is played on a record at the beginning of Scene 15, "Swank Restaurant." There are no doubts, though, that the incidental music selection had a strategic role in this script. For instance, figure 4.4, which reproduces a page from *Triple A Plowed Under,* shows the carefully planned positioning of the musical cues to help divide scenes, build action, create mood, or announce that something is about to happen.

If Wainer's expertise in the selection of incidental music helped to strategically draw attention to the content of *Triple A Plowed Under,* Virgil Thomson's original score for *Injunction Granted* added also a layer of musical sophistication to the practical result.

The music for *Injunction Granted* was not Thomson's first collaboration with a unit of the FTP. In 1934, while he was in Paris enjoying the Broadway success of *Four Saints in Three Acts,* the composer was contacted by John Houseman, who had directed that opera, who proposed that he join a new Off-Broadway project, the Phoenix Theater. Thomson accepted the offer and collaborated with Houseman, providing the incidental music for Countee Cullen's version of Euripides's *Medea* (the work was eventually canceled, but later Thomson arranged the choruses as a concert piece, *Seven Choruses from the Medea of Euripides*), Archibald MacLeish's *Panic,* and Kathleen Connell's production of *Romeo and Juliet* before collaborating with Houseman and Orson Welles in the *Macbeth* production of the Negro Theater of the FTP. For this adaptation of the play to

	Music	Lights and curtain
		CURTAIN AND LIGHT PLOT
SCENE 1.	Overture	House lights out after overture
		News flashes over loudspeaker
		Turn red lights on soldiers
		On four beats of marching music, soldiers start on stage.
		After four counts from soldiers (8 beats in all), curtain open.
		Close portals on cue "Farmer, save the world"
		Leave scrim in
		Clear stage quickly
	Music for curtain to tie into Scene 2	
		Open curtain
		Loudspeaker announcement
	End of music	
SCENE 2.		Open portals
		Light up on first platform
		On cue "I don't see a damn thing," count 1-blackout.
	Incidental music between scenes.	
		Light up after music
		After Scene C close portals—fly scrim
	Incidental music	
		Loudspeaker announcement
		Open portals as quickly as four men are set—
	End of music into	
SCENE 3.		Light up on four men
		1 – "I can't buy that auto" 1-blackout
		2 – "I can't take that shipment" 1-blackout
		3 – "I can't use you anymore" 1-blackout
		4 – "I can't eat" 1-2-blackout finish
		(no close in)
	Incidental music	
		Loudspeaker announcement
SCENE 4.		Milo Reno enters stage right in dark.
	On immediate finish of music	
		Light from balcony spot up on Milo Reno. (Have platform ready stage left for entrance with desk and committee men on cue "1776")
		Send on platform in the dark (stage left)
		On last cue from Reno "if I tried," count 1-2-blackout.
		Spot up from left balcony on to stage left.
		Milo Reno walks to platform
		As he walks voices call "Strike, strike," on mike, off stage.
		After Reno signs, 1-2-blackout
	Music	

Figure 4.4. From the original scripts of *Triple A Plowed Under.* George Mason University, Mason Archival Repository Service, Federal Theater Project Materials Collection, http://digilib.gmu.edu:8080/dspace/handle/1920/3478

modern time with Black actors, which opened on April 14, 1936, the authors chose to set Shakespeare's play on an island (possibly Haiti) at the time of the Black emperor Jean Christophe. Anthony Tommasini reports that Thomson had to provide incidental music (arrangements of waltzes, military marches, trumpet fanfares) and also sound effects, including the music for a percussion ensemble backstage comprising bass drum, thunder sheet, wind machine, and gongs.[40] He also mentions that Thomson used these effects to amplify the actors' voices during the stormy scenes underlying words with thunder claps, rattling drums, and wind effects, but that he did not write any original music, because he felt Houseman was ordering what he should compose and he would not accept this subordination to the producer.

The experience with percussion instruments in *Macbeth*, though, combined with the influential interest of Cowell in the medium, might have contributed to Thomson's choices for the original music he wrote later that year for *Injunction Granted*, a chronicle in twenty-eight scenes of two hundred years of the American labor movement history and its struggles with the court system, which, according to Stuart Cosgrove, brings to mind Vladimir Mayokovsky's circus play in the Soviet Union.[41] Thomson, who apart from the *Macbeth* production had until then not shown particular fascination with percussion instruments, provided a score that complements the original nature of this living newspaper and experimented with form and musical devices that were rather unusual to his style, which at the time favored folk melodies, dance idioms, and American hymnody. To portray the opposing social forces, he juxtaposed traditional fife and drum corps and modern percussion instruments: piccolos, fifes, trumpets, sixteen drums, sixteen snare drums, sixteen Bronx cheers (a lip buzzed instrument that produces a sound similar to a "raspberry"), and a battery of percussion instruments and objects used more to create sound effects and noise than rhythm (including thunder drum, rattle machine gun, railroad train effect, ratchet machine effect, rumble cart, thunder sheet box, train bell, fire department bell, electric bell, factory whistle, locomotive whistle, ocean steamboat whistle, wind whistle, washtub for glass, and cuckoo call).

With this score, Thomson intended to match the forceful denunciation of the struggle of unionism against capitalism and the court system, and to punctuate with 496 musical cues, "every exit and entrance, almost every remark, with percussive comment and ironic framing."[42] The explosive introduction seems indeed to support this claim. The first fourteen cues call for work whistles, snare drum (with handbell on stage), bass drum, and cymbals performing loud ostinato rhythmic patterns, leading to cue 15, which features a *fff* 2-measure solo of two piccolos. Thereafter, there is a sudden change in dynamics; the snare drum plays a *ppp* ostinato march-like rhythm to start another crescendo to *fff* with the reprise of the

138 · CHAPTER 4

two piccolos' entrance. These opening musical blasts, as they are described in the script of *Injunction Granted*, with their repetitive percussive and piercing crescendo statements could symbolize the recurring and never solved struggle of the labor movement throughout history and would have indeed captured the attention of the audience. After this peremptory opening, Thomson indulged in a section filled with sound effects: over the ostinato background of police sirens and the sound of a telegraph key we hear a simple tune in the trumpets, trombone glissandos, and eventually chaotic sounds produced by ratchets, snares, train whistle, police whistle, work whistle, bass drum, and cymbals.

This introduction set the stage for a quite modernist take on incidental music, but despite the astonishing amount of percussion called for in the score, the basic instrumentation of Thomson's music relies mostly on cymbals, snares, and bass drums. Even the sound effects that he employed lost their revolutionary quality and have roots more in the American variety show and silent film theater tradition than in the percussive music of Varèse and Cowell.[43] Moreover, as shown in figures 4.5, 4.6, and 4.7, the melodic instruments (in these cases piccolos but often also bugles and trumpets) interject brief motives on the rhythmic tapestry of rudimental riffs that are more reminiscent of military bugle signals than of a modernist approach to percussive music.[44] The minimalist repetition of these rhythmic/melodic patterns and the absence of a prominent melody, which could have heightened the modernist provocation, appear flimsy based on Norman Lloyd's account:

> One day, Peggy and I ran into Virgil on the 6th Avenue bus.
> "Virgil," I accosted him. "You know I appear and reappear in this play all evening as a clown. Are you going to give me a theme for whenever I come on? A musical theme?"
> "Certainly not," replied Virgil agreeably. "I'm going to write on the score, 'T.T.T.'"
> "T.T.T.? What does T.T.T. mean?"
> "Tunes Take Time," he said briskly.[45]

Lloyd's request seems appropriate, given that he played the role of a mute clown (based on the character of Harpo Marx) whose actions provided a visual commentary to the staged events. Who knows if Thomson justified the absence of melodic interludes to keep up with the quick pace of the action, or if he simply and sardonically referred to the time (and creative energy) that he did not want to squander on such a production?

Nonetheless, Thomson's contribution certainly fulfilled the function that the Living Newspaper Unit requested. According to Ethel Aaron, the score perfectly matched the needs of the staging:

Figure 4.5. Virgil Thomson, *Injunction Granted*, Cue No. 17. NARA II, Record 69—Records of the Work Projects Administration—Records of the Federal Theater Project, Living newspaper research materials ca. 1936–39, Box 555, Folder "Injunction Granted 3"

Figure 4.6. Virgil Thomson, *Injunction Granted*, Cue No. 44. NARA II, Record 69—Records of the Work Projects Administration—Records of the Federal Theater Project, Living newspaper research materials ca. 1936–39, Box 555, Folder "Injunction Granted 3"

In the new production, "Injunction Granted!," Mr. Virgil Thomson, who is composing the score, has an even more difficult job. Mr. Thomson, as you know, is one of the foremost of contemporary American musicians. His score for "Injunction Granted!" is written largely for percussive instruments. There will be at least twelve drums in the orchestra pit. These men as well as those playing other instruments will have many different sound effects to operate. We will use everything from a factory whistle to a cow-bell. The director, Mr. Roman, actually will have a cue book very much like the Stage Manager's, since every

Figure 4.7. Virgil Thomson, *Injunction Granted*, Cue No. 121. NARA II, Record 69—Records of the Work Projects Administration—Records of the Federal Theater Project, Living newspaper research materials ca. 1936–39, Box 555, Folder "Injunction Granted 3"

scene will require many different effects. This kind of writing allows for a perfect synchronization between the score and script. It would be impossible for Mr. Thomson to write this score in any other way, since the scenes are too short to allow any interesting melodic development, and also since the music must be an unobtrusive part of the production and not stand out in any way.[46]

Indeed, Thomson succeeded in creating loud noises and sounds, as Lloyd recalls: "the sound he achieved was marvelous; on opening night, the police burst into the theatre to investigate the apparent catastrophe."[47] But, even if the score could have acquired—at least conceptually—a modernist patina from its use of percussion instruments, it was criticized for what it did not accomplish. For instance, Frederick Jacobi noted in *Modern Music*:

> For this [*Injunction Granted*], Virgil Thomson has written the orchestral accompaniment; to call this "music" is unfair both to it and to music. The shrieking sirens and Klaxons give an effective opening. But when, later, the dialog is punctuated point for point (somewhat in the nature of Walter Winchell's "Flash!"), by beats on the bass-drum, occasionally varied by rolls on the snare-drum, and when

this process is continued regularly for the better part of a long first act, the effect becomes both monotonous and nerve-wracking. Further along there is music of slightly greater pretense in which roll-calls on trumpets and fife play a considerable part. But on the whole it cannot be said that this "score" will add greatly to the reputation of the author of *Four Saints*. It lacks his light hand and his usual ingenuity. No doubt he will claim that it is just the right thing as a commentary on the Living Newspaper and perhaps this is so.[48]

The questionable artistic quality of the score resides in its unconvincing juxtaposition of modernism and tradition. If the dense assembling of percussion and sound effect instruments recalls Varèse's *Ionisation*, the music lacks the experimental nature of this composition.[49] The superimposition of musical topoi associated with military life and of disruptive, almost anarchic sounds could have portrayed the struggle between the judiciary system and the working class in an ironic way. But instead of approaching the medium with a modernist curiosity for interlocking rhythms, expansion of rhythmic cells, or contrast of different kinds of percussive timbres, Thomson treated his medium as a fife and drum corps. Ultimately, the composer seemed to have turned a promising modernist opportunity into, as Jacobi argued, a "nerve-wracking" musical experience. However, even if it was not completely convincing, this effort created the possibility to incorporate glimpses of musical modernism into a theatrical production, an effort that after all the audience seemed to have appreciated, as *Injunction Granted* was the third most attended of the productions of the Living Newspaper Unit (see figure 4.3).

Conclusion

The barely concealed activist tone of the Living Newspaper productions led to increasing criticism from the government. The Unit could not avoid political tensions, given that many staff members came directly from the workers' theater: actors, directors, and writers who had nurtured liberal inclinations with the radical appeal of the New Deal and the compromise politics of the Popular Front. For instance, Joseph Losey, director of *Triple A Plowed Under* and *Injunction Granted*, infused his works with Marxist dialectics and ideological commitment to communism and Soviet agit-prop theater.[50] The Living Newspaper became one of the first targets of the House Committee on Un-American Activities created in 1938 to investigate alleged disloyalty, subversive activities, and communist ties on the part of private citizens, public employees, and organizations. But communist infiltrations alone would not have halted the Living Newspaper and the other experimental activities of the FTP.

142 • CHAPTER 4

Its relative popular and critical success, as well as governmental funds that allowed freedom to experiment, exacerbated tensions, as Mordecai Gorelik still vividly remembered thirty years later:

> The Federal Theater . . . was the most vulnerable of the New Deal institutions. Since it functioned as a relief agency while trying to achieve theater of a high standard, it was an anomaly from the beginning. Snarled in bureaucratic red tape and censorship, it found mass support in the country's largest cities, especially New York, but not in the nation as a whole; it faced opposition from know-nothing politicians, the jealousy of the commercial theater interests, the ambivalence of the stage unions, and political pressures of Left and Right within its own ranks.[51]

Still, besides providing a controversial critique to some of the most pressing sociopolitical issues of the time, the living newspapers offered a potential forum for testing original musical content. The approach to non-Western musical culture, which is at the core of the choices for the musical accompaniment of *Ethiopia*, might have been triggered by the desire to adhere to the facts as much as possible. The Unit could have offered a much more accurate account of African culture and musical traditions because it was not constrained by the business aspects that typified Broadway productions and, in so doing, provided a critique to contemporary problematic commercial musical practices. Thomson might not have succeeded in creating a masterpiece with his score for *Injunction Granted*, but his functional and fragmented music certainly complemented and enhanced the experimental nature of the production. In particular, the ostinato rhythmic patterns, the repetitive short melodies, and the recurrent use of loud and chaotic sound effects provided a counterpart to the cyclic nature of the workers' struggle, which was never solved in the two hundred years portrayed in *Injunction Granted*.

In the end, thanks to these contributions, the Living Newspaper Unit proved to be a progressive theatrical and musical endeavor capable of mitigating the friction between experimentation and popular appeal. It also showed that theater could be fertile ground to experiment with the musical innovations that were promoted by Cowell and many other influential modernists and ultramodernists of the 1930s, a path that would typify the experiments in avant-garde music and theater of the post–World War II years.[52]

CHAPTER 5

A Leftist Myth

Marc Blitzstein's *The Cradle Will Rock*

> However paradoxical it may seem, myth hides nothing:
> its function is to distort, not to make disappear.
> —Roland Barthes, *Mythologies* (New York:
> Noonday Press, 25th ed., 1991), 120

If there is one piece of musical theater that could epitomize the trials, errors, and successes of the works of left-leaning individuals and cultural institutions that were active in New York City in the 1930s, it is Marc Blitzstein's *The Cradle Will Rock*. As we have seen in previous chapters, such forums as the Composers' Collective, the Workers' Theater Movement, and the Federal Theater Project had given Blitzstein opportunities to conceptualize a new brand of socially relevant music and theater. There, he experimented with novel—and, according to contemporary critics and audiences, distinctively American—approaches to music and drama that found their culmination in *Cradle*. In this play in music, Blitzstein developed a form of sociopolitical musical theater that, combining modernist and vernacular musical styles, addressed pressing issues and compelled audiences toward a meaningful engagement beyond the theater. In this chapter, we see that the enthusiastic critical response to the premiere of the play celebrated its use of American vernacular idioms but overemphasized the role of its accidental non-realistic staging, thus concealing its actual artistic merits. Relying on Barthes's conceptualization of mythology, the chapter shows that these critics, attaching a different significance to Blitzstein's musico-dramatic structure, froze the meaning of the original form and created a myth of *Cradle* as the quintessential expression of the non-realistic theater of the left rather than

144 • CHAPTER 5

a work that represents the composer's artistic maturity in the balanced union of modernist and popular approaches.[1]

Reconsideration of the contemporary reception of *Cradle*, of Blitzstein's writings from the 1930s about the show and his own dramatic theories, and of his affiliation with the New York leftist theatrical scene (including its ongoing debate about non-illusionary and epic theater) strongly suggests that his socially relevant theater stemmed more from his own artistic and personal development than, as many believed, from emulation of Bertolt Brecht and Kurt Weill's experiments with non-realistic and epic theater. In revisiting Blitzstein's leftist musical and theatrical experience, we see that with *Cradle* the composer succeeded in bringing a distinctively American element to the various streams of German/Soviet agit-prop theatrical practice. Furthermore, a comparison of selected sketches from *Cradle* in their piano version with the original orchestrated version, recently restored by Opera Saratoga, will help highlight Blitzstein's musical inventiveness and support the argument that the sociopolitical climate tainted the future of one of the most meaningful creative works of the decade. Separating the composer's achievements from the ongoing debate about epic and non-scenery theater would also sustain the claim that, with this play, Blitzstein achieved the successful union of experimentation and populist intent that was at the core of much musical activities of the 1930s in New York City.

Blitzstein's Musico-Dramatic Forms Pre-*Cradle*

Blitzstein's attempts to marry new musico-dramatic forms and socially relevant issues date from the earliest years of his career and are already evident in *Triple Sec* (1928), a one-act farcical opera set to a libretto by the British writer Ronald Jeans. This work features a Black singer and cynically mocks the conventions of grand opera by showing the stage action through the eyes of a drunken audience. After an unremarkable premiere in Philadelphia on May 6, 1929, the Theater Guild included *Triple Sec* in the third edition of the musical revue *Garrick Gaieties* in 1930. The Broadway audience and most critics welcomed the sketch (which remained in the production for 150 performances) with praise for its satirical treatment of grand opera and its musical snobbery. *Triple Sec* stands apart from Blitzstein's later political theatrical discourse; nonetheless, it advanced markedly toward his subsequent rebellious style. The dissonant and cacophonic piece employs syncopated jazz rhythms used, at this point of his career, not to render the music more accessible to a wider audience (as Weill did), but rather to provoke listeners and to emphasize the composer's impatience with traditional composition: "I was slamming the smug people and traditions I had been brought up with. It was a philosophy of denial of their values."[2] His angry words manifest the typical intolerance of youth toward the past, but they also show Blitzstein's growing desire to find new ways of artistic expression and new meanings for his work. Indeed, provocation in both musical and theatrical content characterized his work since before his acquaintance with the musico-dramatic world of Weill and Brecht. Additionally, *Triple Sec* assumes relevance in Blitzstein's future output, in that it constituted his first major contribution to musical revue, a genre that he pursued during the 1930s as a cornerstone of the Workers' Theater Movement and his particular brand of agit-prop theater.

Claire Reis commissioned Blitzstein's next foray into musical theater, *The Harpies* (1931), for the League of Composers. This one-act opera, the first work on Blitzstein's own libretto, was scored for eight characters (four women and four men) and an ensemble of eight instruments (winds, double bass, and piano). The work features dissonance and rhythmic vitality indebted to neoclassical modernism, possibly reminiscent of his studies with Nadia Boulanger, but it also introduces distinctive American traits, such as barbershop harmonies and choral parts similar to radio advertising jingles. *The Harpies* signals another clear step toward the form that will characterize his musical theater starting in the second half of the 1930s. As David Kushner argues, the comic subject drawing on Greek mythology is also typically neoclassical and could represent a satire of previous classical and romantic mythological settings.[3] The plot, from Book III of the *Argonautica* of Apollonius, centers on the story of the sightless oracle Phineus whose dinner the Harpies steal. Three Argonauts, led by Jason, promise to help the blind Phineus in exchange for the favor of the gods. He agrees and a battle ensues between the Harpies and the Argonauts. Meanwhile, Iris, a messenger of the gods, intervenes in favor of Phineus, who eventually eats his restored meal. The allegorical content of this topic, especially at the height of the Great Depression, cannot be overlooked. In the character of Phineus, Blitzstein addressed the contradictions between knowledge and action by suggesting that only militant actions can concretize ideas: the oracle knows everything but, being blind, can do nothing. Likewise, the Harpies portray the economic and political conditions of the Depression that so shattered access to basic human needs. In the end, this allegory turned against Blitzstein, as the economic crisis touched the League of Composers, too, and Reis had to release the League's option on the work.

The Harpies represents a formative moment in Blitzstein's transition from elitist modernist to socially conscious theatrical activist, one that continued with *The Condemned* (1932), another one-act opera on the composer's own libretto. The work recapitulates the trial and the controversial story of the two

146 · CHAPTER 5

Italian anarchists Sacco and Vanzetti, an event that exposed many of main-stream America's prejudices, such as the red scare, class conflict, and xeno-phobia, especially anti-Italian sentiment, and became a banner against po-litical corruption and discrimination. Blitzstein's dramatic conception of this work represents a significant milestone in his quest for a new musico-dramatic form. *The Condemned*, essentially a cantata for choruses and small orchestra, has four characters, each scored for chorus: the Condemned (TTBB), who symboli-cally embodies in one person Sacco and Vanzetti, the Wife (SSA), the Friend (BB), and the Priest (TT).[4] The composer chose to represent the two Italians in a single character to epitomize social injustice. He then gave the character a choral voice—an appropriate allusion to Greek tragedy in that the protagonist represents the collectivity of human tragedy. According to Blitzstein's score instructions, all participants must be on stage during the entirety of the opera, with the choruses representing Wife, Friend, and Priest positioned on ramps or platforms and hidden by curtains to be raised only when the characters' presence on stage is requested. They are not allowed to circulate on stage or to change position, and once their presence is no longer necessary, the curtain falls again in front of them. On the other hand, the chorus representing the Condemned can freely move on stage and must exit only once the hour of execution arrives. There is considerable irony hidden in the freedom of movement reserved for the Condemned: although he is the one to die, he is the only one who can de-termine his movements on stage. His freedom of movement, opposed to the inertness of the other characters, emphasizes the social and political message embodied in the opera. *The Condemned* is a manifest example of Blitzstein's so-ciopolitical involvement, but still, despite his effort to address working-class issues, Blitzstein proved unable to set aside the modernist tenets of musical neoclassicism and to find new and more popular sources for his music. This inability showed the limitations of his still inexperienced dramatic talent, and *The Condemned* went unperformed.[5]

The composer's interest in topical commentary, though, found a new outlet when he joined in the mid-1930s some groups of the Workers' Theater Move-ment and started to employ music for propaganda purposes. Blitzstein soon traversed the "underground" world of the workers' theater and attended par-ties and meetings organized by the Workers' Laboratory Theatre and its shock troupe (which included Earl Robinson and Charles Friedman).[6] These events became for Blitzstein a source of professional inspiration and a training ground for comprehension of the union movement in the United States, as he had not personally experienced the hardships of industrial labor.[7] These first steps with the leftist theater, culminating with the sketch "Send for the Militia" for Paul

Peters and George Sklar's *Parade*, helped the composer to define his artistic direction and provided an entrée to agit-prop theater, which reached fruition in the composition of *The Cradle Will Rock*.[8]

Indeed, many of the features we encounter in *Cradle* resonated with the tenets of the Workers' Theater Movement, with which Blitzstein was fully conversant. The use of dramatized songs to promote socialist ideology and display the needs of the working class had deep roots in the American labor movement, especially in the activities of the Industrial Workers of the World.[9] Minstrelsy, vaudeville, and revue had often underscored agit-prop skits of social and political drama in the productions of the New Playwrights Theatre.[10] During his apprenticeship with the workers' theater, Blitzstein learned through these examples. In the ten vignettes of *Cradle*, he described labor issues with vernacular language, popular songs, revolutionary slogans, and stereotyped characters portrayed in an almost cartoonish manner. But he needed more than the pseudo-amateurish experiments of the labor stage to create his new form. Blitzstein achieved it by integrating modernist and vernacular elements taken from patter, jazz, and musical revue to create a musical language that contemporary audiences and critics perceived as quintessentially American.

The Genesis of *The Cradle Will Rock*

Blitzstein conceived *Cradle* in a set of incidental circumstances. In 1935, he had written two songs for voice and piano that eventually would become part of the show: "People" and "Nickel Under the Foot." Both songs, with his own lyrics, display many of the typical traits of the mass songs of the Composers' Collective and militant pro-working-class content. "People" describes stark scenarios of starvation and mortality and portrays the same dark and gruesome character that we found in some sketches from Peters and Sklar's *Parade*:

> Poor people starve—for no good reason, just starve;
> Slow death, quick death, take it as it comes;
> From feeding out of garbage cans and rotting in the slums.
> [. . .]
> One big question inside me cries:
> How many bread-lines, how many flop-joints, hunger-marches,
> How many toiling ailing dying piled-up bodies,
> Brother, does it take to make you wise![11]

Writing specifically for American workers, Blitzstein set his bitter words to a musical idiom that now departed from his modernist style. "People" employs

148 · CHAPTER 5

syllabic text setting, martial tempo and repetitive rhythmic patterns, mostly homophonic texture, and dynamics that increase across the course of the work.[12] However, perhaps realizing that American workers were more familiar with Broadway songs than with European mass songs à la Eisler, Blitzstein communicated this doomsday depiction of poverty in a Tin Pan Alley idiom that had the potential to communicate directly with urban American audiences. As discussed in Chapter 1, other members of the Composers' Collective addressed this issue in a similar way, showing the commonplace use of American popular idiom. Elie Siegmeister, for instance, in his contribution to the "Special Symposium-meeting" on proletarian music on June 16, 1935, suggested that proletarian composers should write mass songs combining the best features of Broadway tunes and progressive music, to build both musically and politically class-conscious workers. The influence of this approach is clearly evident in Blitzstein's song, which subsequently underwent a series of textual and musical revisions and name changes, from "People" to "Poor People" to "Work People" and, eventually, as "Joe Worker," which came to symbolize the abused working class in *Cradle*.[13]

In Blitzstein's lyrics for "Nickel Under the Foot," a prostitute reflects on the harsh reality that one must disregard other people to fulfill one's own needs:

Maybe you wonder what it is,
Makes people good or bad;
Why some guy, an ace without a doubt,
Turns out to be a bastard,
And the other way about.
I'll tell you what I feel:
It's just the nickel under the heel.

Oh you can live like Hearts-and-Flowers,
And every day is a wonderland tour.
Oh, you can dream and scheme
And happily put and take, take and put.
But first be sure
The nickel's under your foot.

Go stand on someone's neck while you're takin;
Cut into somebody's throat as you put—
For every dream and scheme's
Depending on whether, all through the storm,
You've kept it warm.
That nickel under your foot.

And if you're sweet, then you'll grow rotten;
Your pretty heart covered over with soot.
And if for once you're gay,
And devil-may-careless, and oh, so hot
I know you've got
That nickel under your foot.[14]

The musical setting of these words, once again, is based on a mixture of modernist and popular sonorities and shows how Blitzstein was learning to write for a new working-class audience but without dismissing his artistic inclinations. He employed a strophic musical setting—an introduction followed by three 23-measure strophes only slightly modified to suit phrase lengths. The percussive accompaniment features chromatic harmonies saturated by non-triadic sonorities with instances of quartal harmony, while the vocal line, contained largely within an octave, lacks sentimentality and has some bluesy qualities, especially on the words "under the foot" at the conclusion of each strophe.[15] Ultimately, the song, by appearing in multiple scenes, acted as the thematic connecting thread of *Cradle*.

These two songs proved that Blitzstein was conceptualizing his own brand of musical theater in *Cradle*, a play he conceived after an encounter with Brecht in December 1935. At the time, the German writer had first visited the United States to oversee the Theatre Union production of his play *Mother*, based on a story by Maxim Gorky, which shows the gradual radicalization of a working-class mother whose son has been unjustly imprisoned (in Czarist Russia). Blitzstein's wife Eva Goldbeck, who spoke German fluently and had been in contact with Brecht about becoming the official English translator of his oeuvre, organized a meeting of the two artists.[16] Minna Lederman, co-founder and editor of *Modern Music*, joined the group at the Blitzstein's apartment in Greenwich Village. Having admired Brecht's *Lehrstücke* at the 1929 Baden-Baden festival, Lederman wanted to commission from the dramatist an article to clarify some of his radical concepts for American audiences.[17] After discussing the project, they adjourned for a purely social evening, during which Blitzstein played "Nickel Under the Foot" for Brecht, who encouraged him to write a longer musico-dramatic work on the different forms of prostitution contaminating society. Lederman related that a week later Marc told her: "I've taken up his idea and am making an opera of it."[18]

After his wife's death on May 26, 1936, Blitzstein penned the majority of *Cradle* at the Group Theatre Summer Camp in Trumbull, Connecticut. The play concerns workers' efforts to unionize and the capitalistic system's actions taken against them by Mr. Mister, who controls the town and all its activities. The actual story takes place in a night-court of the imaginary Steeltown, U.S.A., on

150 • CHAPTER 5

the night of a union drive. To oppose the workers, Mr. Mister had established a Liberty Committee formed by some "upright citizens" representing church, arts, medicine, and press. In an example of stylized agit-prop theater, the story of Steeltown unfolds before the audience in ten cartoon-like scenes filled with stereotyped characters. Flashbacks present the deeds of these "honorable" individuals and alternate with philosophical commentaries by a prostitute and a broken-down druggist. As religious institutions sacrifice principle for earnings and artists sell their art to the highest bidder, the workers are ultimately victorious over the prostitution of capitalistic society.[19]

The composer submitted the work for the fourth annual New Theatre League One-Act Play Contest in October 1936 and won first prize, thus catching the attention of Orson Welles and John Houseman of Project 891, one of the WPA's Federal Theater Project units. In March 1937, the duo decided to produce the play. Actors and singers started rehearsing soon after, and the orchestra, under the baton of Lehman Engel, first convened in the middle of April.

Voices:	19 singing actors in named roles; 32 chorus members	
	Voice type	**Role**
	Soprano	Sadie Polock
	Mezzo-soprano	Moll
	Mezzo-soprano	Mrs. Mister, Sister Mister
	Alto	Ella Hammer
	Tenor	Editor Daily, Jr. Mister
	Baritone	Gent
	Baritone	Dick, Gus Polock
	Baritone	Reverend Salvation, Larry Foreman
	Baritone	Yasha, Dauber, President Prexy, Professor Mamie, Professor Trixie
	Baritone	Harry Druggist, Mr. Mister
Instrumentation:	Flute/piccolo	
	Clarinet 1/bass clarinet	
	Clarinet 2/alto sax	
	Clarinet 3/tenor sax	
	2 trumpets	
	Trombone	
	Percussion (bass drum, snare drum, suspended cymbals, timpani, suspended cymbals, timpani, bells, triangle, siren, castanets, maracas, claves, tambourine, sand-blocks, slapstick)	
	Piano, accordion, guitar/banjo/Hawaiian guitar	
	14 strings	
	Optional bugles, fifes, side drums	

Figure 5.1. Personnel Requirements for Marc Blitzstein's *The Cradle Will Rock* (play in music in ten scenes for singing actors, chorus, and orchestra)

The original plan to open the show symbolically on May Day had to be abandoned, most likely because Welles and Engel were at the same time also rehearsing Copland's *The Second Hurricane* for the Henry Street Settlement.[20] For the new opening, scheduled on June 16, the Federal Theater Project issued a press release promoting *Cradle* as "a combination of opera, ballet, dance music, vaudeville, modern jazz, and silly symphony technique," and "Blitzstein's first full-length attempt at using musical phrases and forms that are distinctly American."[21] The dress rehearsal took place on June 15 at the Maxine Elliot Theater. The production credits in this performance—and, as things ended up, the only performance of *Cradle* in its original form for decades—included:

- John Houseman, producer;
- Orson Welles, director;
- Lehman Engel, conductor;
- Abe Feder, lighting;
- Jean Rosenthal, production assistant;
- Clarence Yates, choreography;
- Ed Shruers, sets and costumes.

The principal singing roles:

- Blanche Collins, Ella Hammer
- Olive Stanton, Moll
- Bert Weston, Editor Daily
- Howard da Silva, Larry Foreman
- Will Geer, Mr. Mister
- John Adair, Harry Druggist (Blitzstein played this role on opening night at the Venice Theatre)
- Peggy Coudray, Mrs. Mister
- Ed Hemmer, Reverend Salvation (Hiram Sherman played this role on opening night at the Venice Theatre and Charles Niemeyer in the Mercury Theatre production)

The circumstances of the play's premiere are legendary. An abrupt declaration by WPA officials that all productions under its aegis would be halted until July 1 effectively cancelled the scheduled premiere. Officials of the FTP never explained the circumstances that led to this freeze, even though the controversial work's anti-establishment and pro-union theme might have been the unstated cause.[22] On the evening of June 16, an audience unaware of the (ill-publicized) ban waited in front of the Maxine Elliot Theater. Around six hundred ticket holders had gathered outside the theater and were entertained

152 • CHAPTER 5

by Will Geer and Howard da Silva, while Welles, Houseman, and Blitzstein were working on securing a new theater.[23] Eventually, they found an alternate venue, and redirected performers and audience to the Venice Theatre, which held 1,770 seats, almost twice as many as the Maxine Elliot. For that reason, they also encouraged friends to join the show at the Venice Theatre, and they succeeded in this effort: the theater was "jammed to the rafters," as Blitzstein recalled, and many were standing.[24] The premiere of *Cradle* took place, despite the WPA ban; without scenery, costumes, or an orchestra, actors performed from seats in the audience (thereby satisfying the letter, if not the spirit, of the WPA injunction); Blitzstein himself played his score from an upright piano onstage.[25]

After nineteen performances in this format at the Venice Theatre, from June 19 to July 1, Welles, emphasizing the militant topic of the work, took it on tour in the steel districts of Pennsylvania and Ohio and replaced some of the original performers with unemployed actors not on the books of the WPA. At the end of the year, Houseman and Welles decided to give *Cradle* the chance at a longer run and the Mercury Theatre co-produced the show with Sam H. Grisman at the Windsor Theatre.[26] At this point, the show could have been fully staged, with orchestra accompaniment, yet Welles capitalized on the agit-prop new aesthetic of the show and opted for the no-scenery production. The singing actors, wearing street clothes, sat in parallel rows of chairs on the back part of the stage and moved to the forefront only when, accompanied by Blitzstein at the piano, they presented their sketches.[27] After previews in December 1937, the show officially opened on January 3 and lasted until April 1938 for 180 performances, a relatively short (in Broadway contexts) yet much discussed run.

The Reception of *Cradle*

Cradle, after the unplanned circumstances of its premiere and mostly during the Mercury Theatre run, triggered a shower of enthusiastic reviews, articles, and commentaries focusing on its non-realistic qualities and overstating the effect of the scenery-less production. Reviewers noted that the plot, character types, and themes were common to many other propagandistic plays of the time: a wicked capitalist and his entourage of corrupted lackeys exploit the working class and fight against unionization and a noble labor leader. At the same time, many of the same reviewers commended Blitzstein's innovative way of communicating a familiar narrative and started making connections between *Cradle* and the theater of the left. As eminent a critic as Brooks Atkinson of the *New York Times* wrote:

After drifting from pillar to post since last July, Marc Blitzstein's "The Cradle Will Rock" had an official opening at the Mercury last evening. Written with extraordinary versatility and played with enormous gusto, it is the best thing militant labor has put into a theatre yet. Although Mr. Blitzstein's story of big industry corruption and labor union gallantry is an old one in the working-class theatre, he has transmuted it into a remarkably stirring marching song by the bitterness of his satire, the savagery of his music and the ingenuity of his craftsmanship. At last the comrades of the insurgent theatre can feel sure that they have a fully awakened artist on their side. What "Waiting for Lefty" was to the dramatic stage, "The Cradle Will Rock" is to the stage of the labor battle song. [. . .]

Most of it is caustically satiric in rhyme and score. He can write anything from tribal chant to Tin Pan Alley balladry; the piano keys scatter scorn, impishness and pathos according to the capricious mood of his story. And when Mr. Blitzstein settles down to serious business at the conclusion, his music box roars with rage and his actors frighten the aged roof of the miniature Mercury Theatre.[28]

John Mason Brown's critique in the *New York Post* seconded Atkinson's favorable response:

Yet, familiar as Mr. Blitzstein's ingredients may be, they acquire a new and irresistible force as he states them—in prose, rhyme, and music. . . . Mr. Blitzstein's writing is often crude and uneven. He mixes realism and stylization, tragedy and farce, burlesque and passionate propaganda at will—but to good effect. His shopworn theme gains by its originality of treatment, by the bitter savagery of its laughter, by the glib ferocity of its rhyming, by the strength of its author's convictions, and by the constant illumination of Mr. Blitzstein's interesting and ever-helpful music.[29]

On December 6, Richard Watts, theater critic of the *Herald Tribune*, commented that the play "combines a modernistic musical score with the most sardonic methods of the political cartoonist."[30] Two weeks later, he again praised *Cradle* and its creator:

The humor of "The Cradle Will Rock" is scornful and bitter and ironic. It snarls as well as sings at its entrenched enemies. . . . Marc Blitzstein is a man of ideas and talent, who can provide a score that is bitter and sardonic, defiant and even a bit tender, capturing the mood of American industrial strife in terms of modern rhythms. Above all things, "The Cradle Will Rock" has about it the great quality of excitement. . . . I trust that saboteurs from Hollywood will not soon lure the Messrs. Blitzstein and Rome away from the theater. Now that it can mix humor, tunefulness and gaiety with its partisanship, the Left Wing becomes a force to be reckoned with in the drama.[31]

154 • CHAPTER 5

To no one's surprise, Eric Englander, a reviewer for the left-wing press, emphasized the sociopolitical message, but he also applauded the story for its wit, and the exhilarating and stabbing music for its "extraordinary combination of the quickly singable and the hauntingly difficult."[32]

When critics and reviewers were not making connections with the labor theater, they often found ways to assess *Cradle* against the works of Kurt Weill. As Minna Lederman noted, the unplanned "skinned-down manner" of the first production of *Cradle* "had the immediate air of a Weill-Brecht *Singspiel*" and triggered more associations with Weill's music than Blitzstein might have wanted.[33] Mary McCarthy, for instance, argued in the *Partisan Review* that although the setting and subject matter of *Cradle* are American, "it is essentially a non-indigenous plant" as "musically, it is very much indebted to the German Kurt Weill."[34] Yet *Cradle* was also hailed as the quintessential new American musical form, and some critics set a clear boundary between the two composers' approaches. For instance, John Gassner in the *One Act Play Magazine* compared Blitzstein's play and Weill's *Johnny Johnson*, which had been presented by the Group Theatre in November 1936 and closed after sixty-eight performances, and emphasized a freshness and dramatic continuity in *Cradle* that was absent in Weill's work:

> The climaxes constitute a warning and a challenge. . . . For nearly a year it has been customary to announce the death of the left-wing theatre movement. The Cradle Will Rock proves that it still retains its vitality and unique attractiveness when there is genius in the effort. Genius is perhaps little more than the power of illumination. Nothing that Blitzstein says is original or novel. . . . It is his manner that gives his matter freshness, vigor and beauty. His perfect amalgamation of drama and music has a curiously dynamic effect. In last season's *Johnny Johnson* many of the solo numbers seemed superimposed upon the dramatic incidents. In The Cradle Will Rock the music grows out of the intensity of the scene and is at one with it.[35]

Gassner's commentary still reverberates almost two years later, as Philip Barr dismissed Weill's influence and called Blitzstein's play "people's art":

> Critics have pointed out similarities with Kurt Weill. These things are irrelevant beside the fact of Blitzstein's essential originality—the form, the continuity or whatever is the secret of his unique dramatic power. A few measures from "Frankie and Johnny" inserted in the Nickel sound so different in the new surroundings as to become his own by inalienable right.
>
> It expresses the people, it can be enjoyed by the people and it can also pass before a more severe critical tribunal. . . . It is like seeing the life of our times

A Leftist Myth • 155

laid out on a line; after you have been to it often enough, everything around you seems oddly to be moving to the sound of music. It has made me less nostalgic for other places, other times; all that seemed most contemptuously raw and unattractive in the modern American scene suddenly has become incandescent.

The popular music idiom becomes a new language: poetic, full of harmonic audacities, with the most diverse ingredients in close conjunction—something as remote from the average jitterbug's experience as it is from the average music critic's—yet still unmistakable American vernacular music.

It was as if you and they [the characters on stage] were together, taking part in some ceremony. This communal feeling, as of a friendly atmosphere, grew. . . . We feel intimate with them, too; they speak our language. This feeling is heightened by Blitzstein's use of untrained voices, the rapid alternation of speech and singing, the queer bits of music going on under the spoken dialogue (it is more like "music conversation" than anything I have ever heard).[36]

Amid this sampling of at times contrasting but mainly enthusiastic responses, George Jean Nathan's review for *Scribner's Magazine* presented a very different and blistering analysis of "Blitzstein's opera in déshabillé" and challenged the novelty and artistic value of the work. Nathan perceived the largely positive reviews from his colleagues as an irrational critical response:

Emphasis was laid by the reviewers on its "excitement." Defects, they here and there freely allowed, it had. But, they proclaimed, what matter when, first and foremost, it instilled in its audience so great a degree of this excitement? Now, no one likes excitement in the theater more than the man hired to conduct this critical department. But it still seems to him that there are different kinds of dramatic excitement and that the species engendered by Mr. Blitzstein is hardly to be distinguished, either critically or artistically, from a theater cry of "Fire!"

That the exhibit, with its minstrel-show technique adapted to pseudo-opera, is novel, we may agree. But novelty purely as novelty is exciting only to bub criticism. That its defiant shout of labor propaganda from a stage apron slam-bang against an audience's ears is aurally jouncing, we may also agree. But excessive noise, whatever its quotient of meaning, is exciting only to admirers of melodrama, jazz, Negro revival meetings, aviation movies, and the novels of Zane Grey. That it dismisses all the conventional accoutrements of the musical-show stage, that it abandons scenery and costumes, and that it confines itself to a single piano played by its composer, we may further agree. But so did the celebrated *London Follies*, which, when shown at Weber's theater some years ago, got such a blast of ridicule from both press and public that it was overnight driven in humiliation back to England. Surely, these things could not account in the reviewers' minds for its exciting quality. That its lyrics are in one or two instances amusing, we may still

156 · CHAPTER 5

further agree. But Lorenz Hart's and Ira Gershwin's lyrics are generally amusing in four or five instances, and I have yet to hear them called exciting.[37]

In retrospect, Nathan's harsh assessment of the play demonstrates how the critical reception played a crucial role in the elaborate and ongoing redefinition of the significance of *Cradle*.

Blitzstein, while enjoying success and fame after the Mercury Theatre's production of *Cradle*, also felt the need to set a limit to the critics' associations with non-realistic theater and Weill and to justify his musico-dramatic choices and use of vernacular idioms as his unique attempt to address the American audience in a language it would recognize. In the *New York Times* on January 2, 1938, just a few weeks after the opening at the Mercury Theatre, Blitzstein argued that his artistic approach was primarily a consequence of his own critique of the contemporary state of American musical theater and his continuous search for a new theatrical form.[38] Stressing that musical comedy and revue in the 1930s were in an "alarming" decline, he associated the decay with the incapability of composers and writers to match the needs of a changing society. He claimed that he wanted to write a "colloquial piece" to fit the topic and the presence on stage of a much-diversified group of American citizens, from steel workers to middleclass shopkeepers, from streetwalkers to professionals and steel magnates. In the end, he argued, "[I]f you still have the desire to write for the musical theatre you must find a new form, one which will work in a new way and yet manage to offend nobody by its newness."[39] The form he had in mind, though, had very little to do with epic theater, the unplanned stripped-down premiere, or the scenery-less Mercury production. The question then is why has *Cradle*, with very few exceptions, appeared on professional, amateur, and labor stages only in its *déshabillé* form with piano accompaniment? Undeniably, the critical reception of the play invites a closer look at several issues that had provoked these conflicting opinions and calls for a more in-depth analysis of the circumstances surrounding the critical response.

Theatre Workshop and the Debate on "Scenery or No Scenery"

After the attention that reviewers gave to the scenery-less production of *Cradle*, a handful of theater practitioners, predominantly active on the stages of the Federal Theater Project (FTP) and the Workers' Theater Movement (WTM), began to misinterpret, even willfully manipulate, the radical but unplanned "un-staging" of the first productions of the show. On the night of the Mercury premiere, writer and dramatist Archibald MacLeish overstated the effect of the scenery-less production: he told the audience that they had just shared in the creation of a historic event, namely the elimination of the barrier between audience and performers.[40] He subsequently clarified his view in the foreword to the published script in a comparison of the *Cradle* to Brecht's *Mother* and Elliot's *Murder in the Cathedral*, two plays that, in fact, have little in common with Blitzstein's:

> Brecht and Eliot, however, are merely the most eminent of the assassins of the audience. They are not the most recent. Nor are they the most successful. The most successful must be put down as Marc Blitzstein. Mr. Blitzstein's operetta, *The Cradle Will Rock*, is direct enough, candid enough, and sharp enough to reduce any audience ever collected to its human components. Under Orson Welles' direction and John Houseman's production at the Mercury the present edition of the play is so arguably a piece *of* theatre *for* theatre that the theatrical illusion—the illusion, that is, that what occurs upon the stage is "real"—never has a chance to establish itself. The actors are at all times actors: when they are not down stage acting they are at the back of the stage on their chairs. The play is at all times a play. And the effect upon the observer is the human and humanly becoming effect of the work of art upon the man who faces it.[41]

The connections between *Cradle* and epic and agit-prop theater became a cornerstone also for Hallie Flanagan, the director of the FTP. In 1935, she had encouraged playwrights, designers, and directors to abandon realistic scenery and costumes and rethink how professional theater could reach as many potential theatergoers nationwide as possible. In a letter to the personnel of the FTP, in order to support her advocacy of scenery-less staging, she relied on the success of the Mercury Theatre's *Cradle* and *Julius Caesar*, both produced sans scenery and costumes.[42] Ironically, Flanagan was pleading her case for the development of a non-illusionary stage technique by hailing the non-realistic qualities of *Cradle*, a play that, as director of the FTP, she knew Blitzstein never conceived that way and whose premiere with scenery her organization had blocked. Still, Flanagan and the radical left's theatrical movement took advantage of the success of the accidental staging of Blitzstein's play to support their goals. Deeming the development of innovative theatrical forms to address a new middle- and working-class audience a necessity, they investigated the cause of the increasing number of non-illusionary productions by cross-examining the example of *Cradle*.

The discussion reached its peak in 1938, when the New Theatre League launched an investigation to determine whether the new trend might supersede the late-nineteenth-century development of naturalistic theater and thus herald "the passing of an era in perhaps both playwriting and production forms."[43] The editors of *Theatre Workshop*, the New Theatre League's quarterly journal,

158 · CHAPTER 5

invited a select group of "progressive theater workers" involved with the FTP, the WTM, and the Group Theatre—including Blitzstein—to comment on the previously mentioned letter that Flanagan had addressed to personnel of the Federal Theater in hopes of promoting non-illusionary staging techniques.[44] Participants were asked to respond to the following questions:

1. Do you agree with Mrs. Flanagan's main contention that there is a necessity for the elimination of 19th century realistic scenery in contemporary theatre?
2. Do you believe that the development toward a non-illusory stage technique as exemplified in *Cradle Will Rock* and *Our Town* is to be encouraged?
3. Do you believe that the non-realistic stage technique is the most desirable form of expression for a peoples or labor theatre, which is necessarily limited in production funds and in staging and acting talent and which is trying to win new audiences for a new type of drama?[45]

An analysis of the contributions to this debate, published in the April—June 1938 issue of *Theatre Workshop*, will shed some light on the origins of *Cradle*'s revisionist reading.

Most of the debate focused on the preservation of realism in American theater and on the (mistaken) equation of the non-illusionary approach with cheap and/or unprofessional staging; some respondents seemed reluctant to accept, or even consider, the potential artistic benefits of this approach. Essentially, they did not agree with the epic theater premises that in non-illusionary theater—which has a long history on Western and Eastern stages—non-realistic elements functioned as visual devices not conforming to perceptible reality and capable of producing emotional alienation from the action onstage, thus encouraging the audience to approach objectively the issues presented. However, all participants, in considering the new trend one of the many available possibilities, did concur with Charles DeSheim:

> The development of a non-illusory stage technique is certainly desirable so long as it serves the play adequately. . . . Scenic realism as a formula has no more creative validity than any other single scenic technique which may be set up as universal. The play, its interpretation, the values to which the audience has been conditioned, and the prevailing production circumstances should certainly speak louder than the tradition.[46]

Many feared that American theater was becoming too frugal. Howard Bay, for instance, maintained that the lower artistic quality of many of the productions of the 1930s vulgarized the theater as an art form.[47] He condemned the separation

A Leftist Myth • 159

of scenic design from the "deeper reality of the given production" as the consequence of a selling-out of artistic breadth to a narrower popular demand.[48] Bay blamed this new trend in American theater on the Federal Theater Project:

> A preoccupation with the ways and means of scenic technique should follow rather than precede a wholesale overhauling of the contemporary American Theatre. The Federal Theatre, by its definition of Peoples Theatre, has dragged to the light of day the urgent necessity of junking our dramatic and pictorial stencils and going more than half way to meet this great American public who are, at the present writing, irritatingly unconcerned about the fate of the theatre.

Theater critic John W. Gassner stressed the same naiveté in the activities of the Federal Theater Project and disagreed with Flanagan's enthusiasm for scenery-less productions:

> The finest plays of the past sixty years have been, with few exceptions, realistic in structure and quality, and have required realistic treatment. . . . I should like to see whether the techniques of *The Cradle Will Rock* and *Our Town* can bear even a fraction of the repetition to which the realistic theatre has been subjected. I doubt it. The production of *Our Town* is excellent for this particular play, but it would look like a stunt, and a pretty threadbare one, if it were repeated indiscriminately—which I am sure neither Mrs. Flanagan nor any other intelligent theatre worker would actually countenance.[49]

While he appreciated some aspects of non-realistic treatment, above all its capacity to stimulate imagination and extend the boundaries of the theater, Gassner argued that American audiences valued realism. Even labor audiences, he claimed, had shown more admiration for such realistic plays of the Theatre Union as *Stevedore* and *Let Freedom Ring* than for the intellectualism of Brecht's agit-prop *Mother*, or the "bourgeois-biting *rive gauche* tendencies" of *The Cradle Will Rock*, which "have barely touched the common man."[50]

Stage director Mordecai Gorelik, in defense of his own profession, maintained that the relative success of no-scenery productions relied on their novelty, which intrigued the audiences, but that in the long run "the public demand for richer (by which I also mean more significant) settings of the non-illusory type will grow rapidly, demanding the best effort of scenic artists."[51] Arguing that a non-realistic set could be as heavy, expensive, and complex as a realistic one, he stressed that the elimination of scenic elements does not liberate the actor; rather "the proper use of relevant and functional scenery . . . gives dramatic life to the actor's function in space." To keep audiences interested, Gorelik encouraged companies to better familiarize themselves with the nature and theories

160 · CHAPTER 5

of non-illusionary theater—an admonition that emphasizes how poorly his colleagues on the American radical left understood this staging technique. Lee Strasberg, the leading exponent of Stanislavskian acting in New York, contributed to the debate, too.[52] He noted that in the second half of the 1930s non-realistic productions helped theater workers to trust their imaginations and encouraged playwrights in their search for a modern dramatic form.[53] But he emphasized the experimental nature of scenery-less productions and maintained that they are but a starting point for young playwrights and for writers in search of a form beyond the realistic, a new form in which to present their new content.

Indeed, the search for a new form associated with scenery-less productions became the goal of a generation of young American directors and playwrights of the leftist theater, but not necessarily Blitzstein, whose contribution to the debate addressed specifically this issue. His opening remark in the debate must have chilled the enthusiasm of the proponents of "no-scenery" staging, as his peremptory statement undermined the argument set forth by Flanagan:

> Modern drama, by and large, is written for realistic presentations, and we must admit that it will require almost a new era in playwright [sic] to alter this and lead the theatre beyond the limitations of stage realism.[54]

In calling for a less dogmatic approach to theater, he argued that the play itself must dictate the balanced use of scenery, lights, and music, and the director's interpretation of the play ought to shape the nature of the acting and staging. Blitzstein mentioned Brecht in an attempt to draw a distinction between American agit-prop political theater and the intellectualized aspirations of the non-illusionary theater in Brecht's hands. While he recognized that the German playwright-director had contributed to the contemporary development of non-realistic theater, he cautioned that his drama "has all the earmarks of becoming *artsy*" and undesirable, as "it is inviting danger when the labor audience is allowed to feel that its artists are presenting lessons rather than entertainment."[55] The barely veiled reference to the uproars caused three years before by the Theatre Union's production of Brecht's *Mother* shows that Blitzstein deemed this direction unsuitable for American theater: it would be "extremely snobbish . . . to veer deliberately to a diet of 'scenery-less' plays." The proverbial "final straw"—his comments on the fortuitous circumstances that led to the "no-scenery" production of *The Cradle Will Rock*—revealed Blitzstein's thoughts about scenery-less theater and his belief in the necessity of the musical component to salvage such scanty productions:

A Leftist Myth · 161

It is well known that my play, *The Cradle Will Rock*, came by its recent form of production entirely as a result of certain exigencies. Dropped by its government sponsors shortly before curtain-time opening night, the audience and the show's company repaired quickly to another theater where, with the aid of only a piano and a worklight, we gave the public a reading of our production-denied opera. At that time, more than half of our cast, not being members of Actors Equity, was required to perform from various points of advantage in the house off the stage. As we soon learned, however, the enthusiasms and imagination that our audience brought to this hasty adaptation of our meager resources combined to enrich the results of our efforts beyond expectation, and the show as such survived to become a success.

Most people overlooked the fact that in its original Federal Theatre production, *The Cradle Will Rock* had been greatly enhanced by set-constructions, lighting designs, and orchestrations. In the form by which it finally became known, the show hardly represented a full-blown or a true theatre production. It was really only a heightened reading and, as such, had no intended relation to the theories of Brecht or anyone else. On the basis of our success with this type of presentation, I believe it might be recommended for trial by labor theatres and all groups with limited funds as a practical, worth-while medium for their use. Needless to say, the employment of music has proved to be an essential and invaluable asset in this type of approach to the audience.[56]

As Blitzstein's comments highlighted, the invited experts mounted their arguments for or against non-illusionary theater in relation to the needs, aspirations, and limitations of contemporary American society, rather than authorial intention.

In the published transcripts, the editors recognized that their questions might have influenced the answers, as they "tended to stress the problem of scenery as separate from that of both the play and production conceived by the director."[57] The editors, though, failed to acknowledge that they, as well as Flanagan, had overstated the interest in non-staged productions and misinterpreted some playwrights' choices regarding non-illusionary techniques. It is true that Thornton Wilder had explicitly opted for a non-illusionary production of *Our Town* by maintaining "our claim, our hope, our despair are in the mind—not in things, not in scenery."[58] Yet Blitzstein clearly stated in his response that he did not conceive *Cradle* as a scenery-less play and considered nothing but an unfortunate accident what they deemed as the most influential feature of his play.

The "Scenery or No Scenery" Symposium situates the reception of Blitzstein's *Cradle* in a new context, and the debate on scenery-less productions, as

162 · CHAPTER 5

inconclusive as it appears, reveals a theater of the left engaged in the search for a "form" that a new post-Depression middle- and working-class American audience would recognize as its own and with which it could identify. Many leftist playwrights and directors believed that the answer rested in the improvement of the workers' agit-prop theater of the late 1920s with a more artistic use of non-illusionary techniques and American vernacular idioms: a formula that the unplanned events of the *Cradle*'s premiere offered on a silver platter. Even if Blitzstein protested that the elaborate staging of the Federal Theater's original production would have enhanced the play, *Cradle*'s new identity provided the basis of a myth for the left theater. In *Mythologies*, Barthes argued that a myth, which is an act of signification, is the result of a deformation of the original connection between signifier and signified. Eventually, this new meaning becomes naturalized and takes over reality. A myth, then, is defined more by intention than its actual intrinsic value, as its function is to allow its creators to present their own ideas and interests as a universal truth, even if this truth is foreign to the original signifier.[59] The theater of the left, by mythologizing the unplanned premiere of *Cradle*, went against Blitzstein's intents and changed the scope of his work. Insistence on highlighting its non-scenery and non-illusionary features eventually diverted attention from Blitzstein's artistic achievement—the successful combination of experimentation and populist approach—and created a myth of those theatrical aspects that were the result of a fortuitous circumstance and indeed absent from the original work.

The performance history of *Cradle* supports this claim. For almost a quarter of a century after the Mercury Theatre production, *Cradle* appeared on amateur, student, and labor stages (mostly for just a handful of performances in each instance) only in its *déshabillé* form with piano accompaniment.[60] Not until 1947 did a young Leonard Bernstein direct a concert version with reduced orchestra and trained singers at the New York City Center honoring the twenty-fifth anniversary of the League of Composers.[61] Eventually, in 1960, and only for four performances from February 11 to 17, the New York City Opera produced the show as originally conceived, with Lehman Engel as conductor, Howard Da Silva as director, and David Hays as sets designer. By then, the show had lost its political bite, and finally it could have elicited criticism regarding its artistic merits. Blitzstein himself implicitly maintained that, stripped of its agit-prop context, the piece may not be viable:

> The production given now in 1960 by the New York City Opera is full-scale; this is the way I wrote the piece, how I meant it to be staged. By now, of course, the theme and the treatment—the rise of unionism in America, seen from a brash,

exuberant, idealistic viewpoint—make the work something of a period piece. But I still feel as I did about the subject; and I have nothing to apologize for in the music. Let it take its chances, say I; let it prove whether it remains an engrossing and entertaining musical stage piece.[62]

Paul Henry Lang of the *Herald Tribune* did not think it did: "the issues are gone, and what we see is a sort of vaudeville, at times of a very low grade."[63] But Olin Downes had a different view of the variety qualities of the show:

Electrifying performance. [W]ith masterly stagecraft, with astonishing gifted singing actors . . . [i]t catches fire, it blazes, it amuses, moves and grips the listener until with the really masterly, if unconventional structure of the finale— screaming trumpets in the orchestra, the drum beats, the sounds of fifes and voices chorusing from far and near—the listener wants to beat his palms and shout as the curtain falls. . . . The house was packed and the audience went wild. . . . "The Cradle Will Rock," so presented, has qualities of genius.[64]

Once again, though, *Cradle* seemed to have been insulated against major criticism, as most reviewers, instead of analyzing the play from a musical point of view, tended to focus on the past, on the circumstances of the infamous Venice Theatre premiere, and on its sociopolitical message. Would a negative critique of *Cradle* have been perceived as un-American? An implicit endorsement of government censorship? This assessment becomes plausible if we consider that the sporadic piano version revivals of the production paid homage to the show as part of American history, not as a piece of theater for theater's sake. In the end, *Cradle* never acquired the dramatic significance Blitzstein had hoped for, as the myth that the leftist theater created around the circumstances of its premiere became not only its legacy but also a part of its content.

If we revisit *Cradle* as the piece of musical theater that Blitzstein originally conceived, and not as a piece of American history, we may be surprised. Cues to this "alternate" reality of *Cradle* are already present in some commentaries published after the composer's death in 1964, which focus primarily on Blitzstein's ingenuity and the American qualities of the show. For instance, Minna Lederman claimed:

A less superficial approach to the work will discover its compelling inspiration in Brecht's poetry of rebellion. For it was the force of Brecht's impact upon Marc's youthful *Weltanschauung* which effected the synthesis of his disparate resources—his awareness of the American scene, his feeling for popular speech and music idioms, his militant social consciousness and his skill as a serious composer.[65]

164 · CHAPTER 5

Similarly, Aaron Copland stated in his obituary of Blitzstein:

> He could be sarcastic, parodistic, and at times even derisive; but he could also be gentle, tender, and tragic. Most important of all, he was the first American composer to invent a vernacular musical idiom that sounded convincing when heard from the lips of the man-in-the-street. The taxi driver, the pan-handler, the corner druggist were given voice for the first time in the context of serious musical drama. This is no small accomplishment, for without it no truly indigenous opera is conceivable.[66]

And again, Lehman Engel, in his book *The American Musical Theater*, stated:

> The words and lyrics are as monosyllabic as possible, and the songs are, at least outwardly, as plain as folk music. From the inside, however, the music has a subtle complexity, and every melody—it abounds in melody—is full of surprises. The simplicity seems to be indicating where the music is going and what is going to happen—but not quite. It announces its intention to be banal, but this avowal is only flirtatious—the girl who leads you to her bedroom and, without warning, closes the door in your face.[67]

Engel, who was the conductor of the cancelled original Federal Theater production and thereafter conducted the first staged version with the original orchestration in 1960, was evidently familiar more than anybody else with the orchestral version of *Cradle*. Perhaps the "subtle complexity" of the music he refers to can be found in Blitzstein's orchestral score more than in the piano version. An analysis of these subtleties as they appear in the orchestration, thus, could challenge the often-accepted view of *Cradle* as an outdated piece of theater and offer valid reasons to reconsider the topicality of the script and Blitzstein's musical creativity.

The events narrated in *Cradle* certainly did not seem obsolete to the audience of the 2017 Opera Saratoga Summer Festival who witnessed the production of the first complete performance of the work, that is, staged and with full orchestral accompaniment, after that of the New York City Opera in 1960.[68] Almost as an answer to Blitzstein's comment, "let it prove whether it remains an engrossing and entertaining musical stage piece," this revival uncovered a work filled with brilliant theatrical ideas and musical solutions and, ultimately, a very entertaining musical stage piece. The play has not lost its political bite, as the rather exuberant and idealistic treatment of themes such as unionism, corruption, working-class struggle, and anti-immigrant sentiments finds many parallels in current events in American political life. The ironic and parodic portrayal of the capitalist and chauvinistic behavior of Mr. Mister and his Liberty Committee cannot help but remind us of the many *Saturday Night Live* sketches of political satire, which entertain millions of American viewers. Musically, Blitzstein filtered dramatic situations of *Cradle*, sometimes seriously and sometimes jokingly, through the most appropriate and available American musical match for the characters on stage. He treated the members of Mr. Mister's Liberty Committee like vaudeville characters, portraying them with ironic and funny, almost corny musical numbers, including satirical quotations of Bach and Beethoven. It is indeed in the orchestration and in the rhythmic and melodic choices of these numbers that we can appreciate the complex subtleties and the energetic power of the music of *Cradle*.

In productions without orchestra, the singers are often competing with the piano to bring out Blitzstein's musical nuances. However, the composer's instrumental palette—including flute, two clarinets, alto and tenor saxophones, two trumpets, trombone, piano, accordion, various strummed instruments including banjo, guitar, and Hawaiian lap steel guitar, a large percussion section, and strings—provides a rich and imaginative instrumental accompaniment that allows the singers to project in a more effective way the sometimes ironic, parodic, or empathetic intertextual commentary. Howard Pollack recognized, for instance, that as the two saxophonists at times double on clarinet, Blitzstein's score "occasionally features a clarinet trio, which helps provide some of the music for the Polocks and Ella Hammer with a special pathos."[69] The same attention to detail is present throughout the whole score. Indeed, the quite unique instrumentation combined with effective rhythmic and melodic gestures stands as evidence that Blitzstein intended to take advantage of the sonic qualities of each instrument to add layers of meaning and interpretations.

For instance, let us consider some excerpts from Scene 3, "Mission," the hilarious number in which Mrs. Mr. convinces Reverend Salvation to justify the war, or not, according to steel market demands. In his orchestral score, Blitzstein highlights the paradox in the behavior of this sold-out priest as well as the capitalist plots of Mrs. Mr. on the brilliant and at times mocking timbre of the woodwinds. As seen in figure 5.2, the ironic use of syncopated rhythms in clarinets and saxophones offers an ambiguous and wobbly counterpart to Mrs. Mr. stating "I rely on you to implore that we stay out of the war." The excerpt ends with a twisted dotted gesture in the solo flute followed by the same contorted pattern in the clarinet but in a lower range and ritardando, almost to accentuate Reverend Salvation's thoughts as he plans how to please her. This comedic passage leads to the first chorale section when the priest adheres to the request and sings "Thou shalt not kill" before intoning a chorale. Of course, a good pianist could bring out these musical moments, but not the timbre of the wind instruments, which is part of what Engel called subtle melodic complexities.

166 · CHAPTER 5

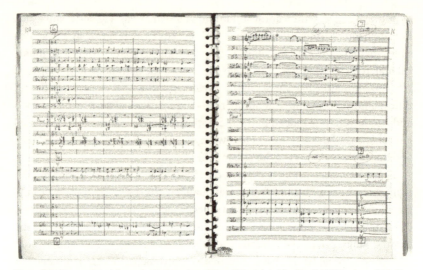

Figure 5.2. Manuscript of the orchestral version of Marc Blitzstein's *The Cradle Will Rock*, pp. 108–9. Copyright by and reproduced with permission from the Blitzstein Music Company

In the following chorale, see figure 5.3, the somber sonorities of double bass and trombone solemnly accompany Reverend Salvation's chanting doubled by the accordion. The typical voice of the accordion, though, adds a different layer of meaning to the priest's words, as its cabaret-like sound seems to finely lampoon the situation. The possibility of this ironic twist is soon mitigated by the harmonized chorale melody in the strings, which highlights how the priest is trying to build a façade of respectability after all.

As the number unfolds, and Mrs. Mr. turns from against war to supportive of it because of capitalist reasons, the orchestration gets thicker and more intriguing as, for instance, in the second chorale iteration where there is a substantial change in texture, see figure 5.4. Blitzstein now gives the chorale melody to accordion and bass clarinet, with low strings playing a modified version; the priest, doubled by the trombone, sings a much more nervous, almost patter-like vocal line. At the same time, the solo flute, doubled on piccolo, performs an over-the-top ornamented variation of the tune. With the much more, using Engel's words, "subtle complexity" in the orchestration at this moment of the scene, Blitzstein portrayed the acrobatics of the priest to please Mrs. Mr. and highlighted his discomfort in having to say yes to whatever she asks him to do.

Another section in *Cradle* that acquires new life in the orchestral version is "Joe Worker," the song in which Ella Hammer is seeking justice for the death of her brother. The martial tempo, recurrent dynamic bursts to *forte*, and repetitive

Figure 5.3. Manuscript of the orchestral version of Marc Blitzstein's *The Cradle Will Rock*, pp. 111–13. Copyright by and reproduced with permission from the Blitzstein Music Company

rhythmic patterns combined with the syllabic text setting could turn the song into a rather monotonous piece, especially when accompanied only by a piano. But when these features are highlighted in the orchestration, they acquire a quite different effect, as they help Ella draw attention to her story. In figure 5.5, for instance, she sings the words "Low class, low down, the thing you never care to see until there is a show-down" on a dramatic crescendo, which ends with a *fortissimo* on the words "here it is." There is no doubt that the singer can achieve

168 · CHAPTER 5

Figure 5.4. Manuscript of the orchestral version of Marc Blitzstein's *The Cradle Will Rock*, pp. 128–29. Copyright by and reproduced with permission from the Blitzstein Music Company

a different level of emotional depth with the strings harmonizing her melody. The song also becomes more powerful when the clarinets enter in the crescendo section and intensify the meaning of the words, thus dramatizing even more the end of the musical phrase. These timbral subtleties of the orchestration and their emotional impact are lost in the piano version, which offers a very limited depiction of Blitzstein's gifted musicianship.

It is undoubtedly true that *Cradle* became the poster play representing the sociopolitical climate of the time. This is, indeed, a significance that some segments of society continue to recognize and value, as the show's sporadic revivals continue to pay homage to it more as part of American history than as a viable theatrical piece. This legacy still endures in American collective consciousness, as in 1999 a much-acclaimed film written and directed by Tim Robbins presented a fictionalized account of the unplanned premiere of *Cradle*. The movie received many nominations, including one for the *Palme d'Or* at the 1999 Cannes Film Festival, for best director at the 2001 London Critics Circle Film Awards, and for best supporting actor and actress at the 2000 Chlotudris Awards. Ironically, the movie suffered the fate of the show itself, as it did not score a box office success (the Internet Movie Database reports that on opening weekend the film made $93,998 and a gross revenue of only $2,899,970). Yet it received prestigious accolades and became something of a cult movie, thus confirming that the myth of *Cradle* is still alive.[70]

Figure 5.5. Manuscript of the orchestral version of Marc Blitzstein's *The Cradle Will Rock*, pp. 141–42. Copyright by and reproduced with permission from the Blitzstein Music Company

If we scratch this surface and search for the artistic value of the play, though, we will agree that Paul Henry Lang missed the essence of *Cradle* when he wrote that it "is a sort of vaudeville, at times of a very low grade." Lang failed to recognize that by integrating multiple styles and genres within a single piece and exploiting the usefulness of the song as an effective dramatic tool, Blitzstein established his own musical creativity. Indeed, the composer went even beyond this goal—by successfully combining experimental theater with modernist and vernacular musical idioms, the play came to embody the aspirations of a generation of leftist artists and intellectuals who during the Great Depression believed in the socially relevant role of art. One hopes, though, that more theaters will start producing *Cradle* in its original staged orchestral version and bring to life its dramatic and musical weight, too. The work itself, as well as Blitzstein's legacy, should be divested of the myth created around the circumstances of its premiere and be appreciated as one of the highest artistic accomplishments of the American Workers' Theater.

Epilogue

> The Renaissance lasted three centuries, the Age of Pericles and the Augustan Age each a half century; for the "cultural birth of a nation" the government allows less than two years.
>
> —Elizabeth McCausland, "Save the Arts Projects," *The Nation* (July 17, 1937): 67.

The political and economic circumstances in which many artists operated in the 1930s opened possibilities to experiment with new forms and contents. They also helped shape a new relationship with the audience, one that would be fundamental for the future of American art even after the federal government, by the end of the decade, withdrew its financial support. As the United States was slowly emerging from the Depression and all the main economic indicators had regained the levels of the late 1920s, Congress proceeded to cut the appropriations for the WPA by 25 percent even though unemployment remained high. The curtailment especially affected Federal One, as congressmen doubted that so much money should be given to the arts. Elizabeth McCausland addressed these drastic cuts in *The Nation* and warned that "[t]he arts in America are on their way back where they came from, to the status which made necessary the WPA and white-collar projects" and that cuts in the job-relief program could potentially bring the unemployment rates in the arts back to those at the beginning of the Depression.[1]

The article, though, draws attention also to another major issue associated with the curtailment—one that, more than on job losses, focused on the end of the socialist dream of a federally supported art, one that could have enriched the lives of Americans. After all, in less than two years Federal One had brought to American audiences thousands of cultural activities. The Federal Theater had played to more than 25 million people (85 percent free and 13 percent paid

Epilogue • 171

admissions), and 60 million people had listened to more than 81,000 perfor-mances of the Federal Music units. But, as McCausland noted, the Roosevelt administration, under pressure from Congress, had to prioritize recovery and economy over the spiritual and cultural enrichment of the nation. Howard Han-son, who contributed to the Federal Music Project not only as a composer and conductor but also in an advisory capacity, explained the situation with detached objectivity some thirty years after the fact:

> Some of us, who had been over-optimistic, believed that we had, finally found a suitable "umbrella for the arts" in the Federal government, but we were wrong. The explanation for that failure is, I believe, very simple. It was because the Federal Music Project was never conceived as a "support" for the arts. It was, primarily, a humane project designed to alleviate un-employment and suffering. The theory, if I may put it brutally, was that a man might as well blow the horn, or paint a picture, as rake leaves![2]

Hanson's comment is, of course, on point, but it fails to acknowledge the fact that many artists who operated under this "umbrella for the arts" developed a new appreciation for the needs of the common man and a desire to address them in their art. Ultimately, the tensions that artists encountered in marrying experimental theater and musical modernism with an accessible way to address sociopolitical issues reflected their struggles to find new ways to address the values of a changing American society. Many artists involved in Federal One then had to find other venues in which to pursue their aspirations and promote art in the name of the people.

The distinction between conscious political affiliation and aesthetic ideol-ogy, which Michael Denning employs to distinguish the actual involvement of artists who made up the cultural front, would also help to explain the drastic changes that occurred at the end of the 1930s, when the big dream of socially relevant music and theatrical endeavors vanished against a growing concern for the unstable international political condition.[3] At this point, those com-posers who had joined leftist movements and workers' theater in response to a historical necessity rather than to a conscious political aspiration began to distance themselves from their "revolutionary" commitments. For some, the social contribution turned into populist rather than political music, one that was inspired by the common denominators of, and addressed to, the American people. For instance, Aaron Copland began composing in a deliberately more accessible style than in his earlier pieces. His ballets and patriotic commissions in particular employed conventional harmonies and a less dissonant musical language than his previous works; he also quoted folk tunes, widely accepted

172 · *Epilogue*

as one of the most authentic forms of indigenous musical expression. These features established him as a composer of American music who could speak to a broader audience, a composer concerned with the "common man." In hindsight, in an autobiographical essay published in the *Magazine of Art* in 1939, Copland attempted to justify the substantial change of compositional direction on the grounds that "we composers were in danger of working in a vacuum."[4]

Curiously, Copland expressed in 1939 the same concept that Blitzstein theorized in 1936, when in *New Masses* he argued that the composer is now an "honest workman among workmen, who has a job to do, a job which wonderfully gives other people joy. His music is aimed at the masses; he knows what he wants to say to them."[5] But while for Blitzstein the goal was to create socially engaged music, Copland's new direction resulted from the need to talk to a broader audience through the radio and the phonograph, to give a music-loving audience what they wanted. As Elizabeth Crist claims, the composer's imposed simplicity—that is, making a work accessible and conceiving of it both as functional and artistic creation—must be seen as an aesthetic orientation more than a political choice.[6] Indeed, this simplistic stance ultimately turned Copland's works populist but hardly leftist.

What remained at the end of the 1930s was the reality of a no longer socially acceptable past; only a handful of composers still associated with leftist institutions or organizations and predominantly concerned with folk music continued to answer to political cultural demands. For instance, Elie Siegmeister, who abandoned the lofty pursuit of proletarian music, began to reconcile folk elements with concert music. He realized artistic arrangements of American folk songs, songs of slavery and emancipation, as well as contemporary working-class and folk songs, and he performed them in a coast-to-coast tour with the "American Ballad Singers," a group that he had founded in 1939.[7] In the post-Depression years, folk music turned decisively political, and songs of protest by popular folk singers such as Molly Jackson, Woody Guthrie, Huddie Ledbetter ("Leadbelly"), and Pete Seeger began to address social, moral, and racial issues. These folk singers anticipated the paramount role that the "protest" folk song played in the 1950s in support of the labor movement against right-wing and anti-communist groups and, again in the 1960s, in support of the Civil Rights Movement and anti–Vietnam War initiatives.[8] Their songs shared roots with the *Little Red Songbook* compiled by the Industrial Workers of the World, but these authors also found new stimuli and social integration in folklore studies and folk song collections sponsored by the WPA and its Resettlement Administration programs.[9]

One of the most palpable heritages of the decade and its political and social unrest remains the use of vernacular idioms in theater and art music, a path

Epilogue • 173

that Blitzstein, in the spirit of the early 1930s, pursued in his quest for a musical theatrical form that would speak to the needs of the working class. At first, he capitalized on the attention given to *Cradle* and in 1937 wrote another agit-prop piece: the radio song-play in one act, *I've Got the Tune.* Commissioned by the Columbia Broadcasting Corporation and dedicated to Orson Welles, the work premiered on October 24 over the Columbia Workshop broadcast, WABC, with Bernard Hermann as conductor, Irving Reis as director, Blitzstein in the title role of Mr. Musiker, and Lotte Lenya as the suicidal woman. The one-act play tells the story of a composer, possibly Blitzstein himself, who has a tune, but is seeking the words to give it meaning. After a series of cartoon-like encounters with a sophisticated patron of the arts, a group of fascists, a suicidal woman, and Tin Pan Alley writers, a group of high school kids finally transforms Mr. Musiker's tune into an agit-prop anthem:

Because this is our day!
We're singing songs of May!
That's why we sing today!
Because we'll rule the world tomorrow, we can sing today![10]

The plot of *I've Got the Tune* portrays Blitzstein's belief that art music can change the world, an ideal that the composer soon realized to be quite naïve, as he depicted a rather different scenario in *No for an Answer* (1937–40), the two-act labor opera that concludes his excursion into the agit-prop theater of the 1930s. This piece tells the story of seasonal Greek American workers at a resort on the East Coast who, during their period of winter unemployment, seek relief and comfort in communal and social activities at the Diogenes Club, especially choral singing. As Blitzstein argued, "it is the life and fate of the Diogenes Club and its little people which forms the opera; tragic episodes, comic interludes, individual love stories, plans, anguish, determinations, setbacks, triumphs."[11] The circumstances become more complicated when, to secure the workers' continuous employment, a trade unionist incites them to get involved in class struggle, while a couple of liberal-minded wealthy citizens want to convert the resort into a year-round facility. Yet these conflicting efforts generate a series of dramatic situations that deal less with unionism and labor issues than with character and plot development, thus answering more to artistic demands than to sociopolitical struggles. Blitzstein himself commented:

After I finished it [*The Cradle Will Rock*], I wanted my next work to try to develop real people, very much themselves, with special personal qualities. I wanted to try characterization in depth and in musical terms. So I set about writing and composing *No for an Answer.*[12]

174 · *Epilogue*

Lacking the heroic quality of the unionism of the steel workers of *Cradle*, this work seems to signal the end of a period, especially with the war on the horizon and unionism taking a back seat to patriotism. Such a hypothesis would also explain the lack of commercial production history of *No for an Answer*: after three experimental semi-staged Sunday concert version performances at the Mecca Auditorium in New York, starting on January 5, 1941, it took sixty years before the production of the first staged performance of the labor-opera on October 22, 2001, at the American Conservatory Theater in San Francisco.

Some reviewers, such as Ralph Warner of the *Daily Worker*, criticized the 1941 performances of *No for an Answer* for the lack of stage setting, thus unequivocally marking the end of an era; something that Blitzstein himself recognized, as he never completed the planned orchestration of the musical score and instead turned his energy to the war efforts, as did many other contemporary composers, eventually enlisting in the United States Army in August 1942.[13] After World War II, still believing that art must aspire to social relevance, Blitzstein adjusted his agit-prop protest to better fit the social issues of the day. He denounced capitalism and social decay in the Southern aristocracy of the early twentieth century (*Regina*, 1948) and tried to dramatize a famous episode of intense political activism from earlier in the century (the unfinished opera *Sacco and Vanzetti*). But his politics frequently trumped his artistic instincts, and his social view of music, coupled with the innate compositional struggles that too often prevented him from completing a coherent large-scale dramatic work, deprived him of the success that smiled on other contemporaries who turned their backs on the leftist idea of socially engaged music.

In the end, most composers were quick to abandon professed political ideals and social aspirations, even if audiences had shown interest in some of such endeavors, especially those that successfully married experimentation with vernacular styles. After all, if the songs of the *Workers Song Books* failed to become the new anthems of the American working class, many of the productions of the Workers' Theater Movement achieved a quite substantial fame among the American proletariat. The success of works of the New Playwrights Theatre, such as Gold's *Hoboken Blues*, Lawson's *The International*, and Sinclair's *Singing Jailbirds*, was indeed associated with the group's ability to merge innovative theatrical approaches, political message, and elements of the American musical vernacular, features that were embraced by the movement in the 1930s. Even *The Cradle Will Rock*, albeit in its no-scenery production, reached a considerable number of Americans and prompted a string of positive reviews, which focused primarily on Blitzstein's skill in addressing the debated issue of unionism with a vernacular idiom that, according to Maxine Block, turned him from "an unorthodox composer whose experiments in new forms and tonalities once made him one of the more difficult moderns to listen to" into "one of America's popular musicians."[14] There was also the famous and successful skit "Sing Me a Song with Social Significance," included in the original version of *Pins and Needles*, which embodied the desire to find irony and humor in contemporary American life and articulated the most genuine expression of the political involvement of music in the 1930s.

Why then are most of these contributions, which expressed polemical and socially relevant issues and played a central role in the sociocultural and political life of the decade, now either forgotten or diminished in their effectiveness? Art music and musical theater inspired by the struggles of the Great Depression were surely topical, a product of the time as many say, but this does not justify dismissing them on artistic and cultural grounds. As Carol Oja maintained, the experiments of the Composers' Collective of New York and, this author would add, of the Workers' Theater Movement, set the stage for Blitzstein to grow "richer in substance and communicability" and explore a style that allowed him to speak to a wider audience.[15] The answer lies in the changing political situation. Once the United States moved out of the Depression years, the strong bond of music and theater with the audience was largely redefined, and leftist political messages were either suppressed or actively distorted on the grounds of suspected communist infiltration. During and after World War II, the American left had to contend with increased repression at home, and right-wing movements were still raising their voices against labor groups, social minorities, and communism.

Starting in October 1947, the House Un-American Activities Committee (HUAC) began targeting left-wing organizations and individuals, many of whom ended up listed in *Red Channels*, a book published in June 1950 by *Counterattack*, an anti-communist organization founded by a group of former FBI men.[16] The publication of *Red Channels*, which contains an alphabetical list of 151 individuals, including their affiliations with left-wing or communist associations, became an incendiary affair for artists such as Aaron Copland, Leonard Bernstein, Earl Robinson, Arthur Miller, Irwin Shaw, Dorothy Parker, Pete Seeger, Langston Hughes, and Marc Blitzstein. The allegations against them were at times preposterous; for instance, Blitzstein's four-page dossier included a performance of *I've Got the Tune* at Carnegie Hall on a benefit program for the National Council for the Arts, Sciences and Professions, and many citations of concerts in which Blitzstein participated, petitions and protests he signed, organizational letterheads in which his name appeared, his contributions to benefit auctions, citations of his articles printed in *New Masses*, his endorsements

176 · Epilogue

to various committees, and professional conferences he sponsored. No matter how ludicrous some of these allegations were, being listed in *Red Channels* was ruinous for many artists as, threatened by the possibility of HUAC purges, producers refused to employ personalities cited therein. Consequently, many rejected or distanced themselves from those endeavors. Famous is the case of Copland's turn to the abstractness of 12-tone music when he found himself trapped between his 1930s activities, which as we have seen showed him vaguely interested in leftist thought, and the consequences these activities carried for him during the Cold War era, including the withdrawal of his *Lincoln Portrait* from the Eisenhower inaugural concert due to his suspected communist affiliations.[17] Because of this backlash, most of the "songs with social significance" from the 1930s enjoyed no posthumous social significance of their own. Idealist experiments overpowered by a changing political framework, they ended up being messages in a bottle that most music lovers and political activists alike were happy to put afloat unopened. These works thus became as little known to most Americans as the modernist pieces that some of them were so eager to critique and supplant.

As demonstrated in this book, though, if we look at the reception history of the works of these 1930s artists and go beyond an interpretation that focuses only on their artistic value, we can appreciate the liveliness of an American society intent on promoting major cultural and political changes. Indeed, these socially oriented works highlighted tensions resulting from the delicate search for balance between idealism and reality, but these tensions are fundamental to understanding the intricate relationship between creators and intended audiences. Through the trials and errors of the leftist cultural movement we can understand how ideas propagated and the relevance they had for contemporary society. The sociopolitical engagement of many composers was much more complex than what has been portrayed in hindsight. No matter if moved by, using Denning's distinction, a conscious political affiliation or a vague political awareness, they undeniably attempted to connect with the new audiences and give them an artistic product to help them overcome struggles. Ultimately, left-oriented composers contributed, each in their own way—and as substantially as their contemporary ultra-modernists, neo-romantics, and cowboy-style Americanists—to the kaleidoscopic musical world of the 1930s in New York City. After all, this may be the only period in American history where theater and music were so deeply involved in everyday life that they became an intrinsic part of American culture.

Notes

Introduction

1. Eric Gordon, *Mark the Music, The Life and Work of Marc Blitzstein* (St. Martin's Press, 1989), xiv.

2. Their friendship was characterized by a sort of intellectual love that led, despite Blitzstein's homosexuality, to their marriage in 1932. The union lasted until May 1936, when Eva died of anorexia nervosa.

3. Marc Blitzstein, "Coming—The Mass Audience!," *Modern Music* 13, no. 4 (May/June 1936): 25.

4. Marc Blitzstein, "Coming—the Mass Audience!"

5. Eventually, this surge of interest for leftist and communist beliefs lessened in 1939, when Joseph Stalin aligned with Adolf Hitler against Poland and decreed the beginning of the Cold War period.

6. "Opera Saved as Benefit Nets $30,000," *Brooklyn Daily Eagle* (April 29, 1933): 3.

7. A fifth division, the Historical Records Survey, was eventually added to the FPO in October 1936.

8. Eleanor Roosevelt, "My Day," November 11, 1939.

9. For a detailed contemporary discussion on this issue, see Grace Overmyer, "The Musician Starves," *American Mercury* vol. 32 (June 1934): 224–31.

10. These and the following data from Kenneth J. Bindas, *All of This Music Belongs to the Nation: The WPA's Federal Music Project and American Society* (Knoxville, TN: University of Tennessee Press, 1995), 1–14.

178 · *Notes to Introduction*

11. For comprehensive data, see "Final Report on WPA Program, 1935–1943" (Washington, DC: Government Printing Office, 1946).

12. Nikolai Sokoloff, frontispiece of *The Federal Music Project* (Washington, DC: GPO, 1936). Born in Kiev in 1886, Sokoloff migrated at age 12 with his family to the United States, where he studied violin at the Yale School of Music and became first violin of the Boston Symphony Orchestra at 16. In 1907, he returned for four years to Europe to study with, among others, d'Indy and Ysaÿe in France. After World War I, he became the conductor of the Cleveland Symphony Orchestra until 1933, when he moved to New York City as a freelance conductor, and Hopkins appointed him director of the FMP.

13. Bindas, *All of This Music*, 9–11. The FMP, the most long-lived division of the FPO, ended as a federal program by mid-1939. While still funded by the federal government, its units were for the most part put into the hands of individual states, which continued to carry on certain art music projects (primarily of a nationalistic nature) until June 1943.

14. In Sokoloff's list, classically trained individuals ranked at the top and received better compensations. Academically untrained performers, many of them once employed in the entertainment industry, found themselves at the bottom of this hierarchical ladder with lower wages and higher weekly workloads. This discrimination engendered concerns at the headquarters of the American Federation of Musicians and, eventually, Sokoloff had to change his policy and treat all performing musicians equally. Paradoxically, given the educational goals of the FMP, music educators received the lowest pay scale wages.

15. Bindas, *All of This Music*, 24.

16. Typical examples are the murals titled *The Arts of Life in America* that Thomas Hart Benton painted in 1932 for the Whitney Museum of American Art in New York City. The panels, five of which are now at the New Britain Museum of American Art in Connecticut, depict scenes of American everyday life, with people representing American diversity dancing, performing music, and playing sports, but they also depict images denouncing unemployment, crime, and racism.

17. Virgil Thomson, "In the Theatre," *Modern Music* 15, no. 2 (January-February 1938): 114.

18. Stephen Wade, *The Beautiful Music All Around Us* (University of Illinois Press, 2012); Robbie Lieberman, *My Song Is My Weapon* (University of Illinois Press, 1995).

19. Richard A. Reuss, with Jo Anne C. Reuss, *American Folk Music and Left-Wing Politics, 1927–1957* (Lanham, MD: The Scarecrow Press, 2000).

20. Peter Gough, *Sounds of the New Deal* (University of Illinois Press, 2015).

21. Leta Miller, *Music and Politics in San Francisco from the 1906 Quake to the Second World War* (University of California Press, 2011); Catherine Parsons Smith, *Making Music in Los Angeles: Transforming the Popular* (University of California Press, 2007).

22. Carol Oja, "Marc Blitzstein's *The Cradle Will Rock* and Mass-Song Style of the 1930s," *The Musical Quarterly* 73, no. 4 (1989): 445–75; Elizabeth Crist, *Music for the*

Notes to Introduction and Chapter 1 • 179

Common Man: Aaron Copland During the Depression and War (New York: Oxford University Press, 2005); Melissa de Graaf, *The New York Composers' Forum Concerts, 1935–1940* (Rochester: University of Rochester Press, 2013); Sally Bick, "In the Tradition of Dissent Music at the New School for Social Research, 1926–33," *Journal of the American Musicological Society* 66, no. 1 (Spring 2013): 129–90.

Chapter 1. Bourgeois Modernism for the Proletariat

1. See Beth Levy, *Frontier Figures: American Music and the Mythology of the American West* (Berkeley: University of California Press, 2012); Denise Von Glahn, *The Sounds of Place: Music and the American Cultural Landscape* (Boston: Northeastern University Press, 2003); Elizabeth Bergman Crist, *Music for the Common Man: Aaron Copland During the Depression and War* (Oxford University Press, 2005).

2. *Marc Blitzstein Papers*, State Historical Society, Madison, Wisconsin, Archive Division (from now on SHSW), Box 7, Folder 6: "Composers' Collective Minutes." This author first introduced part of the content of Blitzstein's notes on the debates that followed the presentations of the Symposium on Proletarian Music at the 2009 AMS conference in Philadelphia. In the succeeding years, the transcript has been discussed briefly in Leonard J. Lehrman and Kenneth O. Boulton, *Elie Siegmeister, American Composer: A Bio-Bibliography* (Lanham, MD: The Scarecrow Press, 2010), 19, and Howard Pollack, *Marc Blitzstein: His Life, His Work, His World* (Oxford University Press, 2012), 105. See also Maria Cristina Fava, "The Composers' Collective of New York (1932–1936): Bourgeois Modernism for the Proletariat," *American Music* 34, no. 3 (Fall 2016): 301–43.

3. Pierre Degeyter, a French worker devoted both to music and to the cause of the working class, studied at the Lille Conservatorium of Music. In 1888, he was commissioned by the Lille section of the French Workers' Party to set to music the poem "Internationale" written in 1871 by Eugene Pottier. The song, premiered in July 1888 by the section's chorus "La Lyre des Travailleurs," immediately appealed to class-conscious workers and, following an international Socialist congress in Copenhagen in 1910, it was adopted as the anthem of all socialist parties.

4. Ashley Pettis, "Marching with a Song," *New Masses* (May 1, 1934): 15. Pettis (1892–1970), before joining the communist editorial boards and becoming a sought-after left-wing orator, started his career as composer and pianist. From 1925 to 1931 he was a faculty member at the Eastman School of Music in Rochester, New York, and in 1935 he founded the Composers' Forum Laboratory as part of the WPA Federal Music Project's Music Education Division. Surprisingly, Pettis, a composer and music critic who at the time actively promoted socially relevant music and leftist propaganda, later became a monk and a pro-Catholic propagandist.

5. The Workers Music League was established on June 14, 1931, by members of the American Communist Party.

6. David K. Dunaway, "Charles Seeger and Carl Sands: The Composers' Collective Years," *Ethnomusicology* 24, no. 2 (May 1980): 161.

180 • *Notes to Chapter 1*

7. For other studies on the Composers' Collective, see Ann M. Pescatello, *Charles Seeger: A Life in American Music* (Pittsburgh: University of Pittsburgh Press, 1992); Reuss and Reuss, *American Folk Music*; Barbara Zuck, *A History of Musical Americanism* (Ann Arbor, MI: UMI Research Press, 1980).

8. Dunaway, "Charles Seeger and Carl Sands," 162.

9. *Marc Blitzstein Papers*, SHSW, Box 7, Folder 6: "Composers' Collective Minutes." On occasion, for some composers Blitzstein used two different names; pseudonyms that seem likely to belong to a given composer are in brackets followed by a question mark.

10. "Jacob Schaefer, Composer of Proletarian Music, Dead at 46," *Jewish Telegraphic Agency* 2, no. 101 (Dec. 3, 1936), http://pdfs.jta.org/1936/1936–12–03_101.pdf?_ga=2.234941441.1861810488.1622384239–861774829.1622384239. Reviews on the Freedom Singers' Society's concerts and activities were common in the *Daily Worker*. See David Shapiro, "Schaefer's 'Twelve' and the Freiheit Singing Society," *Daily Worker* (May 27, 1927): 6; Carl Sands (alias Charles Seeger), "The Freiheit Gesang Verein," *Daily Worker* (March 22, 1935): 5.

11. On Cowell's mystical use of clusters, see Michael Hicks, "Cowell's Clusters," *The Musical Quarterly* 77, no. 3 (Autumn 1993): 428–58.

12. *Marc Blitzstein's Papers*, SHSW, Box 97, Folder 10.

13. Ashley Pettis, "Marching with a Song," *New Masses* XI (May 1, 1934): 15.

14. Letter from Charles Seeger to Marc Blitzstein, July 14, 1934, *Marc Blitzstein's Papers*, SHSW.

15. Deems Taylor, "Music," in *Civilization in the United States: An Inquiry by Thirty Americans*, ed. Harold E. Stearns (Harcourt, Brace and Co., 1922).

16. See, among others, Melissa de Graaf, *The New York Composers' Forum Concerts, 1935–1940* (University of Rochester Press, 2013); Ellie Hisama, *Gendering Musical Modernism* (Cambridge University Press, 2001); Catherine Parsons Smith, "A Distinguishing Virility: Feminism and Modernism in American Art Music," in *Cecilia Reclaimed: Feminist Perspectives in Gender and Music*, eds. Susan Cook and Judith Tsou (University of Illinois Press, 1993).

17. Composers' Forum Transcripts, January 8, 1937. NA II, College Park, MD, Record 69—Records of the Work Projects Administration, Records Pertaining to the Composers' Forum Laboratory 1935–40.

18. On this topic, see Melissa de Graaf, "'Never Call Us Lady Composers': Gendered Receptions in the New York Composers' Forum, 1935–40," *American Music* 26, no. 3 (Fall 2008): 277–308.

19. Richard Kostelanetz, ed., *Aaron Copland: A Reader. Selected Writings 1923–1972* (New York: Routledge, 2004), 88–90.

20. Kostelanetz, ed., *Aaron Copland*, 90.

21. Michael Gold, "What a World," *Daily Worker* (October 19, 1933): 5. Joe Hill (1879–1915) was a member of the IWW and a labor activist, and he became a popular songwriter and cartoonist for the union. The term "Wobbly," commonly used to refer to

members of the IWW, reportedly comes from a Chinese restaurant owner in Alberta, Canada, who was criticized for serving food to IWW members and responded to this criticism by saying something that sounded like "Eye like eye Wobbly Wobbly" (i.e., "I like the IWW"); in Melvyn Dubofsky, *We Shall Be All: A History of the Industrial Workers of the World* (Chicago: Quadrangle, 1969), 485.

22. The IWW, founded in 1905 and consisting mainly of itinerant seasonal workers, envisaged a utopian society embracing "One Big Union" that combined both skilled and unskilled workers. The IWW promoted the abolition of capitalism in favor of a cooperative commonwealth free of any distinctions of class and nationality, one in which the workers would control the wealth that they produced. Linking the workers' struggles with class-conscious and revolutionary aims, the Wobblies identified the general strike as the most effective weapon to overthrow capitalism. They condemned militarism and sought to establish a socialist society through workers' actions at the points of production (e.g., factories).

23. David A. Carter, "The Industrial Workers of the World and the Rhetoric of Song," *The Quarterly Journal of Speech* 66 (1980): 369.

24. At first performed everywhere in the United States where there were picket lines, workers pageants, and protest rallies, this song has traveled around the world like a folk song and has been translated into many languages. Joan Baez sang it at Woodstock, bringing it to even wider popular attention. Hill was also the focus of a 1971 feature film (*Joe Hill*, directed by Bo Widerberg) and an opera (*Joe Hill: The Man Who Never Died*, by English communist composer Alan Bush).

25. David Berginkoff, "Why Not Sing" ("Letters from Our Readers" column), *Daily Worker*, (October 11, 1927): 3.

26. Michael Gold, "Toward an American Revolutionary Culture," *New Masses* (July 1931): 13.

27. *Red Song Book*, prepared in collaboration with the Workers Music League (New York, NY: Workers Library Publishers, 1932). The similarity between the title of the WML book (*Red Song Book*) and that of the earlier IWW collections (*Little Red Songbook*) suggests that the WML wished to build upon and expand the experience of the Wobblies. Indeed, the elimination of the qualifier "little" hints that the working-class song movement had grown up, or, more broadly, that the American Communist Party (parent organization of the WML) had surpassed and essentially replaced the IWW.

28. Gold, "Toward an American Revolutionary Culture," 13.

29. Kostelanetz, ed., *Aaron Copland*, 88–89.

30. *Marc Blitzstein Papers*, SHSW, Box 7, Folder 6: "Notes," 1.

31. Carol Oja, in "Marc Blitzstein's *The Cradle Will Rock* and Mass-Song Style of the 1930s," *The Musical Quarterly* 73, no. 4 (1989): 445–75, offers a detailed summary of the early work of the Collective and the use of mass songs.

32. Sally Bick, "In the Tradition of Dissent. Music at the New School for Social Research, 1926–33" *Journal of the American Musicological Society* 66, no. 1 (Spring 2013): 139.

182 · *Notes to Chapter 1*

33. *Marc Blitzstein Papers*, SHSW, Box 7, Folder 6: "Notes on the Work of the Composers' Collective of NY," 3.

34. Hanns Eisler, *Hanns Eisler: A Rebel in Music. Selected Writings*, edited and with an introduction by Manfred Grabs (London: Kahn & Averill, 1999).

35. Dunaway, "Charles Seeger and Carl Sands," 162–63.

36. Charles Seeger, "On Proletarian Music," *Modern Music* 11, no. 3 (March/April 1934): 121.

37. Seeger, "On Proletarian Music," 122.

38. Karl Marx, *Capital: A Critique of Political Economy*, edited by Frederick Engels (New York, International Publishers, 1967).

39. *Workers Song Book No. 1* (New York: Workers Music League, USA Section of International Music Bureau, 1934); *Workers Song Book No. 2* (New York: Workers Music League, USA Section of International Music Bureau, 1935).

40. This and the following citations are taken from *Workers Song Book No. 1*, 2–3.

41. Oja, "Marc Blitzstein's *The Cradle Will Rock*," 458.

42. Elie Siegmeister, script for a radio show about his music, broadcast on WNCN, April 25, 1971, 6. Quoted in Oja, "Composer with a Conscience: Elie Siegmeister in Profile," *American Music* 6, no. 2 (Summer 1988): 166.

43. *Workers Song Book No. 1*, 3.

44. *Workers Song Book No. 1*, 12.

45. Seeger, "On Proletarian Music," 125.

46. In the performance notes, the Collective described the round as an "old form of English folk music," even if rounds are surely common in other folk singing traditions (i.e., French, Italian, German, etc.). The emphasis on the English quality of the music would seem to be another attempt, like the use of English-sounding pseudonyms, at cleansing the American communist left of ethnic coloration.

47. *Workers Song Book No. 1*, foreword.

48. On back of the front cover of *Workers Song Book No. 2* (New York: Workers Music League, USA Section of International Music Bureau, 1935).

49. In the second *Workers Song Book*, Wolpe's name is spelled as it is pronounced: Volpe—a choice that may also have had the advantage of making him sound Italian rather than German-Jewish.

50. Judith Tick, *Ruth Crawford Seeger: A Composer's Search for American Music* (New York: Oxford University Press, 1997), 191–92.

51. Oja, "Composer with a Conscience," 170.

52. Interview with Mordecai Baumann, November 17, 2007, Manhattan.

53. Elie Siegmeister, "The Strange Funeral in Braddock," words by Michael Gold. *New Music Quarterly Recordings* vol. 3, no. 3 (1936). Mordecai Baumann, baritone; Elie Siegmeister, piano. R646, 78 rpm recorded by Reeves Sound Studios, New York.

54. *Marc Blitzstein Papers*, SHSW, Box 7, Folder 6: "Notes on the Work of the Composers' Collective of NY," 1–2.

55. Blitzstein's most notable contribution to proletarian music is a children's cantata in eight sections called *Workers' Kids of the World Unite!*, which is often referred to

as *Children's Cantata* (1934–35). The text, full of proletarian rhetoric and imagery more suitable for adult workers on the pickets than for children, is set to a modernist musical language full of harsh harmonies. Blitzstein's at times catchy tunes are often set against a sophisticated dissonant accompaniment that hardly helps the children to sustain the vocal line. The piece remained unpublished and the composer himself, as Oja argued, must have realized that the work was too ambitious for its practical use and in the holograph version he made changes to render the piece more accessible. See Carol Oja, "Marc Blitzstein's *The Cradle Will Rock* and Mass-Song Style of the 1930s," *The Musical Quarterly* 73, no. 4 (1989).

56. *Marc Blitzstein Papers*, SHSW, Box 7, Folder 6, 2.

57. Ibid.

58. Ibid., 3.

59. Interview with Mordecai Baumann, November 20, 2007, Manhattan.

60. Arthur Berger, *Reflections of an American Composer* (University of California Press, 2002), 10–11. Berger was not listed among the members of the Collective, but he was a member of the Young Composers' Group led by Aaron Copland, which also included some composers who later joined the Collective, such as Siegmeister.

61. The names in parenthesis, with corresponding addresses, are possibly those of new members of the Collective who joined during the meeting. The presence of four new female members is rather noteworthy, considering the misogynist attitudes showcased by many male members.

62. *Marc Blitzstein Papers*, SHSW, Box 7, Folder 6: "Composers' Collective Minutes." In the minutes there is no indication if these last three papers were discussed in a successive meeting/symposium.

63. Ibid.

64. *Marc Blitzstein Papers*, SHSW, Box 9, Folder 11: "Lectures-Articles, October 1934–1961."

65. *Marc Blitzstein Papers*, SHSW, Box 7, Folder 6: "Notes on the Work of the Composers' Collective of NY," 4.

66. Ibid.

67. This hesitancy about adopting the Soviet Union as an over model foreshadows the self-distancing of the American left from the USSR that began to occur when Stalin signed his infamous mutual non-aggression pact with Hitler.

68. Eisler, *Hanns Eisler: A Rebel in Music*, 59–60.

69. "L'Humanité Interviews Hanns Eisler" appeared in *L'humanité d'Alsace*, Strasbourg, France (June 1935); reprinted under the title "Problems of Working-Class Music" in *Hanns Eisler: A Rebel in Music*, 95–100.

70. *Marc Blitzstein Papers*, SHSW, Box 9, Folder 11: handwritten notebook. The notebook summarizes each presentation and the ensuing discussion and indicates the name of the participating composers followed by their respective comments.

71. Marc Blitzstein, "Music Manifesto," *New Masses* 19, no. 13 (June 23, 1936): 28.

72. Eisler, *Hanns Eisler: A Rebel in Music*, 53.

73. Ibid., 59–60.

184 · *Notes to Chapter 1*

74. Ibid., 100.

75. Initially the IWW published song cards, which were small, four-page card brochures containing songs of revolt, such as "The Red Flag [*Die Rote Fahne*]," "Hold the Fort," and even "The Marseillaise," linking the Wobblies' mass songs of protest to those of revolutionary France and Germany and of the nineteenth-century American labor movement. Given the success of these card songs, in 1909, the IWW started publishing the *Little Red Songbook*, a collection of mostly contrafacta written to popular melodies from sentimental ballads and vaudeville tunes. Among the many tunes borrowed in the various editions of the *Songbook*, those of Stephen Foster and hymns were the favorites. For example, Joe Hill set his "We Will Sing One Song" to Foster's "My Old Kentucky Home," and "Nearer My Job to Thee" to "Nearer My God to Thee," a very popular nineteenth-century Christian hymn with lyrics by Sarah Flower Adams and music by her sister Eliza Flower. See Richard Brazier, "The Story of the I.W.W.'s *Little Red Songbook*," *Labor History* 9, no. 1 (Winter 1968): 91–105. This article is probably the most reliable primary source on the origins of the *Little Red Songbook*, though Brazier penned these reminiscences half a century after his experience with the Wobblies.

76. Eisler, *Hanns Eisler: A Rebel in Music*, 59–60.

77. For a thorough discussion on Soviet music during the Lenin years, see Amy Nelson, *Music for the Revolution* (Penn State Press, 2004).

78. Berger, *Reflections of an American Composer*, 10.

79. The American Communist Party established the *Daily Worker* newspaper in 1924. It generally reflected the prevailing views of the party. However, there were attempts to make it a paper that reflected the wide spectrum of left-wing opinion. At its peak, the newspaper achieved a circulation of 35,000.

80. George Maynard, "Appreciation among Workers," *Daily Worker* (January 23, 1934).

81. Lan Adomian, "What Songs Should Workers' Choruses Sing?," *Daily Worker* (February 7, 1934).

82. Carl Sands, "For Revolutionary Music Criticism in Our Press," *Daily Worker* (March 5, 1934); "Proletarian Music Is a Historical Necessity," *Daily Worker* (March 6, 1934); "The Broad Scope of Revolutionary Music Criticism," *Daily Worker* (March 7, 1934); "The Function of Revolutionary Music," *Daily Worker* (March 8, 1934).

83. Seeger, "On Proletarian Music," 121–27.

84. Michael Gold, "Change the World," *Daily Worker* (June 11, 1934).

85. On this topic, see Kim Kowalke, "Carl Orff and His Brecht Connection," in Albrecht Riethmüller ed., *Brecht und seine Komponisten* (Isarpost, Landshut, Germany: Laaber Verlag, 2000). Kowalke argues that music is incapable of being "left" or "right" by demonstrating that Carl Orff's setting of Brecht's "leftist" songs anticipates the musical style of his *Carmina Burana*, a work inspired by Nazi aesthetic.

86. Robert Shulman, *The Power of Political Art: The 1930s Literary Left Reconsidered* (Chapel Hill, NC: The University of North Carolina, 2000), 15.

87. Dunaway, "Charles Seeger and Carl Sands," 164.

88. Ibid., 165.

Notes to Chapters 1 and 2 • 185

89. *Marc Blitzstein Papers*, SHSW, Box 9, Folder 11.

90. On Blitzstein and *The Cradle Will Rock*, see Chapter 5.

91. For a detailed account of Blitzstein's approach to the new form, see Oja's "Marc Blitzstein's *The Cradle Will Rock* and Mass-Song Style of the 1930s."

Chapter 2. The Workers' Theater Movement and the Politicization of the Musical Revue

1. See Chapter 4 for a discussion of the FTP's living newspapers.

2. Ilka Saal, *New Deal Theater: The Vernacular Tradition in American Political Theater* (New York: Palgrave MacMillan, 2007), 9–24.

3. Richard Watts Jr., "The Theaters—Proletarian Fun," *New York Herald Tribune* (December 13, 1937): 8.

4. The complete text of the sketch is included in the IWW files in the *Labadie Collection*, University of Michigan Library, Ann Arbor, Michigan. Mutt and Jeff were the characters of a newspaper comic strip created by Bud Fisher in 1907, which is regarded as the first daily comic strip.

5. On March 25, 1931, two white runaway women traveling on a freight train through northern Alabama accused nine young Black men on the same train of rape. After a hasty and decidedly not impartial trial, an all-white jury in the town of Scottsboro, Alabama, convicted them, and the judge sentenced eight of the nine defendants to death. The case of the "Scottsboro Boys" became an international symbol of corruption and discrimination, much like the Sacco and Vanzetti trial. Inspiring an outpouring of poems, full-length plays, film scripts, fiction, political cartoons, visual art, political chants, agit-prop skits, and songs, the Scottsboro Boys became a cause célèbre for the radical left of the 1930s.

6. Led by IWW, the strike of the silk mill workers in Paterson, New Jersey began on February 1, 1913. The strikers demanded eight-hour workdays and improved working conditions. The pageant held at Madison Square Garden was one of various efforts undertaken to support the strike financially, but despite the long holdout and the fundraising efforts, the strike ended in failure on July 28, 1913. On this topic, see Steve Golin, *The Fragile Bridge: Paterson Silk Strike 1913* (Philadelphia: Temple University Press, 1988); Anne Huber Tripp, *The IWW and the Paterson Silk Strike of 1913* (Urbana: University of Illinois Press, 1987).

7. John Reed, *Ten Days that Shook the World* (New York: The Modern Library, 1935).

8. "The Pageant as a Form of Propaganda," *Current Opinion* (June 1913), cited in Joyce L. Kornbluh, ed., *Rebel Voices: An IWW Anthology* (Ann Arbor, MI: The University of Michigan Press, 1964), 212–13. *Current Opinion* was an American magazine published in New York in the early twentieth century, which ceased publication in 1925.

9. Douglas McDermott, "The Theatre Nobody Knows: Workers' Theatre in America, 1926–1942," *Theatre Survey* (May 1965): 67. On Artef, see also Edna Nahshon, *Yiddish Proletarian Theatre: The Art and Politics of the Artef, 1925–1940* (Westport: Greenwood Press, 1998).

186 · *Notes to Chapter 2*

10. A. B. Magil, "Artef Theater Opens," *New Masses* (November 1931).

11. William Weinberg, "Proletarian Drama," *New Masses* (July 1930).

12. Ben Blake, *The Awakening of the American Theater* (New York: Tomorrow Publishers, 1935), 15–16.

13. Excerpts from *Tempo Tempo!* (1930) translated from the German by B. Stern of the Workers' Laboratory Theatre, originally published in *Workers' Theatre Magazine* 1, no. 8 (November 1931).

14. For a contemporary report on the music, see Blake, *The Awakening of the American Theatre*, 17.

15. John Howard Lawson (1894–1977) made a significant contribution to twentieth-century American drama as a playwright in the 1920s-30s, a screenwriter during the development of "talking" movies during the 1930s-40s, and as an analyst of writing techniques for stage and screen. A member of the "Hollywood Ten," he was blacklisted during the McCarthy period and played advocate for social reform in American politics and culture. Ida Rauh co-founded the Provincetown Players, and actor and director Jasper Deeter founded the Hedgerow Theatre in Philadelphia.

16. Malcolm Goldstein, in *The Political Stage: American Drama and Theatre of the Great Depression* (Oxford University Press, 1974), refers to the group as the "Workers' Theatre" and does not cite the source of his information; however, the contemporary writer Ben Blake, in *The Awakening of the American Theatre* (1935), calls it "Workers' Drama League."

17. Michael Gold, "Strike!: A Mass Recitation," *New Masses* (July 1926): 19–21.

18. Em Jo Basshe was one of the pioneer members of the Provincetown Players and an author of short plays; Francis Edwards Faragoh acquired some fame as author of the controversial play *Pinwheel*. Information on members and program drawn from *New Playwrights Theatre*, a promotional booklet published for their Third Season and available at the New York Public Library for the Performing Arts, "New Playwrights Theater," NWEZ + n.c. 25,366 #18.

19. "New Playwrights Theater," New York Public Library for the Performing Arts, NWEZ + n.c. 25,366 #18.

20. *Loud Speaker* (1927), play in three acts by John Howard Lawson, staging by Harry Wagstaff Gribble, setting by Mordecai Gorelik; it opened on March 7, 1927 at the 52nd Street Theater and ran forty-two performances.

21. J. Brooks Atkinson, "The Play. Steeplechase Drama," *New York Times* (March 3, 1927): 27.

22. Vsevolod Emilyevich Meyerhold (1874–1940) was a Soviet theater director, actor, and producer known for his experiments in nonrealistic theater and constructivist productions, including Fernand Crommelynk's *The Magnificent Cuckold* and Alexander Sukhovo-Kobylin's *The Death of Tarelkin*. Constructivism for Meyerhold was an attempt to achieve a setting that would be practicable rather than decorative. He employed platforms, ramps, turning wheels, and other devices to turn the stage into a machine for acting and let the actors move in a three-dimensional space.

23. Scripts of the various versions in *Lawsons Papers Collection*, Box 68, Special Collections, Morris Library at Southern Illinois University Carbondale.

Notes to Chapter 2 · 187

24. Roberta Lynne Lasky, "The New Playwrights Theater, 1927–1929," PhD diss., University of California, Davis, 1989, 63–64. As Lasky states, besides jazz dance and song, the show made copious use (more than half of the scenes) of incidental music composed by Eugene L. Berton.

25. As Malcolm Goldstein notes (*The Political Stage*, 17), Lawson's technique resonates, to some degree, with Brecht's use of stage devices to distance the audience from the action (*Verfremdungseffekt*). In fact, though, the New Playwrights did not try to emulate the German author.

26. John Howard Lawson, *Loud Speaker* (New York: The Macaulay Company, 1927), 76.

27. Atkinson, "The Play. Steeplechase Drama," 27.

28. *Hoboken Blues* (1928), play in three acts by Michael Gold, staging by Edward Massey, music by Edward A. Ziman; it opened on February 17, 1928, and ran thirty-five performances.

29. Michael Gold, "Theater and Revolution," *Nation* (November 11, 1925): 536–37.

30. Gold, "Theater and Revolution," 536.

31. Michael Folsom, "The Education of Michael Gold," in *Proletarian Writers of the Thirties*, ed. David Madden (Carbondale: Southern Illinois University Press, 1968), 234. Curiously, at the time of the run of *Hoboken Blues*, Robeson was in the cast of the play *Porgy*, a dramatization of DuBose Heyward's novel that served also as the basis of Gershwin's *Porgy and Bess*, another controversial portrayal of blackness.

32. Michael Gold, "Hoboken Blues: or The Black Rip Van Winkle: A Modern Negro Fantasia on an Old American Theme," in *American Caravan: A Yearbook of American Literature*, eds. Van Wyck Brooks et al., (New York: Literary Guild, 1927), 549.

33. *The International* (1928), play with music written and directed by John Howard Lawson, settings by John Dos Passos, incidental music by Edward A. Ziman; it opened on January 12, 1928, and ran twenty-seven performances.

34. J. Brooks Atkinson, "'The International' Full of 'Realism,'" *New York Times* (January 16, 1928): 24.

35. This and following direct quotations from John Howard Lawson, *The International* (New York: Macaulay, 1927), 7–8.

36. Jonathan L. Chambers in *Messiah of the New Technique. John Howard Lawson, Communism, and American Theatre, 1923–1937* (Carbondale, Southern Illinois University Press, 2006), 110.

37. *Singing Jailbirds* (1928), play in three acts written by Upton Sinclair, directed by EmJo Basshe; it opened on December 6, 1928, and ran seventy-two performances. Sinclair wrote *Singing Jailbirds* in 1924; it tackled controversial issues of class, unionism, and the worker's movement. The incident that inspired the play occurred at Liberty Hill in San Pedro, California in 1923. The text of the play is available online at the New York State Library Digital Image Project at http://nysl.nysed.gov.

38. On this topic, see Raphael Samuel and Tom Thomas, "Documents and Texts from the Workers' Theatre Movement (1928–1936)," *History Workshop* 4 (Autumn 1977): 103–12.

188 · *Notes to Chapter 2*

39. Virginia Hagelstein Marquardt, "Centre Stage: Radical Theatre in America, 1925–1934," *RACAR: revue d'art canadienne/Canadian Art Review* 19, No. 1/2, Art as Propaganda (1992): 113.

40. Kenneth Fearing, "Hoboken Blues," *New Masses* (April 1928): 27.

41. Autobiography, *Lawsons Papers Collection*, Box 94, Folder 10, p. 331a, cited by Chambers in *Messiah of the New Technique*, 88.

42. Goldstein, *The Political Stage*, 32.

43. Blake, *The Awakening of the American Theater*, 18.

44. In 1935, the League of Workers Theaters changed its name, too, and became the New Theatre League, an organization aligned with the program of the Popular Front. It started promoting not only a communist agenda but liberal causes as a struggle against war, fascism, and censorship. Indeed, the new name, eliminating the word "workers," evinced the desire of the movement to define itself as representative of the whole American theater.

45. Blake, *The Awakening of the American Theater*, 27.

46. Morgan Y. Himelstein, *Drama Was a Weapon: The Left-Wing Theatre in New York 1929–1941* (Westport: Greenwood Press, 1963), 25.

47. Blake, *The Awakening of the American Theater*, 23.

48. Jack Shapiro, member of the Workers' Laboratory *Theatre* and chairman of the Repertory Committee for the LoWT, gained fame within the movement as author of *Sweet Charity*, a play that won the second prize at the "Spartakiade," a contest organized as part of the Workers' *Theatre* Conference convened in 1932 in New York City to establish a central organization to coordinate the various groups of the WTM (the first prize went to the Prolet-Bühne's *15 Minute Red Revue*). This play is unrelated to the Broadway musical of the same name (1969).

49. The Group Theatre was a theater collective based in New York City and formed in 1931 by Harold Clurman, Cheryl Crawford, and Lee Strasberg.

50. The economic collapse that had almost paralyzed the United States at the beginning of 1933 contributed to a period of inactivity for the Group Theatre and increased its members' sympathy for the workers' cause. On this topic, see Wendy Smith, *Real Life Drama: The Group Theatre and America, 1931–1940* (New York: Knopf, distributed by Random House, 1990).

51. Jack Shapiro, "The Theatre Collective," *New Theatre* (October 1934): 15.

52. In this particularly troubled period of American history, however, misery and social unrest did not belong to only a communist discourse, and social drama became a topic cherished by many playwrights, even those who did not show an overt communist or leftist affiliation.

53. Paul Peters, "On Writing and Selecting Plays for Workers," *Daily Worker* (February 27, 1935): 5.

54. Plays produced by the Theatre Union: *Peace on Earth* by Sklar and Albert Maltz (1933); *Stevedore* by Peters and Sklar (1934); *The Sailors of Cattaro* by Friedrich Wolf,

Notes to Chapter 2 · 189

tr. by K. Wallis, adapted by M. Blankfort (1934); *Black Pit* by Maltz (1935); *Mother* by B. Brecht and H. Eisler, adapted by Peters (1935); *Bitter Stream* by V. Wolfson (1936); *Marching Song* by Lawson (1937).

55. John Howard Lawson, "Towards a Revolutionary Theatre: The Theatre—The Artist Must Take Side," *New Theatre* (June 1934): 6–7.

56. Lawson, "Towards a Revolutionary Theatre," 7.

57. Lawson, Autobiography, Lawson Papers, Box 99, Folder 6, pp. 879–80, cited by Chambers in *Messiah of the New Technique*, 183.

58. Saal, *New Deal Theater*, 19–24.

59. Margaret Larkin, "Theatre Union—Its Tasks and Problems," *Daily Worker* (May 15, 1935): 5.

60. Robert Garland, "*Parade* Alive and Kicking," *New York World Telegram* (May 21, 1935).

61. In this pursuit, the Guild continued the goals of the Washington Square Players and the Provincetown Players, two companies founded in 1915 to support modernist drama.

62. Goldstein, *The Political Stage*, 102–3.

63. Paul Peters and George Sklar, "Sketches from Parade," *New Theatre* 2, no. 6 (June 1935): 9.

64. Cited in Jay Williams, *Stage Left* (New York: Scribner, 1974), 184. Williams (1914–78), actor and novel writer, took an active part in the workers' and experimental theater movements during the years of the Great Depression and reported his experience in *Stage Left*.

65. Program of the opening night at the Colonial Theater in Boston on May 6, 1935. New York Public Library for the Performing Arts.

66. Peters and Sklar, "The Tabloid Reds," sketch from *Parade*, *New Theatre* 3, no. 6 (June 1935): 5.

67. Helen Eager, "*Parade* Has Premiere at the Colonial—The Guild's First Musical Deals with the Depression," *Boston Traveler* (May 7, 1935).

68. Elinor Hughes, "Theatre Guild Presents *Parade*, New Musical Show," *Boston Herald* (May 7, 1935).

69. "*Parade* in Boston," *New York Post* (May 11, 1935).

70. Lawrence Langner, *The Magic Curtain* (New York: Dutton, 1951), 263.

71. Hughes, "Theatre Guild Presents *Parade*."

72. George Holland, "*Parade* Has Stage Possibilities," *Evening American* (May 7, 1935): 18.

73. Elliot Norton, "Jimmy Savo Proves a Hit at Colonial, But Guild's 'Parade' Doesn't Shape Up as Good Show," *Boston Post* (May 7, 1935).

74. Garland, "*Parade* Alive and Kicking."

75. Minna Lederman, in "Memories of Marc Blitzstein, Music's Angry Man," *Show* 4, no. 6 (June 1964), directly related this number to the events of the insurrection of October 1934 in Spain.

190 • *Notes to Chapter 2*

76. Script at the NYPL for the Performing Arts in NCOF+ Moross, Jerome. Parade Libretto 1935 (1 volume, various pagings).

77. There does not exist a score of the piece, only the orchestral parts at Yale's Beinecke Library. See Leonard Lehrman, *Marc Blitzstein: A Bio-Bibliography* (Westport, Connecticut: Praeger, 2005), 212–14.

78. See Chapter 5 for *The Cradle Will Rock*.

79. On this sketch and its relationship to *The Cradle Will Rock*, see Howard Pollack, *Marc Blitzstein: His Life, His Work, His World* (New York: Oxford University Press, 2012), 151–53.

80. Percy Hammond, "Guild Takes a Left Turn, but Bourbons Get a Laugh," *New York Herald Tribune* (May 26, 1935). The "land of the heel and the home of the knave" phrase is an adroit play on the final words of "The Star-Spangled Banner": the land of the free and the home of the brave.

81. Jerome Moross, "New Musical Reviews for Old," *New Theatre* 2, no. 10 (October 1935): 12–13, 33.

82. On *The Cradle Will Rock*, see Chapter 5.

83. The International Ladies' Garment Workers' Union, founded in 1900 in New York City and one of the largest labor unions in the United States, had a primarily female membership and was a key player in the labor history of the 1920s and 1930s. The Princess Theatre, an intimate 299-seat playhouse on 39th Street, between Broadway and Sixth Avenue, opened in 1913 as the home for one-act plays, but soon it turned to small-scale musical comedies, known as "Princess shows," written principally by Jerome Kern, Guy Bolton, and P. G. Wodehouse. During the Depression, it turned into a movie theater until the ILGWU bought it and renamed it Labor Stage. Information on the Labor Stage and the production of *Pins and Needles* is drawn from Harry Goldman, "Pins and Needles: An Oral History," PhD diss., New York University, 1977.

84. Victor Wolfson had directed the Theatre Union's production of Brecht's *Mother*.

85. Goldstein, *The Political Stage*, 206. At first independently produced in 1931, *Steel* ran for only fourteen performances because, as Goldstein argues, it was too dogmatic and entrapped in Third Period ideologies.

86. Arthur Arent supervised, edited, and assisted in the writing of the scripts of the Federal Theater Project's living newspapers *Ethiopia, Triple A Plowed Under, 1935, Injunction Granted, Power*, and *One-Third of a Nation*.

87. Ben Irwin, "The A.F.L. Theatre Presents," *Daily Worker* (June 17, 1936): 7.

88. Moross, "New Musical Reviews for Old," 33.

89. Goldman reports that several other songs and sketches presented that night did not survive. "Pins and Needles: An Oral History," 59.

90. Goldman, "Pins and Needles: An Oral History," 64. For a detailed analysis of the legal battles with Actors Equity, the League of New York Theatres, and the State Division of Placement and Unemployment Insurance, see chap. IV, "Legal and Managerial Difficulties," of Goldman's dissertation).

Notes to Chapter 2 • 191

91. "Leftist Revue," *The New Yorker* (December 25, 1937): 11–12.

92. Robert Gordon was, like Charles Friedman, a radical who belonged to the Popular Front and directed some sketches of Cabaret TAC.

93. In the end though, considering the size of the average musical theaters and those where *Pins and Needles* was performed, the show had the same audience as a production on Broadway.

94. Actually, *Pins and Needles* had two national road tours—one from April 1938 to January 1939 and the other from July 1940 to May 1941.

95. Strauss, "After a Year of the Industrial Revolution" *New York Times* (December 11, 1938): 4.

96. Strauss, "After a Year of the Industrial Revolution," 4.

97. J. G. (Jack Gould), "The Play," *New York Times* (November 29, 1937): 18.

98. Robert Reinhart, "New Talents' 2 of 3 B'way Hits: Borscht Circuit Endorsed as Training Ground for Intimate Revue Authors and Stagers," *Variety* 128, no. 13 (December 8, 1937): 53f. This section of the review is headed "*Parade* Made It Poison."

99. Richard Lockridge, "The New Play," *New York Sun* (November 29, 1937): 24.

100. Eric Englander, "Sparkling Revue on Labor Stage," *Daily Worker* (November 28, 1937): 7.

101. Burns Mantle, "Labor Stage Troupe Romps Through New Pins and Needles," *New York Daily News* (November 29, 1937): 33.

102. Richard Watts Jr., "The Theaters—Proletarian Fun," *New York Herald Tribune* (December 13, 1937): 8.

103. John Mason Brown, "Two on the Aisle. An Exciting Week-End for Propagandistic Drama," *New York Post* (December 3, 1937): 14.

104. Saal, *New Deal Theater*, 141–42.

105. Mary McCarthy, "Theater Chronicle," *Partisan Review* (April 1938): 52.

106. N. C., "Somebody Has Given the Revised 'Pins' the Needles," *Daily Worker* (November 30, 1939).

107. Saal, *New Deal Theater*, 144.

108. The revue underwent many changes to ensure resonance with the latest sociopolitical events. From time to time, its name changed as well: *Pins and Needles 1939* opened on April 21, 1939, and *New Pins and Needles* opened on November 20, 1939.

109. Michael Denning, *The Cultural Front: The Laboring of American Culture in the Twentieth Century* (New York: Verso, 1996), 306.

110. Goldman, "Pins and Needles: An Oral History," 252. See Trudi Ann Wright, "Labor Takes the Stage: A Musical and Social Analysis of *Pins and Needles* (1937–1941)," PhD diss., University of Colorado, Boulder, 2010, for an analysis of all nineteen original sketches and songs.

111. In her dissertation, Wright breaks down the nineteen songs into three categories: political songs and sketches, sketches about the economy and its effects on workers, and sketches and songs with social consciousness. Her musical analysis concludes that all songs were written in popular forms borrowing from opera,

192 • *Notes to Chapter 2*

sentimental songs, dance traditions, parlor songs, Tin Pan Alley songs, and labor choruses (mass choruses).

112. There are only some available published songs (copyrighted in 1937 by Florence Music Company and Chapel Company), programs, and other primary material from the road company stage manager Kendall Cole's production book from April 18, 1938 to January 28, 1939 that is available at the Education Research Department of the International Ladies' Garment Workers' Union in New York City. Information drawn from Eric W. Trumbull, "Musicals of the American Workers' Theater Movement 1928–1941: Propaganda and Ritual in Documents of a Social Movement," PhD diss., University of Maryland, 1991.

113. While the complete script of the sketch survived, only a few musical fragments of Blitzstein's scene are available at the Wisconsin Historical Society in a folder marked "The Cradle Will Rock: Ten Sketches to Music."

114. On the FTP's Living Newspaper Unit, see Chapter 4.

115. Gordon, *Mark the Music*, 160.

116. Trudi Wright, "Lost in *The Cradle*: The Reconstruction and Meaning of Marc Blitzstein's 'FTP Plowed Under' (1937)," *American Music* 34, no. 3 (Fall 2016): 344–64.

117. Wright, "Lost in *The Cradle*," 348–49.

118. Richard Watts Jr., "The Theaters—Proletarian Fun," *New York Herald Tribune* (December 13, 1937): 8.

119. Richard Watts Jr., "The Theaters—Revues, Past and Present, Including 'Pins and Needles,'" *New York Herald Tribune* (June 5, 1938): 8.

120. Sidney B. Wriffle, "The Rich Cleverly Satirized," *New York World-Telegram* (December 30, 1937): 6.

121. Heywood Broun, "It Seems to Me," *New York World-Telegram* (January 6, 1938): 17.

122. Heywood Broun, "It Seems to Me," *New York World-Telegram* (February 17, 1938): 21.

123. Gordon, *Mark the Music*, 161.

124. Goldman, "Pins and Needles: An Oral History," 26.

125. Denning, *The Cultural Front*, 297.

126. Interview with Charles Friedman in Goldman, "Pins and Needles: An Oral History," 71.

127. Harold Rome, *Pins and Needles*, 1962 Revival Cast Recording (1962), Sony BMG Music Entertainment. Recording personally supervised by Harold Rome.

128. Other famous songs on fashionable dances of the period are "The Varsity Drag" (1927), "The Continental" (1934), and "Begin the Beguine" (1935).

129. Theodor W. Adorno, *Essays on Music*. Selected, with introduction, commentary, and notes by Richard Leppert. New translations by Susan H. Gillespie (Berkeley: University of California Press, 2002), 460.

130. Adorno, *Essays on Music*, 460.

131. For a detailed discussion of the social impact of the revue, see Wright, "Labor Takes the Stage."

Notes to Chapters 2 and 3 • 193

132. Goldman, "Pins and Needles: An Oral History," 200.

133. Ibid.

134. This and the following statements are part of interviews reported in Goldman, "Pins and Needles: An Oral History," 200. Gene Barry, pseudonym of Eugene Klauss, was a professional who joined the show when it moved to Broadway, and there were three different companies performing at the same time. He is, according to Goldman, the most famous person to come out of the show, as he moved on to act in three television series, appeared in many television shows, and appeared in *La Cage aux Folles* (1984).

135. Goldman, "Pins and Needles: An Oral History," 202.

136. Ibid., 207.

137. Ibid.

138. Denning, *The Cultural Front*, 301.

139. Barrett H. Clark, "Our Most American Drama. Recent Developments, 1930–39," *The English Journal* 28, no. 5 (May 1939): 333–42.

Chapter 3. Keeping Politics at Bay

1. The appointment as director of the German Theater of John E. Bonn, former head in the late 1920s of the workers' theater Prolet-Bühne, offers tangible evidence of the intellectual and sociopolitical continuity from militant to government-sponsored foreign language companies.

2. George Crandall, manager of the Concert Unit of the Federal Music Project in New York, organized the activities of the following ensembles: Federal Music Project Chamber Orchestra, Federal Symphony Orchestra of New York, Festival Symphony Orchestra, Greenwich Concert Orchestra, WNYC Concert Orchestra, Opera Orchestra, New York State Symphonic Band, Manhattan Concert Band, Hudson Concert Band, Waverly Brass Band, Knickerbocker Dance Orchestra, Colonial Dance Orchestra, Capitol Dance Orchestra, Gotham Dance Orchestra, Amsterdam String Ensemble, Riverside Salon Ensemble, Gramercy Chamber Trio, Lenox Chamber Trio, Morningside Trio, Hospital Unit No. 1, Hospital Unit No. 2, Hospital Unit No. 3.

3. Michael Denning, *The Cultural Front: The Laboring of American Culture in the Twentieth Century* (New York: Verso, 1996), 59–60.

4. The program included String Quartet, "Song of Occupation," Piano Trio, and American Overture: "Johnny Comes Marching Home." Curiously, going against the custom of the Forum, all pieces but the Piano Trio were prerecorded.

5. The Forums presented, among others, compositions of students of the Eastman School of Music, Columbia University, New York University, the Juilliard School, and Vassar College.

6. Melissa de Graaf, *The New York Composers' Forum Concerts, 1935–1940* (Rochester: University of Rochester Press, 2013).

7. Quoted in Heidi Waleson, "Composers' Forum at 50," *High Fidelity-Musical America Edition* 36, no. 4 (April 1986): 14.

194 • *Notes to Chapter 3*

8. Ashley Pettis (1892–1970), before joining the communist editorial boards and becoming a sought-after left-wing orator, started his career as composer and pianist. From 1925 to 1931, he was a faculty member at the Eastman School of Music in Rochester, New York. He eventually turned away from left-wing endeavors, embraced Catholicism, and became a priest. Still, he kept alive his interest in music and published *Music: Now and Then. Music in Our Time. Our Musical Heritage from the Bible* (New York: Coleman-Ross Company, 1955), in which he associated the ephemeral nature of contemporary music with lack of faith.

9. Ashley Pettis, "Musical Flashlights from Moscow," *Modern Music* 10, no. 1 (November-December 1932): 49–52.

10. Ashley Pettis, "Music," *New Masses* 11, no. 4 (March 6, 1934): 30.

11. The Civil Works Administration (CWA), created in the fall of 1933 and disbanded the following spring, was the first public employment experiment of the New Deal. At its peak in January 1934, CWA employed approximately 4 million workers. The program initiated many projects that later were absorbed by the Works Progress Administration (WPA, 1935 to 1941).

12. Pettis, "Music."

13. Ashley Pettis, Opening address given on October 30, 1935, before the first concert of the New York City Composers Forum featuring music by Roy Harris. NA II, College Park, MD, Record 69—Records of the Work Projects Administration, Records Pertaining to the Composers' Forum Laboratory 1935–40, General, Fl-Y, E 833, Box 1, Folder "New York City Composers Forum 1935."

14. Ashley Pettis, "Marching with a Song," *New Masses* (May 1, 1934): 30.

15. Pettis, Opening address.

16. Daniel Gregory Mason, letter to Ashley Pettis, September 17, 1935. NARA II, College Park, MD, Record 69—Records of the Work Projects Administration, Central Files: State 1935–1944, New York City 651.311 June 1935-January 1936, Box 2083, Folder June-September 1935.

17. Ibid.

18. Ashley Pettis, letter to Daniel Gregory Mason, September 20, 1935. NARA II, Record 69—Records of the Work Projects Administration, Central Files: State 1935–1944, New York City 651.311 June 1935-January 1936, Box 2083, Folder June-September 1935.

19. Ashley Pettis, letter to Daniel Gregory Mason.

20. Daniel Gregory Mason, letter to Ashley Pettis, September 22, 1935. NARA II, Record 69—Records of the Work Projects Administration, Central Files: State 1935–1944, New York City 651.311 June 1935-January 1936, Box 2083, Folder June-September 1935.

21. Chalmers Clifton to Nikolai Sokoloff, NARA II, Record 69—Records of the Work Projects Administration, Central Files: State 1935–1944, New York City 651.311 June 1935-January 1936, Box 2083, Folder 2/2 October 1935.

22. Nikolai Sokoloff to Ashley Pettis, December 24, 1935, NARA II, Record 69—Records of the Work Projects Administration, Central Files: State 1935–1944, New York City 651.311 June 1935-January 1936, Box 2083, Folder 1/2 November 16–30, 1935.

Notes to Chapter 3 • 195

23. Letter from Ernst Bacon to Bruno David Ussher, September 17, 1936, Bacon Papers, Box 1, Special Collection Stanford University, cited in Leta Miller, *Music and Politics in San Francisco from the 1906 Quake to the Second World War* (University of California Press, 2011), 212.

24. Otto Mueller (1837–1920), American composer. George Frederick Boyle (1886–1948) born in Sydney, Australia, came to the United States in 1910 where he remained active as composer until his death.

25. American composer Thomas Calrow Carver, originally from Great Britain, was active in Milwaukee, Wisconsin in the 1910s-20s. American composer and music teacher Carl Eppert (1882–1962) founded the Milwaukee Civic Symphony Orchestra and composed works for band and orchestra and operas.

26. Harry Hewes to Ashley Pettis, April 20, 1936. NARA II, Record 69—Records of the Work Projects Administration, Central Files: State 1935–1944, New York City 651.311 February-September 1936, Box 2084, Folder March 1936.

27. Waleson, "Composers' Forum at 50," 14.

28. Harry Hewes to Ashley Pettis, April 14, 1936. NARA II, Record 69—Records of the Work Projects Administration, Central Files: State 1935–1944, New York City 651.311 February-September 1936, Box 2084, Folder March 1936.

29. Edwin Gerschefski (1909–92), composer, pianist, and teacher, was born in Meriden, Connecticut. He completed his musical education at Yale University (1926–31), at the Tobias Matthay Pianoforte School in London (1931–33), and with pianist Artur Schnabel and theorist Joseph Schillinger.

30. Transcripts of the concert with music by Edwin Gershefski held on April 29, 1936. NARA II, Record 69—Records of the Work Projects Administration, Records Pertaining to the Composers' Forum Laboratory 1935–40, General, Fl-Y, E 833, Box 2, Folder "New York City Transcripts 1935–1936."

31. Transcripts of the concert with music by Aurelio Giorni held on May 13, 1936. NARA II, Record 69—Records of the Work Projects Administration, Records Pertaining to the Composers' Forum Laboratory 1935–40, General, Fl-Y, E 833, Box 2, Folder "New York City Transcripts 1935–1936." Aurelio Giorni (1895–1938) was an American composer of Italian birth who came to the United States in 1914.

32. Melissa de Graaf, "'Never Call Us Lady Composers': Gendered Receptions in the New York Composers' Forum, 1935–40," *American Music* 26, no. 3 (Fall 2008).

33. For details on the two Forum's concerts with music of Johanna Beyer, see Amy Beal, *Johanna Beyer* (University of Illinois Press, 2015), 21–35.

34. Transcripts of the concert with music by Johanna M. Beyer held on May 20, 1936. NARA II, Record 69—Records of the Work Projects Administration, Records Pertaining to the Composers' Forum Laboratory 1935–40, General, Fl-Y, E 833, Box 2, Folder "New York City Transcripts 1935–1936."

35. Deems Taylor, "Music," in *Civilization in the United States: An Inquiry by Thirty Americans*, ed. Harold E. Stearns (Harcourt, Brace and Co., 1922).

36. Ellie Hisama, *Gendering Musical Modernism* (Cambridge University Press, 2001).

196 · *Notes to Chapter 3*

37. Lazare Saminsky, *Music of Our Days—Essentials and Prophecies* (New York: Thomas Y. Crowell Co, 1932); cited in Pettis, opening remark to the first concert of the second series of the Composers' Forum Laboratory on October 14, 1936. NARA II, Record 69—Records of the Work Projects Administration, Records Pertaining to the Composers' Forum Laboratory 1935–40, General, Fl-Y, E 833, Box 2, Folder "New York City Transcripts 1935–1936." The Gotham Symphony Orchestra, conducted by Saminsky himself, opened the second season in front of a filled to capacity auditorium at the WPA Federal Music Project Headquarters on 110 West 48th Street (more than 200 persons having to be turned away). Lazare Saminsky (1882–1959) studied with Nikolai Rimsky-Korsakov and Anatoly Ljadov at the Conservatory in St. Petersburg, where, in 1908, he was co-founder of the St. Petersburg Society for Jewish Folk Music. In 1920, Saminsky immigrated to New York City where he was co-founder and chairman of the American League of Composers and had a career as a conductor.

38. Nikolai Sokoloff, opening speech to the first concert of the second series of the Composers' Forum Laboratory on October 14, 1936; NARA II, Record 69—Records of the Work Projects Administration, Records Pertaining to the Composers' Forum Laboratory 1935–40, General, Fl-Y, E 833, Box 2, Folder "New York City Transcripts 1935–1936."

39. Transcripts of the concert with music by Aurelio Giorni held on May 13, 1936. NARA II, Record 69—Records of the Work Projects Administration, Records Pertaining to the Composers' Forum Laboratory 1935–40, General, Fl-Y, E 833, Box 2, Folder "New York City Transcripts 1935–1936."

40. Ibid.

41. Transcripts of the concert with music of William Schuman held on October 21, 1936. NARA II, Record 69—Records of the Work Projects Administration, Records Pertaining to the Composers' Forum Laboratory 1935–40, General, Fl-Y, E 833, Box 2, Folder "New York City Transcripts 1935–1936."

42. Transcripts of the concert with music by Werner Josten held on October 23, 1936. NARA II, Record 69—Records of the Work Projects Administration, Records Pertaining to the Composers' Forum Laboratory 1935–40, General, Fl-Y, E 833, Box 2, Folder "New York City Transcripts 1935–1936." Werner Josten (1885–1963), a German-born composer, trained in Munich with Rudolf Siegel (1878–1948) and Engelbert Humperdinck (1854–1921) and then immigrated to the United States in 1920 or 1921, where he became a naturalized citizen and taught composition and fugue at Smith College in Northampton, Massachusetts from 1923 to 1949. Interested in the revival of ancient opera, in 1929 he directed the first staged performance of Monteverdi's *Orfeo* in the United States. His most famous composition, the symphonic poem *Jungle* (1928), takes inspiration from African music.

43. Transcripts of the concert with music by Frederick Woltman and Norman Cazden held on January 27, 1937. NARA II, Record 69—Records of the Work Projects Administration, Records Pertaining to the Composers' Forum Laboratory 1935–40,

Notes to Chapter 3 · 197

General, Fl-Y, E 833, Box 2, Folder "New York City Transcripts 1937." Frederick Woltman, born in 1908, won a Pulitzer Prize in 1937 and an Academy Award for Music in 1941.

44. Transcripts of the concert with music by Lazare Saminsky and Charles Haubiel held on October 26, 1938. NARA II, Record 69-Records of the Work Projects Administration, Records Pertaining to the Composers' Forum Laboratory 1935–40, General, Fl-Y, E 833, Box 3, Folder "New York City Composers Forum—Transcripts 1938."

45. Transcripts of the concert with music by Roger Sessions held on November 29, 1939. NARA II, Record 69—Records of the Work Projects Administration, Records Pertaining to the Composers' Forum Laboratory 1935–40, General, Fl-Y, E 833, Box 3, Folder "New York City Composers Forum—Transcripts 1939."

46. Transcripts of the concert with music by Arthur Cohn held on May 26, 1937. NARA II, Record 69—Records of the Work Projects Administration, Records Pertaining to the Composers' Forum Laboratory 1935–40, General, Fl-Y, E 833, Box 4, Folder "American."

47. Charles Hiroshi Garrett, *Struggling to Define a Nation: American Music and the Twentieth Century* (Berkeley, CA: University of California Press, 2008), 5.

48. Transcripts of the concert with music by Lazare Saminsky and Charles Haubiel held on October 26, 1938. NARA II, Record 69—Records of the Work Projects Administration, Records Pertaining to the Composers' Forum Laboratory 1935–40, General, Fl-Y, E 833, Box 3, Folder "New York City Composers Forum—Transcripts 1938."

49. Leonard Bernstein, "Harvard Bachelor's Thesis," in *Findings* (New York: Simon & Schuster, 1982), 36–99.

50. Alfred "Alf" Mossman Landon (1887–1987) was a Republican who served as the twenty-sixth governor of Kansas from 1933 to 1937. In the 1936 presidential election, Landon was the GOP's nominee for president of the United States, whom Franklin D. Roosevelt eventually defeated in a landslide.

51. Transcripts of the concert with music by Werner Josten held on October 23, 1936. NARA II, Record 69—Records of the Work Projects Administration, Records Pertaining to the Composers' Forum Laboratory 1935–40, General, Fl-Y, E 833, Box 2, Folder "New York City Transcripts 1935–1936."

52. Transcripts of the concert with music by Rosalie Housman and Boris Levenson held on November 18, 1936. NARA II, Record 69—Records of the Work Projects Administration, Records Pertaining to the Composers' Forum Laboratory 1935–40, General, Fl-Y, E 833, Box 2, Folder "New York City Transcripts 1935–1936." Rosalie Housman (1890–1949) was a lecturer and composer active in Washington, Philadelphia, and New York City. Interested in English composers, that is, Vaughan Williams and E. Fellows, she studied composition with Ernest Bloch, among others. Boris Levenson (1884–1947) was a composer and conductor born in Russia, where he studied with Nikolai Rimsky-Korsakov, and became a naturalized American citizen in 1927.

53. Transcripts of the concert with music by Roy Harris held on October 6, 1937. NARA II, Record 69—Records of the Work Projects Administration, Records Pertaining to the

198 · *Notes to Chapter 3*

Composers' Forum Laboratory 1935–40, General, Fl-Y, E 833, Box 3, Folder "New York City Composers Forum—Transcripts October-December 1937."

54. Transcripts of the concert with music by Aaron Copland held on February 24, 1937. NARA II, Record 69—Records of the Work Projects Administration, Records Pertaining to the Composers' Forum Laboratory 1935–40, General, Fl-Y, E 833, Box 4, Folder "American-Forum Study."

55. *Statements for Orchestra* consists of six short movements titled *"Military," "Cryptic," "Dogmatic," "Subjective," "Jingo,"* and *"Prophetic"*; these titles, as the composer stated, should have helped the listener understand the political meaning of the piece. On this composition, see Elizabeth Crist Bergman, *Music for the Common Man: Aaron Copland During the Depression and War* (New York: Oxford University Press, 2005), 34–42.

56. Copland had already started in 1933—see his article "The Composer in America 1923–33," *Modern Music* 10 no. 2 (1933): 87–92—to word his desire to experiment with modes of expression best suited to address contemporary audiences, and indeed his excursions in proletarian music can be seen as one of the tentative directions he explored toward that goal. Interestingly, he started working on *El Salón México* already in 1932, which suggests that he was pursuing different directions simultaneously.

57. Transcripts of the concert with music by Quinto Maganini held on November 3, 1937. NARA II, Record 69—Records of the Work Projects Administration, Records Pertaining to the Composers' Forum Laboratory 1935–40, General, Fl-Y, E 833, Box 3, Folder "New York City Composers Forum—Transcripts October-December 1937." Quinto Maganini (1897–1974) started his musical career as a flutist with the San Francisco Orchestra. In 1919, he moved to New York City and became a member of the New York Philharmonic Orchestra until 1928, when he devoted himself to composing and conducting. He studied at Fontainebleau with Nadia Boulanger in 1926–27 and won a Pulitzer traveling scholarship in 1927. From 1940 to 1967, Maganini was conductor and music director of the Norwalk Symphony Orchestra.

58. Transcripts of the concert with music by Howard Hanson held on March 17, 1937. NARA II, Record 69—Records of the Work Projects Administration, Records Pertaining to the Composers' Forum Laboratory 1935–40, General, Fl-Y, E 833, Box 4, Folder "American-Forum Study."

59. Ibid.

60. The program also included *North-Pole Suite* played by the composer at the piano, and *Lento* from the String Quartet performed by the Federal String Quartet.

61. Transcripts of the concert with music by Elie Siegmeister and Herbert Inch held on October 20, 1937. NARA II, Record 69—Records of the Work Projects Administration, Records Pertaining to the Composers' Forum Laboratory 1935–40, General, Fl-Y, E 833, Box 4, Folder "New York City Composers Forum—Transcripts October-December 1937."

62. Ibid.

Notes to Chapters 3 and 4 · 199

63. The forum presented the following compositions: Sonata for Piano, Op. 1; Klavierstücke, Op. 8, and Four Cantatas for Two Clarinets, Viola, Cello, and Voice.

64. Marc Blitzstein, "Music—Music Manifesto," *New Masses* 19, no. 13 (June 23, 1936): 18.

65. Transcripts of the concert with music by Hanns Eisler on April 6, 1938. NARA II, Record 69—Records of the Work Projects Administration, Records Pertaining to the Composers' Forum Laboratory 1935–40, General, Fl-Y, E 833, Box 4, Folder "Methods—Forum Study."

66. Ibid.

67. *Marc Blitzstein's Papers*, State Historical Society, Madison, Wisconsin, Archive Division (from now on SHSW), Box 3, Folder 4. Text attached to a copy of the letter prepared by Blitzstein for Lee Pattison.

68. Ibid.

69. Letter from Colin McPhee to Marc Blitzstein, no date. SHSW, Box 3, Folder 4. Colin McPhee (1900–1964), Canadian composer and musicologist, is known for his ethnomusicological study of Balinese music, a tradition that has influenced his own music.

70. Letter from Virgil Thomson to Marc Blitzstein, February 20, 1936. SHSW, Box 3, Folder 4.

71. De Graaf, *The New York Composers' Forum Concerts*, 13–15.

72. Olin Downes, "Laboratory for Native Composers," *New York Times* (January 10, 1937): 7.

73. Ibid.

74. Letter from Roy Harris to Ashley Pettis, October 6, 1937. NARA II, Record 69—Records of the Work Projects Administration, Records Pertaining to the Composers' Forum Laboratory 1935–40, General, Fl-Y, E 833, Box 2, Folder "Special Report."

75. Elliott Carter, "Coolidge Crusade; WPA; New York Season." *Modern Music* 16, no. 1 (November/December 1938): 33–38.

76. Ashley Pettis, "The WPA and the American Composer," *The Musical Quarterly*, vol. 26, no. 1 (January 1940): 107–8.

77. Carter, "Coolidge Crusade."

Chapter 4. The Living Newspaper Unit and Innovative Musical Approaches

1. Stuart Cosgrove, *The Living Newspaper: History, Production, and Form* (Hull: University of Hull Press, 1982), 7.

2. Hallie Flanagan, *Arena: The History of the Federal Theatre* (New York: Benjamin Blom, 1965), 221.

3. Sally Bick, "Music at the New School for Social Research," *Journal of the American Musicological Society* 66, no. 1 (Spring 2013), 151. The terms "primitive" and "oriental" are today considered problematic as they perpetuate negative stereotypes about indigenous

200 · Notes to Chapter 4

and East Asian peoples; they are only used here because they are part of the titles of Cowell's courses and lectures.

4. On Cowell and his interest in non-Western music, see Bick, "Music at the New School," in particular pages 163–73.

5. Leta E. Miller, "Henry Cowell and John Cage: Intersections and Influences, 1933–1941," *Journal of the American Musicological Society* 59, no. 1 (Spring 2006): 53–54.

6. Miller, "Henry Cowell and John Cage," 54.

7. On this topic, see Miller, "Henry Cowell and John Cage"; David Nicholls, "Henry Cowell's *United Quartet*," *American Music* 13 (1995): 195–217, and his "Cage and the Ultramodernists," *American Music* 28 (2010): 492–500.

8. Miller, "Henry Cowell and John Cage," 58.

9. Haley Jo Nutt, "The Collegiate Percussion Ensemble: Institutional and Gendered Practices in American Academy," PhD diss., Florida State University, 2020, 18–19.

10. *Ostinato Pianissimo* premiered on February 7, 1943 as part of a percussion concert at the Museum of Modern Art in New York sponsored by the League of Composers.

11. Nicholls, "Henry Cowell's *United Quartet*," 214–15.

12. Hallie Flanagan, *Arena*, 183.

13. Ibid., 19–20.

14. Hallie Flanagan, "A Theatre is Born," *Theatre Arts Monthly* 15 (1931): 908.

15. NARA II, Record 69—Records of the Work Projects Administration—Records of the Federal Theater Project. Living newspaper research materials ca. 1936–39, Box 552, Folder: Ethiopia—No. 1.

16. Arthur Arent, "*Ethiopia*: The First Living Newspaper," with an introduction by Dan Isaac, *Educational Theatre Journal* 20, no. 1, 20th-Century American Theatre Issue (March 1968): 19.

17. Arent, "*Ethiopia*," 22.

18. Flanagan, *Arena*, 65.

19. Kristen Turner, "Back to Africa: Images of the Continent in Early Black Musical Theater." Paper presented on November 1, 2018 at the American Musicological Society Annual Meeting, San Antonio, Texas.

20. For instance, in *In Dahomey* (1903), William and Walker used Africa only as a background setting for their duo numbers reminiscent of ragtime and Tin Pan Alley hits, which had little to do with African culture and music.

21. NARA II, Record 69—Records of the Work Projects Administration—Records of the Federal Theater Project. Living newspaper research materials ca. 1936–39, Box 552, Folder: Ethiopia—No. 1.

22. Memorandum from Jacob Baker to Hallie Flanagan on January 18, 1936. NARA II, Record 69—Records of the Work Projects Administration—Records of the Federal Theater Project. Living newspaper research materials ca. 1936–39, Box 537, Folder: Interdep—Hallie Flanagan.

23. Jacob Baker to Hallie Flanagan on January 18, 1936.

Notes to Chapter 4 • 201

24. Memorandum from Jacob Baker to Hallie Flanagan on January 23, 1936. NARA II, Record 69—Records of the Work Projects Administration—Records of the Federal Theater Project. Living newspaper research materials ca. 1936–39, Box 537, Folder: Interdep—Hallie Flanagan.

25. This and following excerpts from "Statement by Elmer Rice, January 24, 1936, Former Regional Director of the Federal Theatre." NARA II, Record 69—Records of the Work Projects Administration—Records of the Federal Theater Project. Living newspaper research materials ca. 1936–39, Box 537, Folder: Interdep—Hallie Flanagan.

26. Ibid.

27. Flanagan, *Arena*, 66–67.

28. "Statement of Morris Watson, Managing Producer of the Living Newspaper." NARA II, Record 69—Records of the Work Projects Administration—Records of the Federal Theater Project. Living newspaper research materials ca. 1936–39, Box 537, Folder: Interdep—Hallie Flanagan.

29. In his inaugural address on January 20, 1937, Roosevelt claimed that the greatest challenge to American democracy was that one-third of the nation still remained "ill-housed, ill-clad, ill-nourished." Franklin D. Roosevelt, "Inaugural Address, January 20, 1937," in *The Public Papers and Addresses of Franklin D. Roosevelt*, 1937 Volume (New York City: MacMillan Company, 1941), 1.

30. Cosgrove, *The Living Newspaper*, 121.

31. Burns Mantle, "The People's Theatre Grows Stronger," *New York Daily News* (May 24, 1936).

32. Ilka Saal, *New Deal Theater: The Vernacular Tradition in American Political Theater* (New York: Palgrave MacMillan, 2007), 127–28.

33. Arthur Arent, "The Technique of the Living Newspaper," *Theatre Arts Monthly* 22, no. 11 (November 1938): 820–25.

34. Arent, "Technique," 821–22.

35. On this topic, see Chapter 2.

36. Saal, *New Deal Theater*, 129.

37. Ibid., 130.

38. Interdepartmental Memorandum from Ethel Aaron to Miss Powell on June 29, 1936. NARA II, Record 69—Records of the Work Projects Administration—Records of the Federal Theater Project. Living newspaper research materials ca. 1936–39, Box 555, Folder "Injunction Granted 3."

39. The original scripts of *Triple A Plowed Under*, *Injunction Granted*, and *One-Third of a Nation* are available online at George Mason University, Mason Archival Repository Service, Federal Theater Project Materials Collection, http://digilib.gmu.edu:8080/dspace/handle/1920/3478.

40. Anthony Tommasini, *Virgil Thomson: Composer on the Aisle* (New York: W. W. Norton, 1998). Tommasini also mentions that Houseman recruited a troupe of authentic

202 • *Notes to Chapter 4*

African drummers to perform this music. One wonders if they could have been members of the same troupe who should have played in *Ethiopia*.

41. Stuart Cosgrove, Introduction to *Liberty Deferred and Other Living Newspapers of the 1930s*, Lorraine Brown, ed. (Fairfax, VA: George Mason University Press, 1989), xiii.

42. Virgil Thomson, *Virgil Thomson* (New York: Alfred A. Knopf, 1966), 264.

43. For some historical recordings of vaudeville sketches employing sound effects, see Richard T. Martin and Meagan T. Hennessey, *Before Radio: Comedy, Drama, and Sound Sketches, 1897–1923* (Bloomington, IN: Archeophone, 2000). Some of the sketches are also available online from the Library of Congress: *The American Variety Stage, 1870–1920: American Variety Stage Audio Sampler*, http://rs6.loc.gov/ammem/vshtml/vssnde.html (accessed January 21, 2012).

44. All musical examples of Virgil Thomson's *Injunction Granted* are reproductions of the manuscript score housed at the NARA II, Record 69—Records of the Work Projects Administration—Records of the Federal Theater Project, Living newspaper research materials ca. 1936–39, Box 555, Folder "Injunction Granted 3."

45. Norman Lloyd and Francine Parker, *Stages of Life in Theatre, Film, and Television* (New York: Proscenium Publishers Inc., 1990), 35. Norman Lloyd (1914–2021)—not to be confused with composer Norman Lloyd (1909–80)—was an actor, producer, and director who worked for the theater, radio, television, and film under some of the most notable directors, such as Alfred Hitchcock and Charlie Chaplin.

46. Interdepartmental Memorandum from Ethel Aaron to Miss Powell.

47. Lloyd and Parker, *Stages of Life in Theatre, Film, and Television*, 34–35.

48. Frederick Jacobi, "In the Theatre. WPA Shows with Music," *Modern Music* 14, no. 1 (November-December 1936): 42–44.

49. The instrumentation of *Ionisation* consists of three bass drums (medium, large, very large), two tenor drums, two snare drums, tarole (a kind of piccolo snare drum), two bongos, tambourine, field drum, crash cymbal, suspended cymbals, three tam-tams, gong, two anvils, two triangles, sleigh bells, cowbell, chimes, celesta, piano, three temple blocks, claves, maracas, castanets, whip, güiro, high and low sirens, and a lion's roar.

50. Colin Gardner, *Joseph Losey* (Manchester, UK—New York: Manchester University Press, 2004), 2.

Joseph Losey (1909–84) studied medicine before turning his career to the stage. In 1935, after an eight-month trip to the USSR and Europe, where he supposedly met and studied with Bertolt Brecht, he came back to the United States and started his career as director of the Living Newspaper. His theater work culminated in 1947 with the staging of Brecht's *Galileo* in Los Angeles and New York. Thereafter, he devoted himself to the film industry, completing his first movie, *The Boy with Green Hair*, in 1948. Losey was blacklisted for his communist sympathies in 1952 and fled to Britain and France, where he had a remarkable career as film director until his death.

51. Mordecai Gorelik, review of *The Federal Theatre, 1935–1939: Plays, Relief, and Politics* by Jane Dehart Matthews, *The American Historical Review* 74, no. 1 (October 1968): 327–28.

Notes to Chapters 4 and 5 • 203

52. For a discussion on avant-garde music and theater, including political implications, see Robert Adlington, "Music Theatre Since the 1960s" in *The Cambridge Companion to Twentieth-Century Opera*, ed. by Mervyn Cooke. (NY: Cambridge University Press, 2005), 225–43.

Chapter 5. A Leftist Myth

1. Roland Barthes, *Mythologies*, selected and translated from the French by Annette Lavers (New York: Noonday Press, 25th ed., 1991).

2. Charles Glenn, July 5, 1941, from an unidentified clipping in the Marc Blitzstein file, Harvard University Theater Collection. Cited in John D. Shout, "The Musical Theater of Marc Blitzstein," *American Music* vol. 3, no. 4 (Winter 1985): 414.

3. David Z. Kushner, "Blitzstein, Marc," in *Grove Music Online. Oxford Music Online* (accessed February 6, 2011).

4. Blitzstein's original score and libretto for *The Condemned* are in the Archive Division of the Wisconsin Historical Society in Madison.

5. Blitzstein returned to the topic in the unfinished opera *Sacco and Vanzetti*. On this topic, see Maria Cristina Fava, "L'ombra del maccartismo contro *Sacco e Vanzetti* di Blitzstein," *Musica/Realtà* 25, no. 74 (July 2004): 101–17.

6. Charles Friedman (1902–84), producer, director, author, and songwriter, was active in the Workers' Theater Movement in the 1930s. He then moved to a show-business career, directing and producing films with Sam Goldwyn, Arthur Freed, and Darryl Zanuck. He directed on Broadway, among other plays, *Pins and Needles*, *Sing Out the News*, *Carmen Jones*, and *Street Scene*.

7. In the fall of 1935, Blitzstein decided to further his ideological education by taking courses in Marxism at the Workers' School. Simultaneously, he taught a course at the Downtown Music School titled "Social Aspects of Music."

8. For details on the activities of the Workers' Theater Movement and Blitzstein's contribution to the leftist musical revue, see Chapter 2.

9. On the Industrial Workers of the World and their use of songs and drama, see Chapters 1 and 2.

10. On the New Playwrights Theatre, see Chapter 2.

11. *Marc Blitzstein Papers*, State Historical Society, Madison, Wisconsin, Archive Division, Box 17, Folder 2, "Lyrics."

12. For a detailed textual and musical analysis of "People" and of the various revisions that transformed it into the song "Joe Worker" of *The Cradle Will Rock*, see Carol J. Oja, "Marc Blitzstein's *The Cradle Will Rock* and Mass-Song Style of the 1930s," *The Musical Quarterly* 73, no. 4 (1989): 445–75.

13. Baritone Mordecai Baumann premiered the song on May 16, 1936, with choreography by Elsa Findley as part of a radical and anti-Nazi dance and drama workshop held at the Young Mens Hebrew Association in New York.

14. Marc Blitzstein, *The Cradle Will Rock* (New York: Random House, 1938), 97–98.

204 · *Notes to Chapter 5*

15. Blitzstein first performed "Nickel Under the Foot" in February 1936, at a Composers' Collective's concert presented by the New Theatre League.

16. Eva Goldbeck's article on epic theater published in *New Masses* accounts as the first recognition in the United States of Brecht's revolutionary epic theater technique. See Eva Goldbeck, "The Theater Principles of 'Educational' Theater," *New Masses* 18, no. 1 (December 31, 1935): 27–28.

17. Minna Lederman reported on this meeting and its unsuccessful outcome, calling it the "affaire Brecht," in *The Life and Death of a Small Magazine (Modern Music: 1924–1946)* (Brooklyn, NY: Institute for Studies in American Music, 1983), 66–75. She also mentioned the meeting in her article "Memories of Marc Blitzstein, Music's Angry Man," *Show: Magazine of the Arts* 4, no. 6 (June 1964): 21.

18. Lederman, "Memories of Marc Blitzstein," 21.

19. For an intriguing critique of *Cradle* as more of a middle-class allegory than a pro-labor work, see Ilka Saal, *New Deal Theater: The Vernacular Tradition in American Political Theater* (New York: Palgrave MacMillan, 2007), 111–23.

20. Commissioned by Grace Spofford, director of the Henry Street Settlement School of Music of New York, Copland's *The Second Hurricane* is a play opera for high school students on a libretto by Edwin Denby. It premiered on April 21, 1937, with Orson Welles, director and Lehman Engel, conductor.

21. Department of Information, WPA-FTP New York City, "Exclusive to Brooklyn Eagle," June 14, 1937. Box 5, Folder 21, Orson Welles Manuscripts, Manuscript Department, Lilly Library, Indiana University, Bloomington, Indiana. The press release was issued for the series of preview performances of the FTP's originally planned production of the play. Most likely, Blitzstein was here alluding to the series of animated short subjects called *Silly Symphonies* that Walt Disney produced from 1929 to 1939. The original principle behind the basis of the cartoons was musical novelty, and Carl Stalling composed the musical scores for many of them. The series culminated in the famous 1940 film *Fantasia* (which, however, did not use the actual label "silly symphonies").

22. Unionization, especially after the establishment of the Committee for Industrial Organization in November 1935, became a heated issue: unions were invoked by the working class as a means to increase its contractual power, but at the same time the ruling class feared them, because they could profoundly affect economic interests connected with the control of the worldwide market. For a historical view on the Committee for Industrial Organization, see John Raymond Walsh "The Background of a Crisis," in *C.I.O.: Industrial Unionism in Action* (New York: W. W. Norton & Company, 1937), 16–47.

23. For a thorough and detailed description of the events before, during, and after the Venice Theatre premiere, see Howard Pollack, *Marc Blitzstein: His Life, His Work, His World*, chap. 10 (Oxford University Press, 2012), 171–94.

24. Marc Blitzstein, "Out of the Cradle," *Opera News* 24, no. 15 (February 13, 1960): 11.

Notes to Chapter 5 • 205

25. The episode generated many controversies, and Blitzstein attempted to rally popular support, as well as his own spirits, by contributing "FTP Plowed Under"—a sketch centered on the plight of the abandoned *Cradle*—to the musical revue *Pins and Needles*. A performance of *Cradle* with the original orchestration would not occur until the production conducted by Leonard Bernstein on November 24, 1947 at the City Center in New York.

26. Orson Welles and John Houseman founded the Mercury Theatre company in New York City in 1937. A year later, the Mercury Theatre progressed into its best-known period as The Mercury Theatre on the Air, a radio series that included one of the most notable and infamous radio broadcasts of all time, "The War of the Worlds," broadcast on October 30, 1938.

27. The 48th Street Theatre, named Windsor Theatre in 1937, was built in 1912 and demolished in 1955; it had approximately 970 seats. The Venice Theatre, renamed New Century Theatre in 1944, opened in 1923, and was demolished in 1962; it had approximately 1,700 seats.

28. Brooks Atkinson, "The Play: Marc Blitzstein's "The Cradle Will Rock" Officially Opens at the Mercury Theatre," *New York Times* (December 6, 1937): 19.

29. John Mason Brown, "Two on the Aisle: An Exciting Week-End for Propagandist Drama," *New York Post* (December 3, 1937): 14.

30. Richard Watts, "The Theatre: Cartoon with Music," *Herald Tribune* (December 6, 1937): 10.

31. Richard Watts, "The Approach of Christmas: The Theater: Drama on the Left," *Herald Tribune* (December 19, 1937).

32. Eric Englander, "*Cradle* Rocks at Mercury," *Daily Worker* (December 7, 1937).

33. Lederman, "Memories of Marc Blitzstein," 21.

34. Mary McCarthy, "Theater Chronicle—Class Angles and Classless Curves," *Partisan Review* (April 1938): 52–56.

35. John Gassner, "The Theatre—Progress on Broadway," *One Act Play Magazine* (December 1937): 742–45.

36. Philipp Barr, "Opera in the Vernacular, Marc Blitzstein's *The Cradle Will Rock*," *Magazine of Art* 32 (June 1939): 356–57 and 382–83. The *Magazine of Art* was published by the American Federation of Arts (Washington, DC) from 1937 to 1953.

37. George Jean Nathan, "Theater," *Scribner's Magazine* 53 (March 1938): 70–72.

38. Marc Blitzstein, "Lines on 'The Cradle,'" *New York Times* (January 2, 1938): 124.

39. Blitzstein, "Lines on 'The Cradle.'"

40. MacLeish's overstatement, cited in Eric Gordon, *Mark the Music, The Life and Work of Marc Blitzstein* (St. Martin's Press, 1989), 144, is also questionable in that the events at the Venice Theatre were quite different than a scenery-less production that occurs on the stage in a traditional manner. Archibald MacLeish (1892–1982) was an American poet and writer who during the 1930s became increasingly politically active and supported Orson Welles in his plea to the WPA officials to allow *Cradle* to proceed after the premiere at the Venice Theatre. Associated with the modernist

206 • *Notes to Chapter 5*

school of poetry, MacLeish received three Pulitzer Prizes for his work, and from 1939 to 1944 he served as Librarian of Congress.

41. Archibald MacLeish, Foreword to Marc Blitzstein, *The Cradle Will Rock. A Play in Music* (New York: Random House, 1938), 7–8.

42. The letter is published in its entirety in "Scenery or No Scenery—A Symposium," *Theatre Workshop* 2, no. 1 (April-June 1938): 7–8. Orson Welles's innovative reading of Shakespeare's *Julius Caesar* remains the longest-running Broadway production of this play at 157 performances. It opened at the Comedy Theater in the fall of 1937 and then transferred to the National Theater (later Nederlander Theater) on West 41st Street. The production also toured the United States in 1938.

43. "Scenery or No Scenery," 5. The New Theatre League, organized in 1935 in New York City as a federation of little theaters and amateur theatrical groups, produced plays that addressed the political issues of the late 1930s and early 1940s. The organization published the journal *Theatre Workshop* and ran the New Theatre School for actors, directors, playwrights, and stage managers. It ceased its activity in 1942.

44. On the attraction that non-illusionary theater exerted on modernist poets and composers around this period, see W. Anthony Sheppard, *Revealing Masks* (University of California Press, 2001).

45. "Scenery or No Scenery," 6.

46. Ibid., 13. Charles De Sheim worked as stage director and actor for the Federal Theater Project and was associated with the Chicago Workers' Theater. He directed, together with Larry Foreman, the first Midwest showing of Blitzstein's *The Cradle Will Rock* produced by the Chicago Repertory Group in 1938–39 (24 performances).

47. Howard Bay (1912–86) was an American scenic, lighting, and costume designer for stage, opera, and film. For Broadway, he designed, among others, sets and lighting for *Show Boat* (1946 revival), *The Music Man* (1957), and *The Little Foxes* (1967). He won the Tony Award for Best Scenic Design twice (*Toys in the Attics*, 1960 and *Man of La Mancha*, 1966).

48. "Scenery or No Scenery," this and all other quotations by Howard Bay, 9–10.

49. "Scenery or No Scenery," 13–16. John W. Gassner (1903–67) was a theater historian and critic. Yale University, where he served as Sterling Professor of Playwriting and Dramatic Literature, established the John W. Gassner Memorial Prize awarded to the best critical essay, article, or review by a student published in, or submitted to, *Theater* magazine. Interestingly, in his review of *Cradle* for *One Act Play Magazine* in December 1937, Gassner had praised the freshness of the dramatic unity of the play.

50. The Theatre Union produced *Stevedore* by Peters and Sklar, its most successful play, in 1934, and *Let Freedom Ring* by Albert Bein in 1936 (see Chapter 2 on the activities of the Theatre Union within the Workers' Theater Movement).

51. "Scenery or No Scenery," 16–17. Mordecai (Max) Gorelik (1899–1990) was a theatrical designer who also wrote, produced, and directed plays. He served as a research professor in theater at Southern Illinois University from 1960 to 1972 and taught at San Jose State College; the book *New Theaters for Old* (1940), which summarized a

century of modern drama and theater, counts as his most valuable contribution to the field.

52. Lee Strasberg (1901–82), actor, director, and acting teacher, co-founded the Group Theatre in 1931 with Harold Clurman and Cheryl Crawford. In 1951, he became director of the nonprofit Actors Studio in New York, and in 1969 he founded the Lee Strasberg Theatre and Film Institute, where he trained several generations of theatre and film's talents, among others Anne Bancroft, Dustin Hoffman, Marlon Brando, James Dean, Paul Newman, Al Pacino, Robert De Niro, and director Elia Kazan.

53. "Scenery or No Scenery," 19.

54. Ibid., 10–11.

55. Ibid., 11.

56. Ibid., 11–12.

57. Ibid.

58. Cited in Frederick Lumley, *New Trends in 20th Century Drama: A Survey Since Ibsen and Shaw* (New York: Oxford University Press, 1967), 333. Wilder's script, for which he received the Pulitzer Prize for Drama in 1938, tells the story of an average New England town in the early twentieth century as depicted through the everyday life of its citizens, and calls for little scenery, no set, and minimal props (chairs, tables, and ladders). He conceived *Our Town*, which premiered in New York on February 4, 1938, as a metatheatrical play where the stage manager interacts with the audience, thus breaking the fourth wall.

59. Barthes, *Mythologies*, 155–56.

60. Relevant productions of the *Cradle* that followed the Mercury Theatre's: Chicago Repertory Group, twenty-four performances with piano and no scenery, from October 25, 1938 to April 22, 1939; New Theatre of Philadelphia, nineteen performances with piano and no scenery, from November 18, 1938 to August 11, 1939; Boston, Sanders Theater, Harvard student performance, with piano (Leonard Bernstein) and no scenery, May 27 and June 20, 1939.

61. Bernstein conducted the first three, December 26–28, of the twenty-one scheduled performances with reduced orchestra, trained singers, and without sets; thereafter the concert version was conducted by Howard Shanet.

62. Marc Blitzstein, "Program Notes" to the New York City Opera production of *The Cradle Will Rock*, February 11–17, 1960.

63. Paul Henry Lang, "The Cradle Will Rock," *New York Herald Tribune* (February 12, 1960).

64. Olin Downes, "Blitzstein Work Proves Success: 'Cradle Will Rock,' Presented at City Center by Bernstein, Is Laden with Pathos," *New York Times* (November 25, 1947): 38.

65. Lederman, "Memories of Marc Blitzstein," 21.

66. Aaron Copland, "In Memory of Marc Blitzstein," *Perspective of New Music* 2, no. 2 (Spring-Summer 1964): 6.

67. Lehman Engel, *The American Musical Theater* (New York: Macmillan, 1967), 147.

208 · Notes to Chapter 5 and Epilogue

68. In its 2017 Summer Festival, Opera Saratoga produced a staged version of Blitzstein's play in music, *The Cradle Will Rock*, with the original orchestration under the musical direction of John Maucery and the choreography and stage direction of Lawrence Edelson.

69. Pollack, *Marc Blitzstein*, 169.

70. The movie starred Hank Azaria as Blitzstein, Rubén Blades as Diego Rivera, Joan Cusack as Hazel Huffman, John Cusack as Nelson Rockefeller, and in minor roles, Vanessa Redgrave, Susan Sarandon, and John Turturro. Data from http://www.imdb.com/title/tt0150216/ (accessed on October 6, 2021).

Epilogue

1. Elizabeth McCausland, "Save the Arts Projects," *The Nation* (July 17, 1937): 67. The article appeared the day after the tumultuous premiere of Blitzstein's *Cradle* and, even if it does not directly refer to the events that took place at the Venice Theatre, it describes the political situation that was at least partially responsible for the delay of its planned premiere and, more than anything else, shook all activities of the Arts Projects to their foundation.

2. Howard Hanson, speech given on April 16, 1969, for the dedication of the Fine Arts Center of the State University of New York at Albany. Howard Hanson Papers, Accession number 2005/3/25, Box 34, Folder 5, Ruth T. Watanabe Special Collections, Sibley Music Library, Rochester, New York. When the Depression ended so did federal support, and not until 1965, with the establishment of the National Endowment for the Arts, would the federal government again initiate a consistent program for support of the arts.

3. Michael Denning, *The Cultural Front: The Laboring of American Culture in the Twentieth Century* (New York: Verso, 1996), 473–74, n. 9. Denning's distinction is indebted to Alan Trachtenberg, who applied it in an essay on the major Popular Front photographer Paul Strand.

4. Aaron Copland, "Composer from Brooklyn," *Magazine of Art* (1939), reprinted in Copland, *Our New Music: Leading Composers in Europe and America* (New York: Whittlesey House, McGraw-Hill Book Company, 1941), 160.

5. Marc Blitzstein, "The Case for Modern Music," *New Masses* 20, no. 3 (July 21, 1936): 29.

6. Elizabeth Crist, *Music for the Common Man: Aaron Copland During the Depression and War* (New York: Oxford University Press, 2005), 6.

7. Carol Oja, "Composer with a Conscience: Elie Siegmeister in Profile," *American Music* 6, no. 2 (Summer 1988): 158–80.

8. On this topic, see Richard A. Reuss with JoAnne C. Reuss, *American Folk Music and Left-Wing Politics 1927–1957* (Lanham, MD: The Scarecrow Press, 2000).

9. Particularly significant, in this field, were the folk song collections edited by Charles Seeger and Ruth Crawford Seeger. See Judith Tick, "Ruth Crawford Seeger,

Charles Seeger, and *The Music of American Folk Songs,*" in Bell Yung and Helen Rees, eds., *Understanding Charles Seeger: Pioneer in Musicology* (University of Illinois Press, 1999), 109–29.

10. Marc Blitzstein, *I've Got the Tune* (Chappell & Co., 1938).

11. Marc Blitzstein, on *No for an Answer,* http://www.marcblitzstein.com/pages/music/intros/no_plot.htm (accessed October 6, 2021).

12. Marc Blitzstein, "On *No for an Answer,*" *New York Times* (January 5, 1941): X2.

13. Ralph Warner, "*No for an Answer*: A True People's Opera," *Daily Worker* (January 7, 1941): 7.

14. *Current Biography. Who's News and Why—1940,* ed. Maxine Block (New York, NY: The H. W. Wilson Company, 1940): 88–90.

15. Carol J. Oja, "Marc Blitzstein's *The Cradle Will Rock* and Mass-Song Style of the 1930s," *The Musical Quarterly* 73, no. 4 (1989): 473.

16. *Red Channels: The Report of Communist Influence in Radio and Television* (New York: American Business Consultants/Counterattack, 1950), 215.

17. On this topic, see Jennifer DeLapp-Birkett, "Aaron Copland and the Politics of Twelve-Tone Composition in the Early Cold War United States," *Journal of Musicological Research* 27, no. 1 (January/March 2008): 31–62.

Index

Aaron, Ethel, 135, 138
Adair, John, 151
Adomian, Lan, 14, 16, 18, 47, 49
Adorno, T. W., 91–92
Agricultural Adjustment Act, 85, 130
Alfasa, Joe, 92
Americana, 71
American Communist Party, 5, 20–21, 24, 69; Composers' Forum Laboratory and, 99–101; support for proletarian music, 48–50
American Congress for Democracy and Intellectual Freedom, 5
American Folk Music and Left-Wing Politics, 1927–1957, 10
American League Against War and Fascism, 2, 5
American musical identity, 1–2, 14, 106–8
American Musical Theater, The, 164
American Music Festival, 8
American Music League, 2
American Youth Congress, 5
Anderson, Maxwell, 9
Antheil, George, 17, 100
Arden, Eve, 75–76

Arena: The History of the Federal Theatre, 120
Arent, Arthur, 79, 85, 124, 133
Argonautica, 145
Artef Club, 58
art music, 37, 42, 172–73
arts, American: American identity and, 1–2, 14, 106–8; censorship of, 92–93, 129–30; cuts in federal support for, 170–71; emergence of left-leaning, 2–5, 171–72; New Deal relief for workers in, 5–7; Regionalist, 9; sociopolitical expression in, 3–4, 9; technological innovations used in, 4, 6–7; types of audiences for, 9–10. *See also* music
Association for Contemporary Music (ASM), 47
As Thousands Cheer, 71
Atkinson, J. Brooks, 61, 63–64, 152–53

Baker, Jacob, 123, 129
Balber, Amnon, 46
Barber, Philip, 68
Bardansky, Irving, 16
Barnes, Janet, 16, 19, 31, 33
Barr, Philip, 154–55

212 • *Index*

Barthes, Roland, 143
Basshe, EmJo, 61
Bauer, Marion, 19
Baumann, Mordecai, 37, 40, 95–96, 112
Bay, Howard, 158–59
Beach, Amy, 100
Beautiful Music All Around Us, The, 10
Before and After Africa, 127
Benton, Thomas, 1, 9
Berger, Arthur, 40, 48
Berlin, Irving, 71
Bernstein, Leonard, 108, 162, 175
Beyer, Johanna M., 103
Bick, Sally, 10, 122
Biggest Boob in the World, The, 60
Black Americans, 62–63, 127
Blake, Ben, 67, 93
Blitzstein, Marc, 2–4, 10, 19, 51, 72, 152,
   173, 175–76; agenda of the Composers'
   Collective written by, 37–38; Compos-
   ers' Forum Laboratory and, 108, 114–16;
   *The Cradle Will Rock (see Cradle Will Rock,
   The)*; death of, 163–64; on Hans Eisler,
   113–14; as member of the Composers'
   Collective, 14–16; *No for an Answer,* 173–
   74; *Parade,* 75–77, 147; on the people's
   audience, 39; *Pins and Needles,* 79, 85–87;
   proletarian music by, 17–18; on proletar-
   ian music style, 42–44; Special Sympo-
   sium meeting and, 40–41
Block, Maxine, 174–75
Bloom, Allan, 1
Bonn, John E., 58
Bori, Lucrezia, 5
Boston Herald, 75
Boston Post, 76
Boston Traveler, 74
Both Your Houses, 9
Boulanger, Nadia, 3
Boyle, George F., 101
Brecht, Bertolt, 85, 144, 149, 157, 159–60
Bromberg, Joe, 68
Brooks, Irving, 16
Broun, Heywood, 87
Brown, Harold, 16
Brown, John Mason, 153

Cage, John M., 123
Cahn, Sylvia, 92

Cain, 116
Can You Hear Their Voices?, 124
Carter, Elliott, 118
Carver, Thomas Calrow, 101
Cazden, Norman, 15, 17, 116
censorship, 92–93, 129–30
Chalof, Herman, 17
Chambers, Whittaker, 124
Charles, Leon, 16–17
Children's Cantata, 116
choral songs, 22
Civil Rights Movement, 172
Clark, Barrett H., 93
Clarke, Henry Leland, 15, 17
Clifford, Margaret Ellen, 124
Clifton, Chalmers, 101
Cohn, Arthur, 106
Collins, Blanche, 151
Composers' Collective of New York, 2–3,
   14–15, 95; absolute *versus* program music
   of, 46–47; agenda of, 37–38; audience
   of, 26, 50; compared to Soviet music, 47;
   criticism of work by, 49; defining proletarian music and, 21–25; diversity of
   members of, 19–20; female composers
   of, 18–19; members of, 16–17; musical genres promotional pamphlet of,
   22; the proletariat and, 15–21; Special
   Symposium-meeting, 1935, 40–42. *See
   also Workers Song Books*
Composers' Forum Laboratory, 10; American musical identity and, 106–8; artistic
   value of works from, 111–13; attacks on
   government and the wealthy, 114–15;
   communist propaganda and, 99–101;
   connection to contemporary life, 104–6;
   establishment of, 96–97; experimental aspect of, 117–19; female composers and, 103–4; mechanics of works of,
   113–14; politics and, 108–10, 115–17;
   politics of music and, 97–98; post-concert discussions of, 102–18; public benefits of, 117–18; purpose of, 97, 99; social
   modernism and, 111; women composers
   of, 103–4, 108–9
Condemned, The, 145–46
Connell, Kathleen, 135
Cook, Will Marion, 127
Coolidge, Calvin, 72

Copland, Aaron, 10, 151, 175; Composers' Collective and, 17; Composers' Forum Laboratory and, 100, 109; folk music and, 14, 171–72; on free speech, 115; *Hear Ye! Hear Ye!*, 56; obituary of Blitzstein, 164

Cosgrove, Stuart, 120, 137

Coudray, Peggy, 151

Counterattack, 175

Cowell, Henry, 14, 16–17, 21, 37; Composers' Collective and, 108; Johanna M. Beyer and, 103; percussion instruments and non-Western sounds and, 121–23

Cradle Will Rock, The, 2, 10, 51, 77–78, 85–87, 93–94, 143, 173–74; artistic value of, 169; cast and personnel of, 150–51; genesis of, 147–52; musico-dramatic form, 144–47; orchestra instruments used in, 165–68; premiere of, 151–52; reception of, 152–56; sociopolitical climate explored in, 168; *Theatre Workshop* and the debate on "scenery or no scenery" of, 156–69

Crichton, Kyle, 72

Crist, Elizabeth Bergman, 10, 172

Current Opinion, 57

Curry, John Steuart, 9

Daily News, 132

Daily Worker, 20, 24, 48–49, 98, 174; Blitzstein's contributions to, 3; Gold's contributions to, 37; on *Pins and Needles,* 79

Damrosch, Walter, 7

da Silva, Howard, 151–52, 162

Deeter, Jasper, 60–61

Degeyter, Pierre, 26

Degeyter Club, 15, 47, 98

de Graaf, Melissa, 10, 97, 103, 116

Denning, Michael, 83, 93, 96, 111, 171

DeSheim, Charles, 158

Diogenes Club, 173

"Doing the Reactionary," 89–90

"Don't Take My Papa Away from Me," 27

Dos Passos, John, 60–61, 69

Downes, Olin, 117, 163

Downtown Music School, 2–3

Drama Was a Weapon: The Left-Wing Theatre in New York, 1929–1941, 52

Duke, Vernon, 72

Dunaway, David K., 16

Eager, Helen, 74

Eisenberg, Emanuel, 85

Eisler, Hanns, 17, 23, 43–44, 113–14, 148

El Salón México, 109

Engel, Lehman, 150–51, 164

Englander, Eric, 154

Eppert, Carl, 101

Ethiopia, 121, 123–30, 134, 142

Events of 1935, 130

Farragoh, Francis, 61

Farrell, James T., 9

Fearing, Kenneth, 65

Feder, Abe, 151

Federal Music Project (FMP), 6–8, 10, 96–97, 101, 118, 171. *See also* Composers' Forum Laboratory

Federal Project One, 6–8, 95–96, 104, 170–71

Federal Theater Project (FTP), 6, 52, 96, 120, 156, 159; "FTP Plowed Under" and, 85–87; success of, 170–71. *See also* Living Newspaper Unit

female composers, 18–19, 103–4, 108–9

Finney, Ross Lee, 97, 102, 108

Fireman's Flame, The, 90–91

Flanagan, Hallie, 6, 52, 120–21, 123–29, 133; scenery-less productions and, 157–59

folk music, 43, 47, 172

Foster, Stephen, 7

Four Saints in Three Acts, 135, 141

Freeman, Joseph, 69

Freiheit Gesangverein, 17, 21, 25

Friedman, Charles, 79, 83, 88–90

Frost, Frances, 105

Fugue for Eight Percussion Instruments, 123

Gabrielson, Frank, 72

Garland, Robert, 71

Garrett, Charles Hiroshi, 107

Garrick Gaieties, 72, 144

Gassner, John, 52–53, 154–55, 159

Geer, Will, 151–52

German Theater, 96

Gerschefski, Edwin, 102–3

Gershwin, George, 7

Gershwin, Ira, 72, 156

Gettysburg, 8

214 · *Index*

Giorni, Aurelio, 103–5
"God to the Hungry Child," 31, 33–34
Gold, Michael, 112, 174; plays by, 61–63; proletarian music and, 20–21, 37, 48–49, 53; Workers' Drama League and, 60
Goldbeck, Eva, 3, 149
Goldman, Harry, 87–88
Goldstein, Malcolm, 66
Gordon, Eric, 3
Gordon, Robert, 80
Gorelik, Mordecai, 61, 68, 142, 159–60
Gorky, Maxim, 149
Gorney, Jay, 71
Gough, Peter, 10
Grapes of Wrath, The, 1, 9
Great Depression, 1, 4–5; growth of labor movement and communist organizations during, 5, 8–9, 110; impact on musicians, 6–8, 23, 175; impact on theater, 52–53, 93–94, 175; New Deal programs during, 2, 4–6, 95–96, 119, 170; technological innovations in, 4, 6–7; Wobblies during, 20, 54–57, 88; working class suffering during, 87–88
Grisman, Sam H., 152
Gross, Robert, 17
Group Theatre, 68
Gunning, Sarah Ogan, 93
Guthrie, Woody, 172

Hammer, Ella, 165–67
Hammond, Percy, 77
Hanson, Howard, 7, 100, 111–12, 171
Harary, Nettie, 93
Harburg, Yip, 71
Harpies, The, 145–46
Harris, Roy, 14, 100–101, 109
Hart, Lorenz, 72, 156
Hart, Moss, 71
Haufrecht, Herbert, 15–17, 108
Hayes, Alfred, 18, 20
Hays, David, 162
Hear Ye! Hear Ye!, 56
Hemmer, Ed, 151
Herald Tribune, 163
Herbert, Victor, 7
Hermann, Bernard, 173
Hewes, Harry, 101

Highlights of 1935, 135
Hill, Joe, 20, 27
Himelstein, Morgan Y., 52, 67
Hindemith, Paul, 106
Hitchcock, H. Wiley, 122
Hoboken Blues, 53, 62–63, 174
Hopkins, Harry, 5, 123
Houseman, John, 135, 150–52, 157
House Un-American Activities Committee (HUAC), 52, 141, 175–76
Housman, Rosalie, 108–9
Hughes, Elinor, 75
Hughes, Langston, 175

Iceman Cometh, The, 9
imperialism, American, 64
Imperial Serenaders, The, 62
Industrial Workers of the World (IWW), 20, 27, 53–57, 147; national defense fund campaign of, 56
Injunction Granted, 121, 123, 130, 135, 137–42
instrumental music, 22, 44
International, The, 63–64, 174
International Composers' Guild, 22
International Ladies' Garment Workers' Union, 54, 78–83, 92
International Music Bureau, 21
Introduction and Two Songs, 105
Invisible Man, The, 62
Ionisation, 123, 141
Irwin, Ben, 79
I've Got the Tune, 173, 175

Jackson, Molly, 93, 172
Jacobi, Frederick, 100, 140–41
jazz music, 62–64, 107, 144
Jazz Singer, The, 7
Jazz Tragedy, A, 62
Jeans, Ronald, 144
Josten, Werner, 105, 108
Julius Caesar, 157

Kahn, Otto H., 61
Keil, Julius, 17
Kipling, Rudyard, 103
Kushner, David, 145

Lang, Paul Henry, 163

Lange, Dorothea, 1
Lawson, John Howard, 60–63, 65–66, 69–70, 174
League of American Writers, 5
League of Composers, 22, 24, 118, 145, 162
League of Workers' Theatres, 67–69, 71
Ledbetter, Huddie, 172
Lederman, Minna, 149, 154, 163
Lenya, Lotte, 173
Lesan, David, 72
Let Freedom Ring, 159
Lieberman, Robbie, 10
Lincoln Portrait, 176
Little Red Songbook, 20, 27, 172
Living Newspaper Unit, 120–21, 141–42; *Ethiopia,* 121, 123–30, 134, 142; *Four Saints in Three Acts,* 135, 141; *Injunction Granted,* 121, 123, 130, 135, 137–42; music's strategic role and, 134–41; percussion instruments and non-Western sounds and, 121–23; *Power,* 130, 135; success and experimentation by, 130–34; *Triple A Plowed Under,* 130, 135–36
Lloyd, Norman, 138
Lockridge, Richard, 81
Loeb, Philip, 79
Losey, Joseph, 141
Loud Speaker, 61–62

Macbeth, 135, 137
MacLeish, Archibald, 135, 156–57
Maganini, Quinto, 110
Magazine of Art, 172
Magil, A. B., 114
Making Music in Los Angeles: Transforming the Popular, 10
Mantle, Burns, 132
Marching Song, 69–70
Marquardt, Virginia Hagelstein, 65
Marxism, 5, 44, 48, 52, 68, 70, 141
Mason, Daniel Gregory, 99–100
Massey, Edward, 63
mass songs, 22–23
Maynard, George, 17, 46, 48
Mayokovsky, Vladimir, 137
McCarthy, Mary, 154
McCausland, Elizabeth, 170–71
McClain, William, 127

McPhee, Colin, 115
Medea, 135
Menk, Mary, 17
Mercer, Johnny, 72
Meyerhold, Vsevolod Emilyevich, 61–62
Migrant Mother, 1
Miller, Arthur, 175
Miller, Leta E., 10, 122
modernist music, 14–15, 37–38, 44–45, 99–100; American *versus* European, 104
Modern Music, 3, 23–24, 140, 149
Modoi, Evelyn, 17
Moross, Jerome, 72, 77–79
Morrison, Lee, 92
Mother, 53, 149, 157, 159
Mueller, Otto, 101
Murder in the Cathedral, 157
music: American Communist Party and, 20–21, 48–50; art, 37, 42, 172–73; censorship of, 92–93; effect of Great Depression on, 6–8, 14–15, 23, 170–71, 175; folk, 43, 47, 172; instrumental, 22, 44; interactions with politics, early 20th century, 10–11, 104–6, 174–76; jazz, 62–64, 107, 144; labor strikes and demonstrations and, 33; modernist, 14–15, 37–38, 44–45, 99–100, 104; percussion instruments and non-Western sounds in, 121–23; proletarian (*see* proletarian music); Tin Pan Alley, 35; women in, 18–19, 103–4, 108–9. *See also* Composers' Collective of New York
Musical Quarterly, The, 3
Music and Politics in San Francisco from the 1906 Quake to the Second World War, 10
Music of Our Day, 104
Music Vanguard, 46
Mussolini, Benito, 125, 128
My Song Is My Weapon, 10
Mythologies, 143, 162

Nathan, George Jean, 155–56
Nation, The, 170
National Association of American Composers and Conductors, 118
National Committee for American Music, 118
National Negro Congress, 5

216 · *Index*

Negro Songs of Protest, 112
Negro Theatre, 96
New Deal programs, 2, 4–9, 95–96, 119, 170
New Deal Theater, 53
New Masses, 3, 172, 175; Blitzstein and, 40; Composers' Collective and, 98–99; Copland and, 109; on the Degeyter Club, 15; Pettis and, 98; on proletarian music, 18, 20–21, 37
New Music, 37
New Music Orchestra, 123
New Music Quarterly, 123
New Pins and Needles, 85
New Playwrights Theatre, 53, 61–66, 69–70, 147, 174
New School for Social Research, 10, 22, 122, 126
New Theatre League, 157–58
New York Herald Tribune, 54, 77
New York Musicological Society, 16
New York Post, 75, 153
New York Sun, 81
New York Times, 61, 80–81, 152–53, 156
New York World-Telegram, 76, 87
Nicholls, David, 123
"Nickel Under the Foot," 148–49
No for an Answer, 173–74
non-Western sounds in music, 121–23
North, Alex, 17
Norton, Elliot, 76
Nutt, Haley Jo, 123

Odets, Clifford, 9, 68, 93
Of Thee I Sing!, 56
Oja, Carol, 10, 25–26, 175
Oliver, Gene, 17
One Act Play Magazine, 154
"One Big Union for Two," 88–89
O'Neill, Eugene, 9
One-Third of a Nation, 130–31, 135
"On Popular Music," 91
"Onward to Battle," 29–30
Ostinato Pianissimo, 123
Our Town, 159

Panic, 135
Parade, 4, 54, 71–78, 81, 88, 147
Parker, Dorothy, 175

Partisan Review, 154
Pattison, Lee, 115
percussion instruments, 121–23
Peters, Paul, 54, 61, 69, 73, 77, 146–47
Pettis, Ashley, 17–18; Composers' Forum Laboratory and, 98–102, 104, 106, 108, 112, 114–15, 118; on the Degeyter Club, 15
Pins and Needles, 54, 78–94, 175; Blitzstein's contribution to, 85–87; casts of, 92; censorship of songs from, 92–93; composers of, 79; costumes and choreography of, 79; numbers included in, 83–84; original cast of, 80; popular idioms used in, 91; satire and humor in, 88–90; second and third companies of, 80; social and political impact of, 92; structure of music in, 90–92; topics covered in, 84–88
Piscator, Erwin, 60
Plato, 1
Pollack, Howard, 165
Popular Front, 5, 83
Porter, Jacob W., 62
Power, 130, 135
proletarian music, 15, 112, 172; absolute *versus* program music and, 46–47; adaptation of foreign music to, 45–46; audience of, 39–40; Composers' Collective and, 17–18; defining, 21–25; importance of, for strikes and demonstrations, 33; phases of development of, 24; political support for, 48–51; reconsidering the role of, 37–47; types of songs in, 23–24; viewed as social necessity, 40; *Workers Song Books* and, 25–37, 47
Pulse, 123

racial equity and justice, 83
racism, American, 62–63
radio, 4
Rauh, Ida, 60
"Rebel Girl, The," 27–28
Red Channels, 175–76
Red Song Book, 21
Reed, John, 57
Regionalist art movement, 9
Reinhart, Robert, 81
Reis, Claire, 145
Reis, Irving, 173

Republic, The, 1
Reuss, Richard A., 10
Rice, Elmer, 69, 77, 124, 129–30
Riegger, Wallingford, 17, 100, 108, 115
Robbins, Tim, 168
Robeson, Paul, 62–63
Robinson, Arthur, 8, 20
Robinson, Earl, 14, 17, 42–43, 47, 79, 175; *Workers Song Books* and, 25–26
Rodgers, Richard, 72
Rogers, Bernard, 100
Rome, Harold, 79, 89–92
Romeo and Juliet, 135
Roosevelt, Eleanor, 6, 80
Roosevelt, Franklin D., 4–5, 80, 128–30, 171
Rosenthal, Jean, 151
Ruger, Harris Hutchins, 8
Russell, William, 123
Russian Association of Proletarian Musicians (RAPM), 47

Saal, Ilka, 132–34
Salzedo, Carlos, 100
Samimsky, Lazare, 104, 106–7
scenery-less productions, 156–69
Schaefer, Louis, 78–80, 83, 92
Schaeffer, Jacob, 16–17
Schoenberg, Arnold, 3
Schrank, Joseph, 85
Schuman, William, 105
Scottsboro Boys, 56, 72
Scribner's Magazine, 155
Second Hurricane, The, 151
Seeger, Charles, 14, 16–18, 21; folk music and, 43, 47; on the growth of American proletarian musical style, 24, 50–51; as ideological and theoretical mastermind of the Composers' Collective, 23–24; musical training of, 24–25; on romanticism, 24; song structures used by, 29–31
Seeger, Pete, 172, 175
Seeger, Ruth Crawford, 17, 35
Selassie, Haile, 125–26, 128
Sessions, Roger, 106
Seven Choruses from the Medea of Euripides, 135
Shapiro, Jack, 68
Shaw, Irwin, 175
Shostakovich, Dmitri, 111

Shruers, Ed, 151
Shubert Brothers, 71
Siegmeister, Elie, 14, 16–17, 29, 172; on adapting music to the needs of the working class, 45–46; Composers' Forum Laboratory and, 112–15; on performances and workers' audiences, 26; *Workers Song Books* and, 35–36
Sinclair, Upton, 53, 60, 64–65, 174
Sing for Your Supper, 135
Singing Jailbirds, 53, 64–65, 174
Sklar, George, 54, 71, 73, 77, 147
Smith, Catherine Parsons, 10
Smith, Walker C., 56
Social History of Missouri, The, 1
social modernism, 111
Sokoloff, Nikolai, 7–8, 101, 104, 106
solo songs, 22
"Song of the Builders," 31–32
Sounds of the New Deal, 10
Sousa, John Phillip, 7
Soviet music, 47, 98; chants in theater productions, 58–60
Stanton, Olive, 151
Statements for Orchestra, 109
Steel, 79
Steinbeck, John, 1, 9
Stevedore, 159
Still, William Grant, 100
Stokowski, Leopold, 7
"The Strange Funeral in Braddock," 37, 112
Strauss, 80–81
Strike, 60
strikes, labor, 33; theater portrayals of, 57–60, 64–65; Wobblies and, 56–57

"Tabloid Reds, The," 89–90
Taylor, Deems, 18–19, 103
Tempo, Tempo!, 58
theater productions, 52–54; from amateur to professional workers' theater, 61–66; balancing aesthetic and political goals, 68–71; *The Cradle Will Rock (see Cradle Will Rock, The); Parade,* 71–78, 81; *Pins and Needles,* 54, 78–94; scenery-less, 156–69; Wobblies and, 54–57, 88; Workers' Laboratory Theatre, 66–68; Worker's Theatre Movement and, 57–60
Theatre Collective, 68–69

218 · *Index*

Theatre Guild, 72–75, 77
Theatre Workshop, 157–58
They Shall Not Die, 72
Thomson, Virgil, 14, 121, 135, 137–41; on
types of audiences, 9–10; on the WPA,
115–16
Tin Pan Alley music, 35, 54, 78, 90, 93, 148,
173
Tommasini, Anthony, 137
Topics of 1923, 90
Tracy, Thomas H., 56
Triple A Plowed Under, 130, 135–36, 141
Triple Sec, 144–45
Tsiang, H. T., 37
Turner, Kristen, 127

Union of Soviet Composers, 47
United Quartet, 123

Varese, Edgard, 100
Variety, 81
Vermfrendungstechnik, 70
Vietnam War, 172
von Hornbostel, Erich, 122

Wade, Stephen, 10
Wainer, Lee, 134–35
Waiting for Lefty, 9, 93
Walker, Charles, 69
Walker, George, 127
Warner, Ralph, 174
Washington, George, 8
Watson, Morris, 124, 129–30
Watts, Richard, Jr., 54, 86, 153
Weill, Kurt, 144, 154, 156
Welles, Orson, 135, 150–52, 173
Weston, Bert, 151
"We Want the World," 36
Wexley, John, 79
Wiggins, Ella May, 93

William, Bert, 127
Williams, Jay, 72
Wittfogel, Karl, 60
Wobblies, 20, 54–57, 88
Wolfson, Victor, 79
Woltman, Frederick, 105
Wood, Grant, 9
Workers' Drama League, 60–61
Workers' Laboratory Theatre, 66–68, 88
Workers' Music League (WML), 2, 15,
20–22, 33
"Workers of the World Awaken!," 27
Workers Song Books, 4, 14–15, 22, 25–37, 47,
174; audience reactions to, 26; militant
quality of songs of, 27–28; mission of,
25–26; publication of, 25; structure of
songs of, 29–33. *See also* Composers'
Collective of New York
Workers Theater, 66–67
Workers' Theater Movement (WTM), 2, 6,
9, 51, 70–71, 81, 93, 95–96, 121, 124, 156,
174–75; as agitators, 57–60; audience of,
54–55; *The Cradle Will Rock* and (*see Cradle
Will Rock, The*); emergence of, 52–53, 55,
57, 93–94; Wobblies' labor protests and,
54–57
Works Progress Administration (WPA),
2, 4–6, 95, 152, 170; dissolution of, 119;
freedom of speech and, 115; promotion
of music programs by, 101
Wriffle, Sidney B., 87

X Plus Y, 62

Yates, Clarence, 151
Yiddish Theatre, 96
Young Composers' Group, 48

Ziegfield Follies, 90

MARIA CRISTINA FAVA is an associate professor of musicology at Western Michigan University.

The University of Illinois Press
is a founding member of the
Association of University Presses.

University of Illinois Press
1325 South Oak Street
Champaign, IL 61820-6903
www.press.uillinois.edu